International Research Management

INTERNATIONAL RESEARCH MANAGEMENT

Studies in Interdisciplinary Methods from Business, Government, and Academia

Edited by
PHILIP H. BIRNBAUM-MORE
FREDERICK A. ROSSINI
DONALD R. BALDWIN

New York Oxford
OXFORD UNIVERSITY PRESS
1990

Oxford University Press

Oxford New York Toronto
Delhi Bombay Calcutta Madras Karachi
Petaling Jaya Singapore Hong Kong Tokyo
Nairobi Dar es Salaam Cape Town
Melbourne Auckland

and associated companies in
Berlin Ibadan

Published by Oxford University Press, Inc.,
200 Madison Avenue, New York, New York 10016

Library of Congress Cataloging-in-Publication Data
International research management:
studies in interdisciplinary methods from business,
government, and academia /
edited by Philip H. Birnbaum-More , Frederick A. Rossini, Donald R. Baldwin.
p. cm. "Papers presented to the Fourth International Conference
on the Management of Interdisciplinary Research
held in August 1986 at the University of Minnesota . . .
sponsored by the International Association for the Study
of Interdisciplinary Research (INTERSTUDY)"—Pref.
Includes bibliographical references. ISBN 0-19-506252-3
1. Interdisciplinary research—Management—Congresses.
2. Research—International cooperation—Management—Congresses.
I. Birnbaum-More, Philip H. II. Rossini, Frederick A. III. Baldwin, Donald R.
IV. International Conference on the Management of Interdisciplinary Research
(4th : 1986 : University of Minnesota)
V. International Association for the Study of Interdisciplinary Research.
Q180.55.I48I587 1990 001.4—dc20 89-25543

9 8 7 6 5 4 3 2 1

Printed in the United States of America
on acid-free paper

Preface

This book brings together the contributions of practicing research managers and scholars which address the status and future of interdisciplinary research. The theme is developed around three topics: preconditions, processes, and impacts of interdisciplinary research. The book is organized by geographic area and within each area by the organizational setting in which the interdisciplinary research took place. In the section on research in North America, for example, individual papers are grouped by whether they deal with research in governmental organizations, in high technology firms, or in universities.

The book had its origins in the Fourth International Conference on the Management of Interdisciplinary Research held in August 1986 at the University of Minnesota. The conference was sponsored by the International Association for the Study of Interdisciplinary Research (INTERSTUDY) and was the fourth in a series of conferences held at two- to three-year intervals since 1979. Each conference has brought experts together from around the world to share their latest thinking on how to manage this most difficult form of team research. Earlier conferences were held in the Federal Republic of Germany in 1979, in the United Kingdom in 1981, and in the United States in 1984. The published papers from these earlier conferences are cited in the annotated bibliography included in this book.

The editors of this volume have chosen sixteen papers from this conference that, in our opinion, best represent the conference theme: the status and future of interdisciplinary research. These papers form the chapters of this volume and represent views from Brazil, Canada, the German Democratic Republic (East Germany), Israel, Romania, and the United States.

As with any such endeavor, many people and institutions provided help. We could not have completed the manuscript without the help of Nancy Reach and the people of the University of Southern California School of Business Administration Word Processing Service who retyped the manuscripts in their many versions. In addition, Dr. Martha Russell and her colleagues at the University of Minnesota provided superb help before, during, and after the conference, which was moved from Hungary to Minnesota on short notice. Bud Saxberg, unable to attend, was helpful during the planning stages of the conference. In addition, we would like to thank Dr. György Darvas and his colleagues from the Hungarian Academy of Sciences, who put such long hours into planning for the conference at Veszprém, Hungary, only to have it cancelled at the last moment. Finally, we would like to thank our families for their patience over these many months as this final manuscript took shape.

April 1990

P. H. B.
F. A. R.
D. R. B.

The International Association for the Study of Interdisciplinary Research (INTERSTUDY)

The International Association for the Study of Interdisciplinary Research (INTERSTUDY) was formed in 1980 following the first International Conference on Interdisciplinary Research. This first conference was jointly sponsored by the U.S. National Science Foundation and the German Volkswagen Foundation and came about because of a growing international awareness of the importance and difficulty of obtaining successful collaboration across scientific disciplines on increasingly complex research problems. It became clear during the first conference that there was a need for some entity to hold continuing and structured attention on the study of interdisciplinary research.

To meet that need, INTERSTUDY was founded early in 1980. The association provides the organizational structure through which to identify and communicate with persons who are involved or interested in interdisciplinary research. A major element of communication is a newsletter called the "INTERSTUDY Bulletin," issued about three times per year.

The objectives are (1) to advance the art and science of interdisciplinary research; (2) to organize and sponsor meetings, courses, conferences, and symposia to bring together researchers for discussion of problems, demonstrated strengths, and alternative methodologies related to interdisciplinary research; (3) to assemble, compile, and disseminate information concerning all aspects of interdisciplinary research, including its management; and (4) to educate members about the status of interdisciplinary research and its application to various local, regional, national, and international goals and needs.

Contents

International Research Management

Overview and Perspective

Research and development (R&D) is a form of organized creativity. Its institutionalization is one of the greatest achievements of the past century. R&D is and will remain a great engine of scientific, technological, and economic progress. From its beginnings in the small laboratories of independent inventors to the massive government R&D complexes throughout the world, the major research universities, and the great industrial labs that are crossing national boundaries more and more, R&D is the womb of the technological society.

The technological outpourings of R&D have had impacts both directly in the products and processes that have changed our global economy and life-styles and indirectly in changes in the organization and conduct of R&D itself. Some of the most significant impacts have come from the development and widespread use of communications and computer technology. Communications have shrunk the globe, while computers are in the process of creating languages and symbols that span it.

R&D is steadily becoming a transcultural activity. The international dimension has accelerated technology transfer. There is a second transcultural dimension that enriches R&D activity and makes it more complex. This is interdisciplinarity, working across the boundaries of the cultures of intellectual disciplines.

Both transcultural dimensions address critical issues faced by contemporary R&D. Many of the most important scientific and technological problems confronting us cut across the traditional intellectual disciplines. For example, the use of technology in medicine and the improvement of manufacturing processes require substantial contributions from a wide range of disciplines. In addition, these contributions are not intellectually isolated from one another. Biomedical imaging requires the integration of computer science, biomedical science, and computer engineering. Integrating the intellectual and social aspects of disciplinary cultures is analogous to relating R&D across national cultures.

This volume was assembled from papers prepared for the Fourth International Conference on Interdisciplinary Research, held in Minneapolis in the summer of 1986. It stresses the management of the transdisciplinary and transnational aspects of R&D. In so doing, it raises issues involving differences and similarities in R&D in different organizational, national, and intellectual contexts.

Beginning with the interdisciplinary aspects of R&D, it is important to consider the environmental factors or preconditions that set the framework in which R&D is conducted. These can be divided into external and internal conditions. External conditions include problem characteristics, incentives and rewards, resources, and institutional context. Internal conditions involve personnel, leadership, skills, project organization, and team dynamics.

Problem characteristics include degree of technical complexity, degree of predictability of outcome, and type of interaction with users of the work. Incentives and rewards relate to tangible satisfactions, such as compensation and working conditions, as well as intangible satisfactions, such as meeting intellectual and emotional needs. Resources involve time, money, facilities, and personnel. Institutional context especially relates to organizational mechanisms for performing R&D and to structural facilitators and barriers encountered in the R&D process.

Personnel issues for interdisciplinary R&D reflect the intellectual backgrounds, range of skills, cognitive styles, and diversity of the participants. Leadership pertains to the management style used in the R&D effort. Skills involve not only the substantive and research technique expertise of the participants but also their skills in working in a group context. Project organization is simply the internal structure of the effort. Team dynamics involves the communications patterns within the group as well as physical proximity.

Process factors detail the dynamics of the project through stages working to conclusion within the context set by the preconditions. There are various characterizations of the stages of an interdisciplinary project. A typical set is the following:

- problem definition
- determining knowledge and personnel needs
- developing an integrative framework and questions to be investigated
- engaging in role negotiation
- specifying particular studies to be undertaken
- resolving disciplinary conflicts
- gathering current knowledge and searching for new information
- building and maintaining communication through integrative techniques
- collating all contributions and evaluating their adequacy
- integrating the individual pieces
- developing the proposed solution
- determining the future disposition of the results of the project

Clearly these activities are not listed in a fixed order. Nor are they linear in character. That is, the same step may be performed a number of times during the course of the project or not at all.

As the stages of the project are undertaken, integrative techniques are used to move the project toward a synthesis rather than to maintain a collection of discrete components. Such techniques may include interactive group meetings, common data gathering and analysis, iteration, and ongoing interaction with the users/client. Computerized data bases and models have the potential to serve as integrating vehicles. The acceptance of a common assumption set or framework allows a reference point for discourse to which all participants can return.

Projects have stages, in effect a life cycle. Likewise, teams and organizations have life cycles of their own. The stages in a life cycle depend on the paradigm within which the organization views itself. A common set of paradigms for viewing organizations are the Allison models. These can be characterized as the rational model, the organizational decision model, and the bureaucratic-political model. In the rational model, stages are determined by the teleological relationships between inputs, outputs, and objectives. In the organizational decision model, the organization is seen as coping with a complex and uncertain world at high search costs. To cope, the organization develops mechanisms to reduce uncertainty, behaves myopically with threats and opportunities, and initiates search when threatened. The political model views the environment as a power game with stakeholders and role-players.

The rational model suggests that response comes rationally to the demands made by the environment. Thus, if the organization or team is not organized around a core of interdisciplinary methodological research, its existence will be limited in time by the utility of the skills it has developed in responding to external demands. If a general methodology for interdisciplinary research is developed with a learning curve built in, then the organization can respond to a range of external signals, and its lifetime will be extended until it is unable to respond effectively to its environment.

The organizational decision model suggests that the organization will conform its internal structure to the larger environment. It will develop bureaucratic procedures by which it will function. In the absence of environmental shocks it will ossify. These shocks will either kill it or revivify and redirect it.

The political model views institutional dynamics as a game played to enhance relative power. Power is maintained by having available slack resources and satisfying immediate clients so that the external environment produces no threats. Individuals within the organization function best when they balance organizational and individual objectives.

The dynamics of startup, maturation, and senescence of an organization or team can be viewed through any or all of these models or, for that matter, through any other. However, some models explain some organizations better than others. Indeed, the culture of a specific organization may approximate the categories of a particular model.

Interdisciplinary R&D has been most extensively studied through its practice in the United States and Western Europe. The situation of R&D in the United States is exceptionally rich in its organizational contexts. The three principal performing sectors are the government, private industry, and universities. Each of these sectors relates to the others, and each is internally quite complex. There are no single models of institutions that represent a sector adequately.

The funding patterns are quite complex. The government funds R&D in its own labs as well as in industry and universities. Industry funds R&D in universities as well as in house. Universities fund some internal R&D. It is very tempting to approximate government institutions by the political model, industry by the organizational decision model, and the university by the rational model. However, it may be safer to study each situation independently. Because the conditions of employment are different in the three sectors, management's control over researchers varies from almost nil over a tenured university faculty member to substantial over an industrial researcher. In industry and government, conflicts typically arise across functional subunits with disciplinary conflicts being a perturbation on this. Academia, with its disciplinary units, reverses this. However, disciplines can be seen as collections of substantive and technique skills for the performance of R&D. While skill sets cross disciplinary units and vice versa, the relatively stable ideology of academia gives priority to the discipline, as professional organizations typically match well with academic departments.

Of studies in interdisciplinary R&D in the United States and Western Europe, the university context has been by far the most common subject. This has unfortunate consequences in that much cross-disciplinary, cross-organizational R&D takes place in industry and government as well as across all sectors. While R&D organizations that do research in a specific problem area are most common in a technology-based company, such as Honeywell, or in a government lab, they are the exception in the university environment. Much study has been given to these atypical units—interdisciplinary centers or institutes—in the university and their relationships to the disciplinary departments where the academic faculty are based and have their tenure.

Academic departments are quasi-permanent organizations which can offer their senior members lifetime employment. Research institutes and centers are very impermanent organizations which depend on the faculty of academic departments and professional researchers. The latter often do not have faculty status and almost never have the protection of academic tenure. The advantage that institutes and centers bring to the university is that they are topically focused at a time when most large-scale external funding for university R&D is oriented toward problem areas rather than pure disciplinary research. Thus, they act as a magnet or at least a focal point for attracting external funds to the university by providing a nucleus of topical activity to give confidence that the university has both commitment and capability in an area.

There is a trade-off between resources on the one hand and stability and status on the other. Universities and individuals adopt various postures along a continuum toward these poles. Yet the increasing role of centers and institutes in universities is a recognition of the importance of interdisciplinarity.

Because the culture of R&D varies from country to country and from region to region, the majority of studies are limited in their scope. Some regions where relatively less study of interdisciplinary R&D has taken place include Latin America, Asia (especially Japan), and, to a lesser extent, Eastern Europe.

Eastern Europe has typically followed the Soviet pattern of research institutes affiliated with academies of science as the principal performers of R&D. Universities in these countries tend to be relatively more oriented to teaching than they are in North America. These countries make use of a degree of central planning that is unknown in the United States. This requirement of planning provides an orientation to the future that opens up another field of interdisciplinary activity. The intrinsically interdisciplinary character of future-oriented activities such as forecasting, planning, and impact assessment means that the study of interdisciplinary R&D can be enriched by understanding studies of the future from this perspective. The "science of science" is an area of considerable interest in Eastern European intellectual circles, and this focus allows a ready entree into the study of interdisciplinary R&D.

Japan's rapid rise after World War II as a major technological power has spawned considerable interest about the R&D culture of that nation. Most Japanese R&D is performed in industry. Here also, the universities are predominantly teaching institutions. In fact, it would be interesting to know whether more R&D sponsored by Japanese industry is conducted in Japanese or American universities. The Ministry of International Trade and Industry (MITI) has played a coordinating role in focusing industrial R&D on specific sectors, as well as being involved in the formation of cooperative research activities among industrial firms. Because few westerners understand the Japanese language and culture, its unique approach to R&D is poorly understood in the United States and Western Europe.

An anecdote told by a Japanese R&D executive should illustrate one major difference between the R&D cultures of Japan and the United States. After a session on the use of computers in industrial R&D conducted at a meeting of the Industrial Research Institute, a U.S.-based organization of R&D executives from large firms, a representative of Nippon Steel told the following story. A researcher in their corporate R&D lab was interested in developing a particular expert system for use in the company. He submitted his plans and a budget to his management for review. By the time his project was funded, the engineers on the plant floor had the system up and running. This direct link between R&D and production is very uncommon in the United States and Western Europe. Yet there are other areas where understanding needs to increase. These include the diversity of management styles used in Japanese firms as well as the techniques of evaluating the success and failure of projects and the performance of R&D personnel.

In Latin America, much of the R&D is carried on by governmental organizations. Many of the problems encountered here are analogous to those in other countries. However, research cultures are not the same, and unique issues have arisen in this context.

There is a whole range of problems that have not been commonly addressed in cross-national analyses of R&D that relate to the formation and performance of teams and organizations made up of representatives from many nations. As R&D becomes more global, this set of issues should emerge in the context of the multinational corporation and cooperative R&D programs among groups of countries.

We are only beginning to understand some of the basic issues affecting cross-disciplinary, cross-cultural R&D. As both of these dimensions become more important, our understanding of them will need to grow. In particular, empirical studies, rather than anecdotes and case studies, should be the norm. However, case studies may be important and, if well handled, make significant contributions. This volume and the conference on which it is based mark an initial step toward increasing our understanding of transcultural R&D.

I

PRECONDITIONS AND PROCESSES

What is the status and future of interdisciplinary research? This was the question that formed the core of the conference. The first four papers present an overview of the current state of knowledge concerning the preconditions and processes of interdisciplinary research. The first paper, by Julie Klein and Alan Porter, reviews the growing literature from many disciplines on the preconditions for successful interdisciplinary research. In the second paper, Julie Klein reviews the literature on the activities successful projects use as they conduct the interdisciplinary research process. A somewhat different approach is taken in the third paper by Ilan and Patricia Vertinsky to the preconditions of successful interdisciplinary research. The Vertinskys develop three competing explanations of the necessary preconditions from the literature and then use a series of case studies of interdisciplinary research to identify the most accurate predictions derived from the competing models. The fourth and final paper in this section is by Israel Dror, who looks at the interdependence between science and technology and social and economic forces over fifty- to sixty-year long-wave cycles. Dror discusses how activities such as interdisciplinary research coincide with the evolutionary phases of different disciplines.

1

Preconditions for Interdisciplinary Research

JULIE THOMPSON KLEIN
ALAN L. PORTER

There is an old Dutch proverb: *Goed begonnen is halfgewonnen.* "Well begun is half done." Clearly, tending to the preconditions for IDR will enhance the prospects for success. Unfortunately, there are no widely accepted models of IDR, and the "recipe" approach, as Richard Schuller pointed out, is only valid to a limited extent (Schuller 1986). Still, the growing literature on IDR does contain a wealth of observations and lessons about the most favorable preconditions for IDR (Klein 1989). These may be grouped in two broad categories: external conditions (problem characteristics, incentives and rewards, resources, and institutional setting) and internal conditions (personnel matters, leadership, appropriate skills, project organization, and the setting for team dynamics).

EXTERNAL CONDITIONS

Problem characteristics affect IDR in a number of ways. Certain problems require a large-scale effort, greatly increasing problems of project management (Birnbaum 1979). Correspondingly, certain topics are so technically complex that in-depth skills are needed. Yet, because all participants may not master those skills fully, certain management strategies may be precluded and communication made more difficult. The nature of much applied and policy R&D also dictates interaction with intended users/clients of the study, adding further complexity. Some projects can begin with a well-bounded framework and relatively predictable outcomes, yet others must deal with extreme uncertainties. Some projects will also have a sense of urgency that limits the amount of time a team has for developing a shared understanding of their objectives and research capabilities. Basic virological research, for example, may be pressed only by interlaboratory rivalry, but aeronautical and environmental projects may have strict timetables. Finally, while there is an obvious virtue to settling upon a clear research program early in a project, there is, at the same time, a very real danger from imposing a specific conceptual framework without a full grasp of the problem, a lesson learned in several environmental and ecological projects (Bella and Williamson 1976–77; Barmarck and Wallen 1979).

Incentives and rewards are usually based on disciplinary rather than interdisciplinary standards. Whether team members are drawn to a project by their inherent interest in the research problem or the availability of funding, their commitment will be enhanced by negotiating professional rewards in advance, if possible. In addition to such tangibles as salary, promotion, and tenure, these rewards also include satisfaction of the emotional and intellectual needs of individual researchers (Walsh et al. 1975). Project directors should be aware of the problems created by split appointments, which inevitably divide loyalties between disciplinary homes and interdisciplinary projects. Veterans of full-time appointments caution, however, that periodic disciplinary leaves of absence are advisable for maintaining contacts and keeping abreast of current work, especially in long-term projects.

Resources include the obvious necessities of time and money, as well as conducive facilities and appropriate personnel, such as team members, a leader, potential consultants, and extrateam liaisons.

Institutional setting raises a host of issues for IDR. Settings vary (Klein 1985b) from independent "buffer institutions" (Brooks 1977); to established centers at the university, college, and department levels; to individual studies, independent projects, and phantom efforts that exist only on paper. While problems do exist in the industrial setting (Stucki 1979), the literature has tended to concentrate on the academic setting. The concentration of research within U.S. universities contrasts to an emphasis on free-standing research institutes in other nations (e.g., France, China, Soviet Union). In multi-institution projects, the involvement of different types of institutions with differing objectives and personnel characteristics may complicate the research process. Barriers among organizational divisions can also impede collaboration, whether the divisions are discipline-, function-, or project-oriented. Larger organizations tend to reduce flexibility, to the disadvantage of IDR. In studies of technology assessment projects, small contract research firms (with thirty or fewer professionals) provided the most conducive institutional setting (Rossini et al. 1981).

The lowest organizational barriers occur when IDR takes place within one unit. The obvious university model for this is the organized research unit (ORU), usually a center or institute (Teich 1979). Widely regarded as an ideal environment for IDR, the university research center creates a central location for dealing with complex problems, drawing upon a large pool of physical and human resources, while enhancing the social visibility of the university and facilitating interactions across disciplines. However, not all universities can marshall the resources for sizable structures, and there may even be problems with a center, despite its high number of integrating devices. Centers suffer from the vagaries of "soft money" support. They may lean toward certain disciplinary biases and may also fail to confer adequate professional rewards upon participants (Friedman and Friedman 1985). Were ORUs empowered to confer tenure (Campbell and Kimmel 1985) and given permanent funding, most of these problems would disappear, but then ORUs would resemble university departments.

The alternative to establishing ORUs is broadening the accommodation of IDR among existing academic departments. The transformation of U.S. anatomy departments into neuroscience research units provides a useful example (Rossini et al. 1984). These organizational units demonstrate a great openness to desired research skills, regardless of whether they fall within the traditional confines of anatomy, biochemistry, computer science, or zoology. Permanent faculty and postdoctoral personnel are hired to build the requisite techniques and substantive expertise. The phenomenon is not unique to anatomy. Across the disciplines and professions, researchers are following questions and problems across traditional boundaries, as in cellular biology, tumor virology, political behavior, and environmental physics. In some areas, full-fledged "interdisciplines" have developed to consolidate work in an area of cross-fertilization, as in social psychology, biochemistry, physical chemistry, materials science, and American studies. In other areas, the problem communities are less well developed but still constitute recognizable efforts to work beyond monodisciplinary confines, as in immunopharmacology, the study of oral testimony, urban affairs, environmental studies, sociobiology, political gerontology, human population biology, and bioelectrochemistry.

INTERNAL CONDITIONS

Personnel factors include both team members and leaders. There are certain ideal characteristics for personnel: flexibility, patience, a willingness to learn, sensitivity toward and tolerance of others, and a willingness to venture into uncharted waters. White contends that people who tend toward Taylor's category of divergent thinkers are probably more likely to find interdisciplinary research compatible and enjoyable than convergent thinkers (White 1975, p. 384). Mead (1977) felt "digital" thinkers may be too narrow in focus to deal with broad, cross-cutting issues, that "analogic" thinkers can better perform integrative tasks. In the context of interdisciplinary education, Swora and Morrison (1974, p. 50) suggested the ideal personnel are those Jencks and Riesman called "academic intellectuals," people with an eye toward questions of personal and societal importance and thus accountable to a larger audience. All interdisciplinary teams, whether in education, IDR, or medicine, also depend on the willingness of individuals to subordinate their individual interests to a common objective.

Just as there are no algorithms for interdisciplinary work, there are no prescriptions for building interdisciplinary teams. Nevertheless, experience suggests several lessons. Familiarity with general systems theory has proven a benefit in some projects (Sharp 1983; Wasniowski 1983), and many veterans of IDR contend that it becomes easier with experience, though in a study of twenty-four technology assessments, Rossini et al. found that interdisciplinary experience did not relate to team performance. Andrews (1979, pp. 269, 285) observed that research performance, in general, appears positively associated with researcher diversity in terms of professional activities, knowledge of several areas of specialization, engagement in multiple projects, and interdisciplinary orientation. Studies of technology assessment projects also suggest that increased intellectual diversity among team members relates to superior research to a point, then diminishes. Superiority, in this case, relates to validity, utility, and integration. Yet diversity can also be a source of disharmony. Linguistic and epistemological differences, compounded by variances in personality and cognitive style, can engender conflict.

Leadership selection encompasses all the uncertainties associated with heading any research group, plus additional considerations. An IDR leader has been called a ringmaster, bridge scientist, gatekeeper, boundary agent, ombudsman, polymath, dynamo, meta-scientist, specialist/generalist, and strong entrepreneur. Leading IDR demands both knowledge of pertinent specialties and general awareness of other disciplinary paradigms, in addition to problem-solving, communication, and management skills for implementing interdependent schedules, focusing on core tasks, handling difficult budgets, dealing with multiple organizations, setting and monitoring performance standards, and performing public relations. Research on leadership style suggests that status and emphasis on initiating structure (on tasks, authority, control, and providing structure) are important in the early phases of a project. In technology assessments, a democratic leader tended to generate more fully integrated research than either an authoritarian or a laissez-faire leader. Michael Anbar's concept of a "bridge scientist" provides an attractive leadership model of someone able to go beyond the "multidisciplinary" translation of a problem to "interdisciplinary" management and evaluation of terminological and paradigmatic conflicts (Anbar 1973).

Skills, as we mean the term, pertain to substantive expertise and research techniques, not only in disciplinary terms but also "multiple-skill" requirements (Porter and Rossini 1984) as well as interdisciplinary skills. Interdisciplinary skills include knowing what information to seek; participating effectively in collaborative work; acquiring a working knowledge of the language, concepts, information, and analytical skills pertinent to the problem; collating the contributions of individual experts; establishing the adequacy, relevancy, and adaptability of pertinent materials; fitting the pieces into place in order to achieve a pattern of mutual relatedness and relevancy to the overall problem; and knowing how to confirm or disconfirm the proposed solution. Veterans of IDR recommend early training in group interaction skills, and Luszki (1958, pp. 291–98) has outlined activities that cultivate interdisciplinary skills in general.

Project organization straddles preconditions and processes, though we emphasize here structural factors leaning toward the former. Project organization necessarily entails careful planning. The guiding principle is reducing structural barriers to collaboration, while tending to personnel and facilities. Project goals must be articulated and controls established over data, information, and accounting. This can be achieved most effectively through a central project office. Given the typically high uncertainty that characterizes IDR projects, it is important to build in the flexibility necessary for making shifts at later stages. Balancing hard and soft money in the planning stage will promote long-term stability, facilitate flexibility in the later stages, and allow for allocating funds to departments as a form of disciplinary compensation, a factor that enhances negotiation of faculty release time and rewards. It is equally important to anticipate the intellectual and organizational needs of each stage, identifying appropriate combinations of disciplines, existing models and traditions, as well as appropriate literatures (Chubin et al. 1986; Klein 1985a, 1989).

Matrix structures have proven quite supportive of project work in larger organizations, since they superimpose project organization on an existing hierarchy. An IDR matrix structure can facilitate a balance of power and increase intrateam communication and decision making, through lateral channels. Interdisciplinary educators have long made use of matrix structures, building degree programs and clustered course blocks within larger institutions, some taken only by students enrolled in a given program and others open to the general college population. The interdisciplinary medical team offers an even closer analogy, since it is a collaborative community of scientific peers working between and within organizational structures to diagnose health problems and provide coordinated treatment. Taking a task-centered or patient-centered approach, interdisciplinary medical teams promote communication across traditionally segmented specialties, allowing more expeditious approaches to complex problems.

Team dynamics is our final internal precondition. Physical proximity is quite important. White suggests that the ideal physical arrangement is a suite, with each team member's office opening into a conference or lounge area. This arrangement promotes interaction, facilitating the fundamental process of mutual education (White 1975, p. 384). If that is not possible, IDR organizers should devise workable means of fostering regular interactions. Team size should conform to problem characteristics. Relatively small teams appear more likely to achieve integrated results. Studies of technology assessments pointed toward five (plus or minus two) as a desirable team number. Swanson (1982) contends that the most successful interdisciplinary projects at academic institutions appear to be those with external funding and no more than four or five disciplines. Stankiewicz (1979) adds that academic research teams tend to reach optimum size for cohesion and productivity at five to six people. Cohesion tends to fall dramatically in large groups that are poorly organized, although leaders with more than fourteen years of experience had been successful in maintaining productivity in large groups. Large groups, though, as a rule, will tend to inhibit creativity, aggravate communication problems, and provoke a tendency to work at the level of the smallest common denominator. Thus, it would seem wise to divide very large project teams into small working groups. In any such arrangement, though, assurance of "open channel" communication (rather than a "hub and spokes" arrangement) appears highly desirable (Rossini et al. 1981).

Because interdisciplinary groups are status systems that reflect external hierarchies and disciplinary loyalties, they will tend to follow the status system and world outside the team if there is no strong alternative organization, though even a strong alternative structure will not necessarily prevent clashes in different educational backgrounds, career goals, professional styles, disciplinary ideologies, and places in the disciplinary pecking order (Chubin et al. 1979). Consider, for example, the disdain of scientists for engineers, of mathematicians for physicists, and of pure scientists for applied scientists (Mar et al. 1976, p. 651). The technology assessment studies uncovered dissension within teams over quantification (near disdain among some physical scientists for the social sciences and humanities), unwillingness by some to venture beyond data in hand in order to predict the future, and overuse of jargon, overblown modeling, and unrealistic data requirements (the latter problems ascribed particularly to economists). More globally, there is a question of mixing the four academic cultures of the humanities, social sciences, natural sciences, and professional studies (Becker 1984, p. 173). Differences associated with disciplinary training run deep. Studies of forty National Science Foundation IDR projects found relatively little crossing of these cultures (Porter and Rossini 1985). An IDR team including a lawyer, accustomed to adversarial thinking, as well as physical and social scientists, accustomed to quite different operationalizations of the scientific method, may face serious obstacles in trying to reach an understanding of what each considers knowledge, how to obtain that knowledge, and how to apply it. Data from a 1968 questionnaire (Gaff and Wilson 1971) also suggested that professors in fields where the knowledge is more tightly codified (mathematics and the natural sciences) are less favorably disposed to interdisciplinary teaching than professors in less tightly codified fields (humanities and to a lesser extent the social sciences).

CONCLUSION

Gerald Holton (1986, p. 241) once offered a wise principle for making science more coherent: "Try to be a scientist first, a specialist second." However, the organization of research along disciplinary lines does and will continue to undermine interdisciplinary research in universities, reinforcing communication gaps between disciplines and creating a series of social, political, and intellectual obstacles to collaborative work (Hershberg 1981). These problems are only compounded by the lack of widely accepted guidelines on how to approach a problem in an interdisciplinary fashion and the relative paucity forums for interdisciplinary publication. Given these realities, it is essential that existing knowledge about preconditions for interdisciplinary research be brought to bear on IDR projects.

REFERENCES

Anbar, M. 1973. The "bridge scientist" and his role. *Research/Development.* (July):30–34.

Andrews, F. M., ed. 1979. *Scientific productivity.* Cambridge: Cambridge University Press.

Barmark, J., and G. Wallen. 1979. The interaction of cognitive and social factors in steering a large scale interdisciplinary project. In R. T. Barth and R. Steck, eds., *Interdisciplinary research groups: Their management and organization.* Vancouver: IRGIP, pp. 180–90.

Becker, T. 1984. The cultural view. In B. R. Clark, ed. *Perspectives on higher education.* Berkeley: University of California Press, pp. 165–98.

Bella, D. A., and K. J. Williamson. 1976–77. Conflicts in interdisciplinary research. *Journal of Environmental Systems* 6(2):105–24.

Birnbaum, P. H. 1979. A theory of academic interdisciplinary research performance: A contingency and path analysis approach. *Management Science* 25:231–42.

Brooks, H. 1977. Office of Technology Assessment invites comments on health of science. FAS Public Interest Report 30(1):6.

Campbell, D. T., and A. J. Kimmel. 1985. *Guiding preventive intervention research centers for research validity.* Final Report on Contract SSN 552-12-4531. National Institute of Mental Health, Rockville, MD.

Chubin, D., A. L. Porter, F. A. Rossini, and T. Connolly. 1986. Annotated bibliography. In D. Chubin, A. L. Porter, F. A. Rossini, and T. Connolly, eds. *Interdisciplinary analysis and research: Theory and practice of problem-focused research and development.* Mt. Airy: Lomond, pp. 441–70.

Chubin, D. E., F. A. Rossini, A. L. Porter, and I. I. Mitroff. 1979. Experimental technology assessment: Explorations in processes of interdisciplinary team research. *Technological Forecasting and Social Change* 15:87–94.

Friedman, R. S., and R. C. Friedman. 1985. Organized research units in academe revisited. In B. M. Mar, W. T. Newell, and B. O. Saxberg, eds., *Managing high technology.* New York: Elsevier Science, pp. 75–91.

Gaff, J., and R. Wilson. 1971. Faculty cultures and interdisciplinary studies. *Journal of Higher Education* 42(3):186–201.

Hershberg, Theodore. 1981. Epilogue: Sustaining interdisciplinary research. In Theodore Hershberg, ed., *Philadelphia: Work, space, family, and group experience in the nineteenth century, essays toward an inter-disciplinary history of the city.* Oxford: Oxford University Press, pp. 492–95.

Holton, Gerald. 1986. Niels Bohr and the integrity of science. *American Scientist* 74(3):237–43.

Klein, J. T. 1985a. The interdisciplinary concept: Past, present, and future. In Lennart Levin and Ingemar Lind, eds., *Inter-disciplinarity revisited: Re-assessing the concept in the light of institutional experience.* Stockholm: OECD/CERI, SNBUC, Linköping University, pp. 123–36.

Klein, J. T. 1985b. The evolution of a body of knowledge: Interdisciplinary problem-focused research. *Knowledge: Creation, Diffusion, Utilization* 7(2):117–42.

———. 1989. *Interdisciplinarity: History, theory, and practice.* Detroit: Wayne State University Press, pp. 121–39, 243–54.

Luszki, Margaret Barron. 1958. *Interdisciplinary team research methods and problems.* New York: New York University Press, pp. 291–98.

Mar, B. W., W. T. Newell, and Borje Saxberg. 1976. Interdisciplinary research in the university setting. *Environmental Science and Technology* 10(7):650–53.

Mead, Margaret. 1977. Can research institutions accommodate interdisciplinary researchers? Symposium at 143rd Annual Meeting of the Association for the Advancement of Science. Denver, February 20–25, 1977. Taped transcript available from AAAS.

Porter, A. L., and F. A. Rossini. 1984. Interdisciplinary research redefined: Multiple skill, problem-focused research in the STRAP framework. *R&D Management* 14:105–11.

———. 1985. Forty interdisciplnary research projects: Multiple skills and peer review. In B. W. Mar, W. T. Newell, and B. O. Saxberg, eds., *Managing high technology.* New York: Elsevier Science, pp. 103–12.

Rossini, F. A., A. L. Porter, D. E. Chubin, and T. Connolly. 1984. Crossdisciplinarity in the biomedical sciences: A preliminary analysis of anatomy. In S. R. Epton, R. L. Payne, and A. W. Pearson, eds., *Managing interdisciplinary research.* Chichester: John Wiley & Sons, pp. 176–84.

Rossini, F. A., A. L. Porter, P. Kelly, and D. E. Chubin. 1981. Interdisciplinary integration within technology assessments. *Knowledge* 2:503–28.

Schuller, C. Richard. 1986. Three synergistic proconditions for inter-disciplinary research. Paper presented at the Fourth International Conference on Interdisciplinary Research in Minneapolis, August 25–28.

Sharp, J. M. 1983. A method for peer group appraisal and interpretation of data, developed in interdisciplinary research programs. In S. R. Epton, R. L., Payne, and A. W. Pearson, eds., *Managing interdisciplinary research.* Chichester: John Wiley & Sons, pp. 211–19.

Stankiewicz, R. 1979. The effects of leadership on the relationship between the size of research groups and their performance. *R&D Management* 9:207–12.

Stucki, J. C. 1979. A goal-oriented pharmaceutical research and development organization: An eleven year experience. In R. T. Barth and R. Steck, eds., *Interdisciplinary research groups: Their management and organization.* Vancouver: IRGIP, pp. 77–96.

Swanson, E. R. 1982. Working with other disciplines. In M. Russell, ed., *Enabling interdisciplinary research: Perspectives from agriculture, forestry, and home economics.* St. Paul: University of Minnesota, Agricultural Experiment Station, pp. 19–27.

Swora, Tamara, and James L. Morrison. 1974. Interdisciplinarity and higher education. *Journal of General Education* 26:50.

Teich, A. 1979. Trends in the organization of academic research: The role of ORU's and full-time researchers. In R. T. Barth and R. Steck, eds., *Interdisciplinary research groups: Their management and organization*. Vancouver: IRGIP, pp. 244–59.

Walsh, W. B., et al. 1975. Developing an interface between engineering and the social sciences. *American Psychologist* 30:1067–71.

Wasniowski, R. 1983. Futures research as a framework for transdisciplinary research. In S. R. Epton, R. L. Payne, and A. W. Pearson, eds., *Managing interdisciplinary research*. Chichester: John Wiley & Sons, pp. 228–35.

White, I. L. 1975. Interdisciplinarity. In S. Arnstein and A. N. Christakis, eds., *Perspectives on technology assessment*. Washington, D.C.: Academy for State and Local Governments, pp. 380–87.

2
The Interdisciplinary Process

JULIE THOMPSON KLEIN

Interdisciplinarity is neither a subject matter nor a body of content. It is a process that requires clarifying different perspectives and resolving conflicts in order to produce a coherent synthesis. While there are no formulas for achieving synthesis, there are nonetheless valuable descriptions of the process in the literature. These descriptions on problem-focused research, medical care, and education reveal not only how integration takes place but also techniques for enhancing its prospects.

The process begins with a problem, question, topic, or issue. Differences in disciplinary worldviews must then be clarified and conflicts resolved in order for a coherent synthesis to be achieved. This requires a healthy respect for both the core objective and any other participants. There are a number of steps in the general process (Winthrop 1964; McEvoy 1972; J. T. Klein 1986):

- begin defining the problem
- determine all knowledge needs, including appropriate disciplinary representatives, additional consultants, and relevant models, traditions, and literatures
- develop an integrative framework and appropriate questions to be investigated
- engage in role negotiation
- specify particular studies to be undertaken
- resolve disciplinary conflicts by working toward a common vocabulary and focus through reciprocal learning
- gather all current knowledge and search for new information
- build and maintain communication through integrative techniques
- collate all contributions and evaluate their adequacy, relevancy, and adaptability
- integrate the individual pieces to determine a pattern of mutual relatedness and relevancy
- confirm or disconfirm the proposed solution or answer
- decide about future management or disposition of the project/patient/curriculum.

INTEGRATIVE TECHNIQUES

The foremost challenge is ensuring that the end result not be a "multidisciplinary" juxtaposition of separate perspectives but a genuine "interdisciplinary" synthesis. Utilizing integrative techniques will promote interaction among team members who need to shift from a secondary group relationship, reflecting individual self-interests, to a primary group relation, reflecting the team's new corporate identity around a common task (Stone 1969). Individual researchers and educators may also use a number of specific techniques to promote consultation and corroboration (Mar, Newell, and Saxberg 1976; Birnbaum 1978; J. T. Klein 1989):

- regular meetings
- internal and external presentations
- joint organizing and planning
- internal and external seminars
- joint legislative work
- periodic reports and reviews
- joint presentations, papers, and publications
- joint patent work

- common data
- common data gathering and analysis
- common data-reporting forms
- common teaching rounds and staff meetings
- common equipment
- common facilities
- common objective(s)

- letting members articulate their differences to render them clearer
- training in group interation skills
- interdependence in analysis of a common object/objective
- focusing on a common enemy or target (a common concern that will dominate over individual differences)
- involvement of client
- using iterations
- using established techniques (scenario, Delphi, etc.)
- joint continuing education
- informal gatherings
- telecommunication for dispersed members

Members of interdisciplinary teams must be able to translate specialized knowledge into a "synthetic product," acting as filters for each other and for consulting experts. White (1975; pp. 385–86) has demonstrated some of the quality-control measures used to ensure a synthetic product in technology assessments of oil and gas operations on the U.S. outer continental shelf (conducted at the University of Oklahoma). Work began with an interdisciplinary core research team comprised of specialists from the natural and social sciences and engineering. To ensure interdisciplinary quality, assignments were rotated among team members, extensive and intensive internal reviews were conducted, and numerous rewrites were performed. Internal and external reviews were particularly helpful in resolving communication problems. After several internal iterations, outside consultants, an oversight committee, and representatives of various parties of interest were involved. Detailed critiques, White reported, were most likely to come from paid consultants. By relying on this system of review procedures, the core research team was able to produce papers that became the basis for an interdisciplinary rather than multidisciplinary report.

Iteration and negotiation among experts have both proven valuable to the interdisciplinary process. Iteration enables authors to become readers and critics themselves, reacting to one another's work in order to achieve a coherent, common assessment. To facilitate interactions, a project director or commentator can act as synthesizer (Kann 1979). Role negotiation and clarification (Ackerman et al. 1983) allow team members to assess what they need and expect from each other, from consultants, and from users/patients/students. Team members are able to clarify differences in disciplinary language, methods, tools, concepts, role conceptions, and professional identities and ideologies. A team, Koepp-Baker suggests (1979, p. 54), represents in many ways a "polygamous marriage." It is launched by the announcement of intentions, the engagement, considerable publicity, a honeymoon, and, finally, the long haul, which is inevitably threatened by the onset of ennui. Making it through the long haul will be aided by identifying where difficulties lie, where goals are clarified and roles defined (and by whom), what the levels of communication are inside and outside the group, how the group builds and maintains its identity and sense of purpose, what its capacity for change is, and how and by whom points are assessed and achievements measured (Logan and McKendry 1982, p. 884).

Sharp (1984) suggests that fragmentation may be avoided by consigning all available and pertinent data to a computer, then assigning the appraisal, synthesis, and interpretation of those data to a combination of system generalists and disciplinary specialists. This procedure entails a continuous process of appraising and interpreting the collective knowledge of all co-investigators. Data are tested for consistency and then organized into a program data base, where all elements can be readily merged and retrieved. Appraisal and synthesis should occur on at least a semicontinuous basis, with feedback going into disciplinary components. Completing the process involves developing peer-group consensus on the adequacy, consistency, and validity of not only the data but also the types of conclusions that can be supported from data, the range of valid applications, and selection of visual displays and tabulations of data. Iterative judgment and reformulation of hypotheses play an important role in interpretation. Sharp also stresses the value of an "old-fashioned naturalist" or generalist who can appraise data as they relate to system behavior. Depicted diagrammatically in Figure 2.1, degrees of interpretation and synthesis may be discriminated: summing the disciplinary results on top versus a less limited summation of component results in the middle versus a total data interpretation and synthesis that depends on having adequate correlatable data and unrestricted database services (on the bottom).

Clearly, a large-scale computerized data base has a profound potential for integration. Elsewhere, Theodore Hershberg (1981) has called the machine-readable data base a kind of "research laboratory" that can also support "mutidisciplinary" and "interdisciplinary" research in the humanities and social sciences as well, an instrument comparable to the microscope in the biological sciences. In the Philadelphia Social History Project (PSHP), a large-scale investigation of how urbanization and industrialization shaped the development of nineteenth-century Philadelphia and the

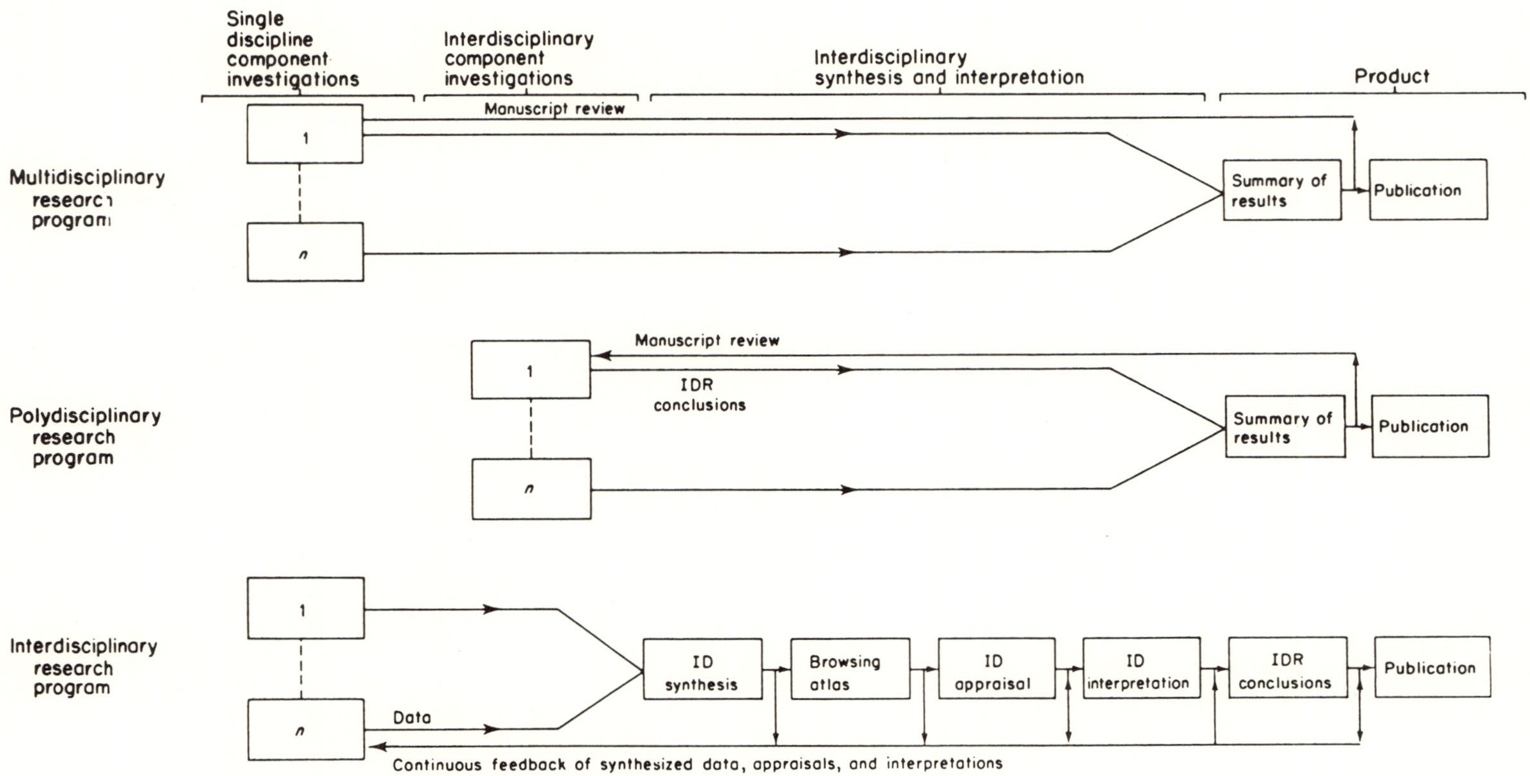

Figure 2.1. Comparison of alternative research schemes

experience of its diverse population, such a data base acted as a "magnet" for researchers from other disciplines. As the project grew, it shifted from strictly disciplinary methods to a "multidisciplinary" focus on four substantive areas, and, ultimately, prior to its termination, the beginning of an interdisciplinary focus on new analytic goals emphasizing integrative over discrete studies. This shift toward an integrative set of analytic goals in the PSHP corresponds to the shift from disciplinary to problem perspectives observed in pharmaceutics (Stucki 1979) and a large-scale ecosystem project (Barmark and Wallen 1979).

Organizing frameworks and key research questions have also played a vital role in integrating knowledge, not only in such problem-oriented projects as coping with increased carbon dioxide levels in the atmosphere and ecosystem research in general (Chen 1981, pp. 437–29) but also in interdisciplinary education. Based on his experience as director of a large-scale project concerned with human effects on Lake Tahoe (Nevada), McEvoy (1972) concluded that the existence of a framework into which diverse data can be arrayed to make conceptual sense is vital, especially in large projects with many subsystemic relations. The framework permits conceptual integration of diverse metrics and the data gathered. In a different context (Klein and Nachbar 1982), an undergraduate course on "Approaches to Value in a Technological Culture," instructors ensured integration in three ways: by establishing four controlling questions, by asking that controlling questions be answered in relation to three areas of a dialectical framework, and by devoting a segment of the course to synthesis. The dialectical framework enabled students to integrate material from separate disciplines (literature, the arts, philosophy, and popular culture) around a thesis (a positive approach to technology), antithesis (a negative approach), and, finally, synthesis (a position that accounted for technology as an integral part of human nature). This example is just one indication of a growing belief that the relationship between disciplinarity and interdisciplinarity is a dialectical one, based on defining connections and resolving contradictions into a coherent synthesis.

MODELS OF THE PROCESS

In describing an interdisciplinary model of general education, Hursh, Haas, and Moore (1983) have diagrammed the process for interdisciplinary study of a given problem, based on two levels. The first level is one of clarification, developing an understanding of both the salient concepts and the skills to be used in evaluating those concepts. *Power,* for example, is a concept relevant to virtually all the social sciences, each with its own definitions. By contrasting the ambiguities and assumptions of those definitions, students can understand and practice the skill of clarification and build higher-order constructions, to accommodate discrepancies. They can gather a list of disciplinary definitions of power and construct a composite meaning consistent with the disciplines under consideration. The second level is one of resolution, centered on a more thorough integration of the different perspectives identified by the definitions of *salient concepts* in the different disciplines involved. Students can challenge their conclusions by combining input from more than one discipline and working toward a more comprehensive understanding of the problem at hand. This process (Figure 2.2) depends on using the fundamental interdisciplinary skills of differentiating, comparing, contrasting, relating, clarifying, reconciling, and synthesizing (Newell and Green 1982).

Writing in the context of bioethics, Maurice de Wachter (1982) has conceptualized the interdisciplinary process in a more complex five-phase model based on using methodical epochè, a philosophical technique that calls for the temporary suspension of all known methods. Its purpose is to achieve an interdisciplinary way of stating a global question.

Figure 2.2. Interdisciplinary process

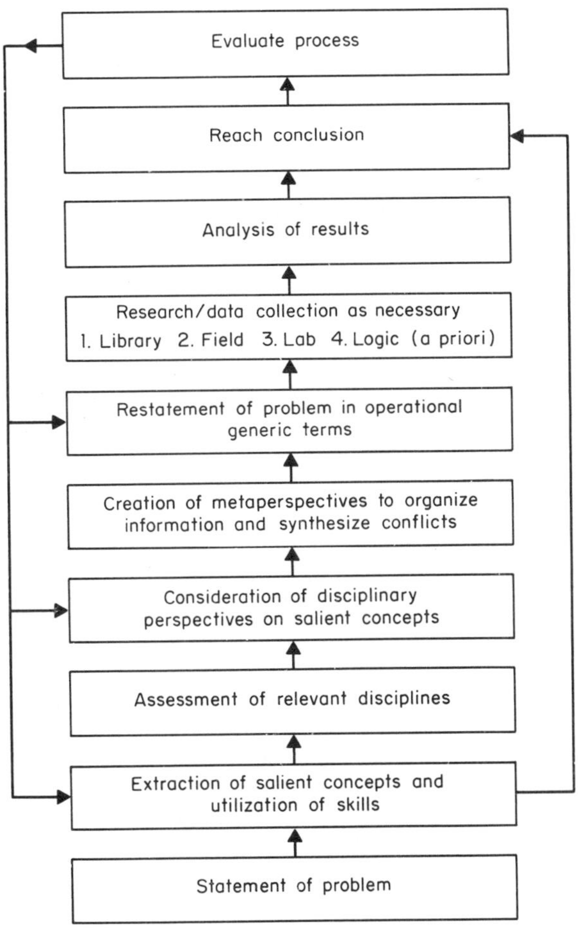

Bioethics, de Wachter explains, does not substitute for the competencies and responsibilities of traditional disciplines. Rather, it confirms and sometimes reinforces the autonomy of other disciplines, putting them into wider perspective, adding new tasks and responsibilities to previous ones. Ideally, there are five phases in the interdisciplinary process: (1) accepting methodical epochè by having all disciplines abstain from approaching the topic along lines of their own monodisciplinary methods, (2) trying to formulate in an interdisciplinary way the global question (acknowledging all aspects as well as the total network), (3) translating the global question into the specific language of each participating discipline, (4) constantly checking the answer to this translated question by checking for its relevance in answering the global question, and (5) agreeing upon a global answer which must not be produced by any one particular discipline but rather integrating all particular answers. This ideal model may be pictured as in Figure 2.3.

This is, however, an idealized model. Realistically speaking, the best chance of succeeding lies in starting at the level of the third phase of idealized interdisciplinarity and trying to work back to the original epochè, as depicted in Figure 2.4.

CONCLUSIONS

When planning to implement integrative techniques and follow models of the interdisciplinary process, it is wise to remember Sjölander's (1985) cautionary description of the ten stages in the typical progression of an interdisciplinary venture. At Stage 1, participants often spend their time singing the old songs, presenting themselves, their work, and their answers to any conceivable criticism. Short-term meetings and workshops attended by larger groups may never get past this stage. At Stage 2, everyone on the other

Figure 2.3. Ideal interdisciplinary model

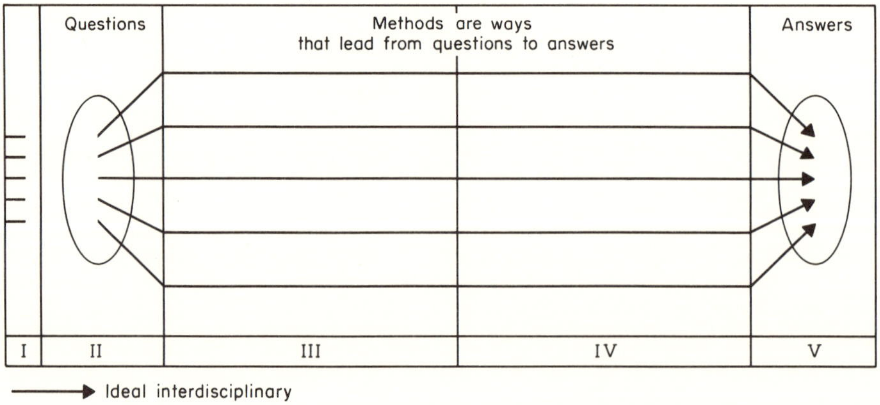

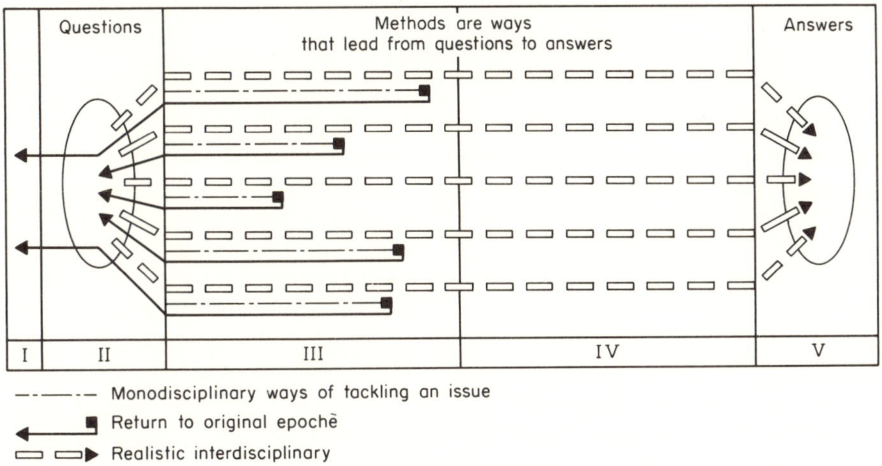

Figure 2.4. Realistic interdisciplinary model

side is an idiot, as individuals begin detecting the deficiencies in each other's position. Many quit the venture at this point, regarding it as a waste of time. At Stage 3, participants may be found retreating into abstractions, as a way of finding common ground for discussions. The more abstract things are, the easier it is to agree. However, while there may be a general feeling of progress, difficulties will return as questions are asked about the more concrete results of discussions. When participants are not able to account for the content and results of discussions, a project may remain indefinitely at this stage. At Stage 4, the definition sickness sets in, as colleagues ask each other to define technical terms and discover that use of more general, philosophical terms varies. Developing a jargon specific to the group has its merits but does make it difficult for new members to join. At Stage 5, participants can begin concentrating on fruitful discussion areas, if the earlier stages have been passed successfully. However, the areas may be quite disparate: one in methods, another in the use of statistics, a third in a general attitude toward experimental work, or in a holistic framework. Discussion will tend to jump from one area to another, much like jumping the tussocks in a quagmire.

At Stage 6, participants will play the glass bead game, building on common jargon and the common group. This is an undeniably positive step, in that a common framework may be the starting point for something really new and fruitful. However, it is a time-consuming process and may prove no more successful than earlier methods; by Stage 7, the great failure surfaces. After wallowing in abstractions and playing glass bead games, participants begin to despair of their time and effort. Yet, when asked to produce some kind of report of the activity and results at this stage, many find their interests rekindled. Projects that stop at this stage are usually considered to have ended just when they could have really become fruitful.

Participants who make it to Stage 8 may well find themselves wondering what's happening to them. They have changed in more ways than they may be aware of consciously. This realization often comes as they return to their original places of work or when they describe the results of a project to colleagues in their own disciplines. In many cases, they have become better advocates or at least "reluctant defenders" of the disciplines with which they have interacted, strengthening and rekindling their interests in further interdisciplinary work. Those who left projects in a pessimistic mood will deplore their failure to spend more time on the project or to have a follow-up activity, a beneficial event months or even years after a project. Evaluations immediately upon termination of a project may be far more negative than evaluations measuring long-term growth, a tactical measure to consider when seeking funds for interdisciplinary projects and institutions. Stage 9 is getting to know the enemy, moving toward a more in-depth knowledge of other disciplines, in terms of not only immediate knowledge for the project but also the discipline's general structures, principles, and ways of thinking. Stage 10 is the real beginning, reached after long-term work or repeated meetings and often productive of results at an astounding rate. The common occurrence of interaction and cooperation that appears long after the termination of a project may even be the starting point for new disciplines and research areas.

Interdisciplinary work is often attacked for lacking rigor. However, rigor is not diminished. Rather, it is shifted from disciplinary criteria to a new interdisciplinary objective, to what Singleton (1983) calls a core sense of "interdisciplinary rigor." There are no clearly defined standards for judging interdisciplinary work, but Stephen Schneider's three criteria for interdisciplinary excellence are quite appropriate. Excellence in interdisciplinary research can be measured in terms of (1) disciplinary clarity, (2) clarity of cross-disciplinary communications, and (3) the utilization and combination of existing knowledge from many fields to help solve a problem or to raise or advance knowledge about a new issue (Schneider 1977). While there is merit to James Beck's contention that the interdisciplinary approach holds all disciplines potentially useful—"the more fields, the better" (Beck 1980)—there can be no such thing as a "light basic dose of interdisciplinary thinking" (Beck 1982). Good interdisciplinary work comes of hard work and a commitment to a core sense of interdisciplinary rigor. There are no guarantees for making it to Stage 10, but having a greater understanding of the interdisciplinary process and using integrative techniques will enhance the prospects considerably.

REFERENCES

Ackermann, Lynne, et al. 1983. Role clarification: A procedure for enhancing interdisciplinary collaboration on the rehab team. Paper presented at the 60th

Annual Session of the American Congress of Rehabilitation Medicine, Los Angeles.

Barmarck, J., and G. Wallen. 1979. The interaction of cognitive and social factors in steering a large scale interdisciplinary project. In R. T. Barth and R. Steck, eds., *Interdisciplinary research groups: Their management and organization.* Vancouver: IRGIP, pp. 180–90.

Beck, J. P. 1980. Theory and practice of interdisciplinary English. *English Journal* 69:28–32.

———. 1982. Thinking across the curriculum. *California English* (Jan.–Feb.).

Birnbaum, Philip H. 1978. Academic contexts of interdisciplinary research. *Educational Administration Quarterly* 14:80–97.

Chen, Robert S. 1981. Interdisciplinary research and integration: The case of CO_2 and climate. *Climatic Change* 3(4):429–47.

De Wachter, Maurice. 1982. Interdisciplinary bioethics: But where do we start? A reflection on epoch as method. *Journal of Medicine and Philosophy* 7:275–87.

Hershberg, Theodore. 1981. Epilogue: Sustaining interdisciplinary research. In Theodore Hershberg, ed., *Philadelphia: Work, family, and group experience in the nineteenth century, essays toward an interdisciplinary history of the city.* Oxford: Oxford University Press, pp. 492–95.

Hursh, Barbara, Paul Haas, and Michael Moore. 1983. An interdisciplinary model to implement general education. *Journal of Higher Education* 54:42–59.

Kann, Mark E. 1979. The political culture of interdisciplinary explanation. *Humanities in Society* 2:195–200.

Klein, J. T. 1989. *Interdisciplinarity: History, theory, and practice.* Detroit: Wayne State University Press.

Klein, Thomas, and Jack Nachbar. 1982. In search of technology. *Science, Technology and Society* [Curriculum Newsletter of the Lehigh University STS Program] 29:1–9.

Koepp-Baker, Herbert. 1979. The craniofacial team. In Kenneth R. Bzoch, ed., *Communicative disorders related to cleft lip and palate.* Boston: Little, Brown, p. 54.

Logan, R., and M. McKendry. 1982. The multi-disciplinary team: A different approach to patient management. *New Zealand Medical Journal* 95(722):88.

McEvoy, James. 1972. Multi- and interdisciplinary research: Problems of initiation, control, integration and reward. *Policy Sciences* 3(2):201–8.

Mar, B., W. T. Newell, and B. Saxberg. 1976. Interdisciplinary research in the university setting. *Environmental Science and Technology* 10(7):650–53.

Newell, W. H., and W. J. Green. 1982. Defining and teaching interdisciplinary studies. *Improving College and University Teaching* 30(1):23–30.

Schneider, Stephen N. 1977. Climate change and the world predicament: A case study of interdisciplinary research. *Climatic Change* 1:21–43.

Sharp, J. M. 1984. A method for peer group appraisal and interpretation of data developed in interdisciplinary research programs. In S. R. Epton, R. L. Payne, and A. W. Pearson, eds., *Managing interdisciplinary research.* Chichester: John Wiley & Sons, pp. 211–19.

Singleton, Rivers Jr. 1983. Interdisciplinary teaching with humanists: Reflections of a biological scientist. *Perspectives in Biology and Medicine* 26(2):304–14.

Sjölander, Sverre. 1985. Long-term and short-term interdisciplinary work: Difficulties, pitfalls and built-in failures. In Lennart Levin and Ingemar Lind, eds.,

Inter-disciplinarity revisited: Re-assessing the concept in the light of institutional experience. Stockholm: OECD/CERI, SNBUC, Linköping University, pp. 85–92.

Stone, A. 1969. The interdisciplinary research team. *Applied Behavioral Science* 5:351–65.

Stucki, J. C. 1979. A goal-oriented pharmaceutical research and development organization: An eleven year experience. In R. T. Barth and R. Steck, eds., *Interdisciplinary research groups: Their management and organization.* Vancouver: IRGIP, pp. 77–96.

White, Irvin L. 1975. Interdisciplinarity. In S. Arnstein and A. N. Christakis, eds., *Perspectives on technology assessment.* Washington, D.C.: Academy for State and Local Governments, p. 284.

Winthrop, Henry. 1964. Methodological and hermeneutic functions in interdisciplinary education. *Educational Theory* 14:118–27.

3

Resilience of Interdisciplinary Research Organizations: Case Studies of Preconditions and Life-Cycle Patterns

ILAN VERTINSKY
PATRICIA VERTINSKY

This paper investigates the relationships between preconditions characterizing the creation of interdisciplinary research organizations (IDROs) and their likely life cycles under alternative environmental scenarios. The paper employs three alternative basic paradigms of organizational behavior and decision processes in order to obtain alternative perspectives and predictions with respect to the resilience of IDROs in coping with changing environments. The three theoretical frameworks follow the classic work of Allison (1971) and include (1) the rational decision paradigm, (2) the organizational behavior/bounded rationality paradigm, and (3) the political/ bureaucratic behavior paradigm. The predictions made on the basis of the implications of the three paradigms are assessed using case studies of three interdisciplinary research organizations.

Specifically, this paper deals with broadly aimed interdisciplinary research organizations, that is, organizations that are not designed to deal with a specific, well-defined problem or a class of problems.

Broadly aimed interdisciplinary research organizations typically evolve in academic environments such as universities, science academies, or publicly funded basic science research establishments. The lack of well-defined objectives and the relatively autonomous position of such organizations present them with the particular challenge of developing the means for legitimizing their activities and claims for resources, as well as developing internally a rationale and framework for decision making. The management of a high level of both the external and internal uncertainties that face such organizations determines, to a large extent, their ability not only to survive but to sustain their interdisciplinary nature.

Our major hypothesis is that a prime danger to the survival of IDROs stems from strategies initiated by their management to reduce external and internal uncertainties. The validity of this hypothesis will be explored through an analysis of three case studies. Those implications concerning the conditions that must prevail externally to the IDRO and the particular features that must be incorporated into its organizational design are also addressed.

THE EVOLUTION OF IDROs

Typically, IDROs are initiated as a response of the scientific community to external opportunities and challenges and/or as a means of dealing with certain problems or opportunities that stem from the nature of the scientific process of knowledge creation itself.

Beam (1982, p. 60) has pointed to the continuing historical trend toward narrower compartmentalization and finer fragmentation of knowledge: "Fragmentation impedes the cross-fertilization of ideas across discipline boundaries and prevents the emergence of more general and more parsimonious conceptual structures." In the search for rigor that characterizes the evolution of scientific disciplines, specialization increases and leads to the proliferation of knowledge-generating units (subdisciplines). Increasing specialization and rigor strengthens boundaries between knowledge units. The fragmented and autonomous nature of the scientific community results in the isolated development of knowledge by different epistemic communities with little coordination among them, creating both duplication and gaps. The development of an IDRO is often viewed as a way of identifying and colonizing researchable areas that have been neglected by the various disciplines, or as a means of interdisciplinary cross-fertilization. The development of IDROs as a fish-scale structure within universities or other departmentalized academic institutions tends to take the form of low-resource organizations inhabited by members whose major institutional role and identification belong to the departmental disciplinary structure.

External opportunities for the creation of IDROs often arise in response to urgent societal missions or problems. Since the traditional modes of scientific knowledge generation are based on a philosophy of knowledge that offers no kind of "justification" for the pursuit of knowledge (Maxwell 1984), the organizational molds that have evolved for the pursuit of scientific knowledge are inadequate for responding to problem-solving tasks. Governments, directly or indirectly (through special funding programs), encourage the creation of new types of research organizations defined (at least initially) in terms of the problem rather than the discipline. Broadly defined problems or problems that are ill defined and in need of definition are multidimensional and uncertain in nature. The safest feasible strategy of initially dealing with a highly uncertain and ill-defined problem is that of diversification. Diversification means attacking a problem from a variety of perspectives and employing a diversified portfolio of research technologies. Funding agencies in many Western countries have deliberately promoted the establishment of IDROs in response to changing national priorities. In doing so, their objectives were (1) to bypass the dysfunctional molds of organization within the academic community that have emerged over generations to protect autonomy and freedom from immediate societal demands, and (2) to mobilize a broad range of research technologies to grapple with ill-defined problems that do "not come in disciplinary-shaped blocks" (Klein 1985). IDROs were established directly as fully funded independent research institutes, or promoted through institutional grants and contracts awarded to universities. The highly visible Manhattan Project in the 1940s provided a salient example of the potential of a mission-oriented interdisciplinary effort. The challenge of Sputnik in 1957 was met by the establishment in the United States of NASA, which promoted the creation of many interdisciplinary organizations within universities (e.g., the Space Laboratory at Berkeley), in addition to its own internal IDROs.

The attention to social problems that characterized the late 1960s and early '70s created incentives and opportunities for IDROs in the social and managerial sciences. The environmental and "limits to resources" challenges of this era led to the emergence of IDROs that linked the biological, social, and managerial sciences. (Indeed, the case studies described in a later section of this paper represent examples of the emergence of IDROs in the late 1960s as a response to a variety of social, environmental, and economic challenges.)

The recognition of the limits of disciplinary science and its underlying philosophy of knowledge created a demand for a new philosophy which, on the one hand, promoted interaction between the intellectual domain of inquiry and the social world (Maxwell 1984) and, on the other, promoted a holistic or systems point of view.

The emergence of such philosophies and their derived methodologies of inquiry (e.g., general systems theories, operations research, systems analysis) provided both direction and a rationale for some IDROs. Fads and fashions, coupled with strong financial incentives, however, gave rise to a number of IDROs that could be characterized as "opportunistic entities" (Teich 1979, p. 242), lacking in philosphical commitment to "generalist" or "unified" knowledge. Klein (1985, p. 119) describes some of the experiences of such IDROs initiated in the early 1970s: "Born of pressures for solving problems outside the narrow scope of the academic world, IDR projects were themselves plagued by disciplinary chauvinism and the psychological, social, and epistemological problems of communicating across specialties."

The internal and external forces that promote "disciplinary chauvinism" are prime ingredients of the decay of IDROs as interdisciplinary institutions and/or causes of their more limited life span. Those organizational design features that help to resocialize members toward acquiring interdisciplinary problem-oriented research norms are critical preconditions for the resilience of IDROs.

PRECONDITIONS TO ORGANIZATIONAL SURVIVAL AND GROWTH

An analysis of organizational survival and growth can be informed by the application of alternative, general paradigms of organizational behavior. In this paper we employ three alternative paradigms to study the relationship among environmental conditions, design features, and the resilience and dynamics of IDROs. The three paradigms suggested by Allison (1971) are: (1) the rational decision model, (2) the bounded/rationality/organizational decision model, and (3) the bureaucratic-political model.

The rational framework views the organization and its clients as rational, purposive entities. Evolutionary organizational paths are examined or predicted in terms of the teleological relationships of inputs-outputs-objectives (or preferences). The bounded rationality/organizational decision model views the organization as an entity that must cope with a complex and uncertain world with high research costs. The organization (1) develops heuristics and mechanisms to reduce uncertainty, (2) behaves myopically in response to threats and opportunities as they arise, and (3) initiates search when threatened or when the status quo becomes unacceptable to its members. This paradigm also recognizes that organizations typically consist of subunits with parochial, sometimes conflicting objectives, differentiated perceptions and experiences, and faulty (or at least noisy) internal communication networks. The third paradigm recognizes that organizations are embedded within a large political game (internally and externally) where stakeholders act to acquire power and use power to defend their stakes. The political model explicitly recognizes the relationship between stakes and stands and the fact that individuals may act as individuals in some circumstances and as specific role holders in others. Analysis must therefore consider the stakes involved for individuals, and for institutions, as well as the environmental triggers that determine which role an individual plays.

Each of the three paradigms implies important preconditions for the creation and resilience of IDROs. First, the rational model suggests that the emergence of an IDRO and its survival depend on the extent to which it provides appropriate technologies for dealing with the legitimate demands of those endowing it with resources. Changing societal priorities cause a change in the nature of the IDRO and its demise. The survival of an IDRO in an environment with changing demands will depend not on the specific portfolio of disciplines and expertise gathered in the organization but on the ability of the organization to manage diverse disciplinary portfolios and focus them upon new types of problems. The rational paradigm thus implies that IDROs need to acquire a unique methodological capacity that can provide bridges between disciplines and match scientific methodologies with problems. The survival of broadly aimed IDROs is contingent upon the existence of such general methodology. If the IDRO is not organized around a core of interdisciplinary, methodological research, its existence as a broadly aimed organization will only be transitory. As ill-defined external challenges and problems are articulated, the focus of the organization will narrow until an optimal portfolio of disciplinary research methodologies and expertise is reached. The solution of the problem signals the optimal term for the life of the IDRO. Indeed, normatively the rational model will prescribe a sunset clause for any broadly aimed IDRO unless a "learning curve" is postulated for general interdisciplinary research (i.e., a core of IDR methodology experts with a peripheral consisting of a changing disciplinary mix of experts).

Second, the bounded rationality/organizational decision process model predicts that IDROs are likely to face strong resistance when grafted onto regular departmental structures (e.g., creating interdisciplinary programs or institutes in universities). The pressure will be intense for molding IDROs to standard procedures and programs of the institution, with little attention to the arrangements that would allow the optimal pursuit of the goals or functions of the IDRO. For example, an IDRO created within a departmentalized institution tends to adopt the reward systems and membership rules of regular disciplinary departments. The incompatibility of these reward systems and functions leads inevitably, over time, to a disciplinary convergence. Representatives of disciplines characterized by a higher degree of rigor will, in the long run, assume leadership. Recruitment patterns will ensure a shift in the mix of disciplines in favor of those characterized by rigor, with little regard for the fit of disciplinary mix and the mission of the IDRO. In contrast, an IDRO designed de novo with standard operating procedures suitable to its task but in discord with rules and regulations operating in the larger institution is likely to become isolated. It will be exposed to forces aimed at detaching it from the organization and its resources. In addition, IDROs are likely to lose, over time, their flexible structure and innovativeness. As any other organizational unit, IDROs develop standard operating procedures, programs, and solutions as a means of coping with complexity and uncertainty. Standardization tends to replace innovation, and the search for new solutions becomes triggered only when crises threaten. Within the IDRO, subunits develop parochial goals and particularized standard operating procedures and programs. The quest for certainty and the reduction of noisy communication lines lead to the creation of informal subunits along disciplinary lines. Over time, these subunits also develop parochial objectives, procedures, and programs leading to the institutionalization of disciplinary chauvinistic forces. The paradigm implies that an important design precondition for promoting the resilience of an IDRO is an internal structure that ensures that nuclear subunits contain an interdisciplinary mix, a counterforce that will exist to counteract the tendency of members from the same discipline to form powerful subunits. The theory also implies that an independent existence of IDROs outside the traditional disciplinary structure of the basic science establishment (e.g., universities) is desirable. Such independence, however, may be developed only at the cost of those economies to scope and scale that existence within a larger structure can offer. The existence of IDROs within a traditional structure must be ensured by the careful design of reward and recruitment procedures, independent funding, and a favorable exchange relationship between the IDRO and its mother institution which will create incentives for both to preserve the links. Finally, the paradigm implies that environmental shocks are the prime means for stimulating innovation. Planned crises such as external, periodic reviews and performance assessments may be an institutional means for ensuring the development of flexible response capabilities which permit IDROs to adapt to shifting environments and changing problems.

Third, the political/bureaucratic paradigm implies that the survival and developmental path of an IDRO depends on the power with which it was initially endowed, the changes that occur in this endowment as a result of external circumstances, or the skills of the organization and its leaders to preserve and build power. The sources of power can be diverse. The ability of an organization to meet the demands of client organizations is a source of power. The desired or valued output of the organization may not be the one specified in its charter or the contract(s) leading to its creation. Some organizations are initiated by governments, not necessarily as means for solving specific social problems but as a way of diffusing pressures upon them to act or excusing delay. Under such circumstances, performance that directly relates to the task environment may reduce rather than enhance the power of the organization. A failure to communicate with client (and potential client) organizations means that organizational output is less visible and consequently less effective in mobilizing support. The ability of an organization to remove or create uncertainty for others is also a source of power (and a source of threat that others may seek to avert and eliminate). Thus, knowledge and information are important strategic resources that can be used to secure organizational survival. Material resources (e.g., funds, space, equipment, support services) are also a source of power, especially if they are used, through exchanges, to develop support for the organization. Abundant scarce resources may attract researchers seeking to acquire them. The strategic advantage offered by material resources depends, to a large extent, on the flexibility and speed with which they can be mobilized. An organization that efficiently uses the resource base with little remaining uncommitted slack is likely to experience internal conflict which can destroy its ability to deal with external threats or opportunities. Indeed, life cycles of many IDROs indicate that an initial resource boom leading to internal overcommitment of resources results, in the longer run, in a loss of flexibility and a process of severe internal fragmentation and territorial defense by subunits. The elimination of slack in resources provides external enemies with a sensitive lever upon organizational activities. Finally, one must consider the power that stems from ideas, symbols, and personalities involved in an IDRO. Some organizations are created as an expression of the messianic missions of their founders. The power of ideas embodied in an organization, usually with a charismatic leader, can attract converts along with a strong commitment to work with and spread these ideas. As the organization becomes more complex and bureaucratic, the messianic mission ideas dim with the power and enthusiasm that stems from them. The size of resources garnered in the first stage, the institutionalization of ideas, and the organizational design that emerges to support them all determine the ability of the organization to survive changes of style and leadership. The political model implies that those preconditions that increase the resilience of an IDRO are (1) an adequate resource base with management that retains slack and flexibility of resource deployment, (2) an initial messianic leadership with a strong commitment to the basic philosophy of IDR followed by the institutionalization of the philosophy and leadership, (3) the capability to monitor demands of client organizations and produce valued outputs for them, and (4) communication capabilities. The political model views institutional dynamics as a game through which units and subunits compete for scarce resources and control on actions and outcomes as well as for power. Power is the ability to affect and control future actions in the system, thus ensuring future claims on resources, actions, and outcomes. Units can garner power by exchange relationships and the formation of coalitions that will shift over time in response to changing patterns of power. Changes in the external environment may result in changes in the power structure. Thus, for example, the Sputnik crisis created unparalleled opportunities for the science establishment in the United States: shifting social priorities triggered shifts in the power base of different scientific communities and contributed to the emergence and the decline of different types of research organizations. The nature of internal politics is an important factor affecting the resilience of an IDR organization. Individuals view organizational life from a variety of perspectives and engage in the political game to defend not only their personal stakes but also the stakes they believe they hold as role-players in the organization (i.e., organizational stakes that are internalized by role-players). The strength of the process of socialization determines, to a large degree, the allocation of effort by organizational members in pursuit of opportunistic (individual) objectives and organizational objectives. Organizations that provide the best match between the two, through reward systems, side payments, or socialization, are more likely to mobilize their resources and ensure organizational survival than are other organizations. When members of an organization do not internalize its values and when reward systems fail to reinforce commitment to such values, one can expect fragmentation and parochialism to emerge. An external threat will ultimately result in personnel desertion and the abandonment of the organization. Thus, the political model predicts that if socialization mechanisms (including reward systems and recruitment patterns) are faulty, organizational resilience will be low.

THREE CASE STUDIES

The predictive power of the general paradigms of organizational behavior just described are illustrated using three case studies of IDROs, each in a different area of the world: (1) the Institute of Animal Resource Ecology, University of British Columbia, Vancouver, Canada (IARE); (2) the International Institute of Management in Berlin, West Germany (IIM); and (3) the Multi-Disciplinary Committee for Research on Health in Cali, Colombia (CIMS). All three institutions were created in the late 1960s. IIM still remains, though with a significantly altered structure and philosophy. IARE was recently closed in anticipation of the emergence of a new interdisciplinary structure with a new focus. CIMS was relatively short-lived. The three units were developed as broad-purpose organizations: IIM to promote the development of management resources in West Germany, CIMS to promote health and social development, and IARE to initiate interdisciplinary research in the management of natural resources.

Establishment and Composition

IIM was the only one of the three institutes under discussion to be established as an independent entity—an independent section of the proposed Science Center of Berlin (but initially the only part). It was incorporated as a private corporation with ownership vested in the Berlin government and the West German federal government. IARE was established as an institute within the University of British Columbia in Canada, with a center attached to it as a means for achieving further flexibility in managing projects exceeding the bounds of the IARE mandate. CIMS was established as an organization within the Universidad del Valle in Colombia and was given little formal organizational structure.

Initially, IARE consisted mainly of zoologists, with the addition of some members from regional planning, the faculty of forestry, and the faculty of business administration. All members of IARE were jointly appointed between the institute and departments representing the "generic fields." In addition to the regular members, members from other faculties ranging from architecture to medicine were associated with the center attached to IARE. The center housed a large interinstitutional, interdisciplinary project focusing on regional systems management. For this project the center coopted members from some of its client organizations (the city, the Ministry of Urban Affairs, and the Regional Development Board). IIM recruited most of its members from a variety of business schools and economics departments, with a minority coming from other social science departments and law faculties. Members (research fellows) were contracted for periods ranging from several months to five years (with renewable contracts). The emphasis on recruiting in the first phase of IIM's growth was on academic excellence, with the idea that interdisciplinary, innovative projects would emerge spontaneously from the presence of a variety of skills and perspectives in the same working space. CIM's membership consisted mainly of doctors from the faculty of medicine and the University Hospital and members of the architecture department. Other participants were drawn from the engineering faculty and some of the social science departments. Membership was defined by commitment to CIMS, its meetings, and research and service activities.

Financial Arrangements

IIM was established with large financial commitments from two levels of government. The establishment of IIM had the political objective (apart from the specific task of conducting management research) of helping develop West Berlin as a vital cultural center of West Germany, thus ensuring the survival and growth of a city geographically isolated from the rest of the republic. International prestige and membership were thus important attributes of the institute.

IARE was funded by a large five-year grant from a foundation. In order to receive the grant, the university committed itself to absorb the budgets of the institute into its regular operating budget. A further large joint government-foundation grant, managed through the center for its major project, provided slack resources in the initial phase of IARE's existence. CIMS was funded mainly from departmental and hospital budgets, though large grants from the World Health Organization were anticipated. (These anticipations, however, were never realized.)

Leadership

The three IDROs all enjoyed charismatic leadership in their initial phases. CIMS's leadership, however, was very soon transferred to those in charge of specific activities. IARE and IIM enjoyed a relatively longer tenure of their founding leaders, permitting the evolution of formal organizational structures of governance before a transfer of leadership. In IARE, the transfer of leadership took place after the effective separation (and basically death) of the attached center. In IIM, the leadership was transferred and broadened to two directors, one German and the other a foreigner. Slack resources were relatively abundant during the transfer.

Internal Structure

The internal structure of the three IDROs preserved, to a large degree, disciplinary nuclei. IARE, however, emphasized a methodological core independent of disciplinary focus-simulation modeling. IIM, while establishing a method group alongside other thematic-disciplinary groups, did not establish channels that might link them together. Interdisciplinary interaction in CIMS was achieved through ad hoc subproject coordination; that is, the task environment dictated the required expertise and interdisciplinary consultations. A regular seminar provided the vehicle for program activity coordination and also facilitated joint research. The CIMS model in this sense was an extension of the team approach in the delivery of health-care services (i.e., a professional cooperative mode).

Developmental Phases

The first phase of each of the three institutes reflected four general characteristics: (1) the type and size of resource endowments, (2) the internal structure, (3) the leadership, and (4) the definition and bounds of the task environment.

The structure of funding for IARE and its associated center led to a dichotomous structure—both permanent and transitory. To become a permanent structure within the university, the institute had to accept existing university standard operating procedures with only minor modifications. Thus, appointments to the institute were regular tenure-track appoints, a fact that required a disciplinary appointment in addition to institute membership. Control over a relatively well-endowed purse implied that the institute, by offering "free" services to departments (i.e., by assuming a disproportional share of salaries), could influence the type of joint appointments—at least in the early stages. Capitalizing on the strength of its ideas and relative freedom from routine teaching duties, the institute attracted senior researchers from both government laboratories and other universities, researchers who otherwise would resist joining regular departments. The institute was thus used by departments as a means of recruiting for their own departmental purposes. The exchange between the institute and departments was floated on the large pool of resources available to the institute. The center attracted associate members from various faculties on the strength of its ideas, its visibility, the use of marginal seed funds, and the provision of shared research services (e.g., support staff, computer facilities, etc.). The dual structure that evolved became a constant source of conflict once the side payments and exchanges between the center and the institute and between the institute and the departments strained the increasingly committed pool of funds. The cementing force at the early stage was the development of a core methodology for integrating diverse sources of knowledge (large-scale simulation modeling). Conflicts between core methodologies (modelers and disciplinary scientists) were lessened over time through co-optation and mutual learning. Exchange relationships developed on the basis of mutual improvement in research effectiveness and general recognition of complementarity. The two organizational cultures that evolved in the center and the institute were reconciled initially by a strong charismatic leader and some overlapping membership. The different task environments, however, led to the evolution of different, dominant disciplinary groups within the interdisciplinary structure. A process of selective recruitment and survival, starting in both camps, gradually led to the dominance of zoologists in the permanent structure and economists in the center, with the modelers playing key but diminishing roles in both. The formal separation between the two marked the end of the first phase of the life cycle of the IDRO. The narrowing focus was dictated both by the demand for rationality (i.e., the more precise definition of tasks and selection of appropriate technologies of production) and the limited processing abilities of individual members and the strong professional standard operating procedures they brought with them, implying clearly defined bounds on attention and interest as well as reduction in perceived uncertainty. The task environment led to a dual structure inviting parochialism and modified by an interunit exchange relationship. An increase in the scarcity of resources, however, led to more conflict and a political mode of interrelationships within the IDRO as well as among the other subunits of the university. Charismatic leadership committed to IDR maintained supportive coalitions. The transition of leadership into a more bureaucratic mold marked the second phase of consolidation followed by fragmentation.

IIM, with a broad and ill-defined mandate coupled with independence and abundant resources, initially evolved as a highly productive academic institution with an opportunistic, diversified research agenda based on individual and small group subjects. The cementing forces were the weekly seminar series, workships, conferences, and a charismatic leader. Members (especially senior members) of IIM largely retained memberships (faculty positions) in other universities and considered their stay in IIM as an opportunity to increase their individual productivity. The forced interaction with members from other disciplines proved to be enriching but led, in the long run, to few truly interdisciplinary research programs. As the institute matured, members, administrators, and the external clients searched increasingly for more coherence and focus in its research programs. The tension created by the quest for a collective rational model for the institution and the rational behavior of individuals characterized the transition to the next phase. The temporary nature of membership for many of the senior members meant that collective goals were not of prime concern to administrators, while scientists tended to pursue their interests opportunistically. Since the acquisition of prestige and visibility was an important latent goal of the client organizations, the conflict between these sets of goals was minimal, allowing the institute continued growth in membership and resources. Collective goals were means for enhancing the external legitimacy of the institute rather than guidelines for action and allocation of resources. Growth in size and complexity, however, created a demand for formal structures and decision processes and led to the evolution of standard operating procedures. These were augmented by rules and procedures that characterized the legalistic German environment and managerial culture. In particular, the period saw the increasing role of the elected research council and an increase in the rigidity of its procedures, especially with regard to recruitment of new members.

CIMS, in its first phase of operations, provided the best fit with the predictions of the rational paradigm. Having a dual research and service focus, the task environment was quickly defined in terms of specific objectives. Interdisciplinary teams were formed in such a way as to be able to pursue objectives with maximum effectiveness. Thus, the flexible structures that evolved and the procedures that were adopted were mainly dictated by constraints on both the objectives and available feasible technologies for pursuing goals. The task orientation and the interdisciplinary structure of the teams broke through the traditional technologies of health-service delivery, seeking a better fit with local target populations and utilizing existing endogenous resources. Indeed, it was the very success of CIMS, in terms of its goals, that created the seeds for its early destruction. The lack of organizational depth and permanent structures, in addition to a political environment that was intolerant of rapid social change (even change fitting expressed political goals), brought about the dissolution of CIMS. CIMS was built on the idealistic commitment of its members and survived the fact that expected funding schemes never materialized. The organization failed, however, to understand and cope with organizational environments other than its own task environment. As it became increasingly successful in accomplishing tasks that established, well-funded programs had failed to accomplish, conservative pressures mounted to block its activities. These efforts eventually took the form of withdrawal of permission to use local health-care facilities, since it was suggested that CIMS operations might inflate community demands for health services that could not, in fact, be met. This rationale was in marked contradiction to the expressed philosophy of a health-care delivery system that proclaimed "awareness and health knowledge" as keystones in the achievement of a healthy society.

The second phase in the life cycle of IIM and IARE illustrates the growing importance of the phenomena predicted by the organizational decision paradigm. As slack in resources and procedures is reduced and the organization matures, parochialism begins to spread. A higher degree of complexity and rigidity in standard operating procedures strongly affects organizational dynamics and performance. The leadership that emerges becomes increasingly burdened with the task of consolidation and the honing of procedures, rather than actively engaging in strategic choices. Recruitment patterns tend to strengthen those units with a critical mass, rather than maintaining a careful balance of strengths or building a diversified portfolio of expertise. In our IDROs, pressures from an external environment to define tasks coherently and accurately led IIM to reexamine its relative competence. It focused on a methodology emphasizing international comparisons and adopted two functional themes, each relating to a particular policy domain and, therefore, specific external clients. IARE, now separated from the center, attempted to develop structures paralleling, in many ways, regular departmental structures. These emphasized interdisciplinarity only in terms of joint marginal products on the periphery, or frontiers, of disciplinary work. The most routine interdisciplinary portfolio involved requirements of substantive technical or methodological expertise (e.g., mathematicians and computer modelers). Multifaceted modeling efforts were almost completely abandoned. However, lack of a formal teaching program and degree-granting authority and dysfunctional reward structure hindered it form becoming a department.

The longevity of IDROs appears to be determined, to a large extent, on their ability to develop a permanent power base and attain legitimacy in a larger system. Legitimacy depends on occupying a niche that best utilizes the distinct competencies of the organization. A high level of sustained performance within the bounds of the niche is a source of legitimacy but not a necessary or sufficient condition for its acquisition. IDROs must fit, or appear to fit, their environment, not only in substance but also in form and procedures.

Legitimacy through system inertia reduces the needs of power acquisition and its use of organizational defense. IIM, in its mature stage, has developed organizational structures and standard operating procedures similar to other science-related institutes in Germany. By developing programs along narrower, thematic lines, it was able to create and maintain clients' support. The international and transitory nature of membership has slowly changed to conform to a pattern common to similar German institutions—more permanent and more German. While the international visibility and the academic producitivity of the institute have declined, the coherence of its outputs in terms of the task environment and relevance to client organizations has grown.

IARE—an unusual organization within a university structure—was subjected to numerous attacks from other units in the university. Its lack of formal degree-granting authority, as well as an internal structure not resembling that of other departments, constantly raised the question of legitimacy. Internal fragmentation, neglect in the maintenance of external client groups, as well as an inability to muster internal support, finally led to the official closure of the institute. This occurred despite the well-recognized outstanding publication record of its members and the continuous flow of large amounts of grant money. The trigger for the closure was a university budget crisis, yet, in fact, the closure did not contribute to the solution of the crisis since all members of the institute and its staff were retained. Indeed, the death of the "old" institute created the opportunity for adjustment and renewal that a rigid IDRO could not accomplish. Those in the institute with commitment to modeling and interdisciplinary work have secured the support of new external clients and the university establishment to launch a new program focusing on the management of natural resources. The future will tell whether the emperor really has a new suit of clothes!

CONCLUSION

External preconditions are important in determining organizational survival in the first period of IDRO development. The task environment and type of leadership determine, to a large extent, the path along which internal structures and standard operating procedures evolve. At the first stage, coping with uncertainty in the task environment requires the assembly of a broad interdisciplinary portfolio of expertise. The maintenance of a complex organization characterized by a diversity of technologies imposes high transaction and communication costs. To reduce uncertainties associated with noisy internal communications, tasks are divided, and organizational fragmentation occurs. Parochial standard operating procedures evolve, reducing local uncertainty. Uncertainties are also reduced through the alignment of organizational subdivisions and disciplinary divisions. The task environment, however, may constraint this process of fragmentation, forcing structures that are adopted to tasks or client groups. Thus, external uncertainty may provide a balancing influence on organizational evolution.

At maturity, organizations whose structures and processes do not conform to standard patterns prevailing in the large system create uncertainty for other units in the system. These organizations must constantly defend themselves. Political side bets and exchange ties can reduce these political uncertainties but require ample resource endowments.

REFERENCES

Allison, G. 1971. *The essence of decision: Explaining the Cuban Missile Crisis.* Boston: Little, Brown.

Beam, D. 1982. Fragmentation of knowledge: An obstacle to its full utilization. In K. E. Boulding and Lawrence Senesh, eds., *The optimum utilization of knowledge: Making knowledge serve human betterment.* Boulder, Colo.: Westview Press.

Klein, J. Thompson. 1985. The evolution of a body of knowledge: Interdisciplinary problem focused research. *Knowledge: Creation, Diffusion, Utilization* 7(2):117–42.

Maxwell, N. 1984. *From knowledge to wisdom: A revolution in the aims and methods of science.* Oxford: Basil Blackwell.

Teich, A. 1979. Trends in the organization of academic research: The role of ORU's and full-time researchers. In R. T. Garth and R. Steck, eds., *Interdisciplinary research groups: Their management and organization.* Vancouver: IRGIP.

4

Long-Wave Patterns Influence Research Attitudes

ISRAEL DROR

Research activity is described as driven by science and technology considerations as well as by social and economic forces. On the other hand, research results have impacts on these same input entities. The forces interplay causes and transfers in cyclical patterns of change, where a typical life cycle may be of the order of fifty to sixty years. History of changes in the frequency of innovations and economic cycles are examples of such patterns. Research modes, especially interdisciplinary research, coincide with the evolution phases of different disciplines. Research takes part in the interplay described, and its characteristics may also change in a similar cyclic pattern.

Meetings of people coming from different disciplines are known to facilitate innovations and new ideas and to promote new disciplines. But once a discipline becomes established and mature, it is very difficult for an outsider to enter and make contributions to it. It seems that building a body of knowledge is governed by different forces along its different phases. We suggest that such life-cycle patterns can be better understood within the broader context of society. There one may find entities that impinge one upon another, forming closed loops. And a closed-loop structure, with its embedded feedback routes, is a sure mechanism for cyclic patterns of behavior. The activity known as research comprises many of the aspects relevant to our approach. Interdisciplinary research, being a meeting place for disciplines at different phases, is especially susceptible to this type of force. Some interesting implications may be drawn in this context.

RESEARCH DRIVING FORCES

One of our basic assumptions is that research is a purposeful activity. Some locus has to be defined a priori, a definition of a research problem and aspects that will be investigated. Consequently, at the end of a research project, one expects to find some impact of the results on the predetermined research area—new knowledge that has been acquired, standing problems that have been solved, and so on.

Those input-output relations allow us to set research as a pivot in a loop diagram such as in Figure 4.1. One loop is the applied-research loop. It aims at human need and is driven by socioeconomic forces, believing that research may reveal knowledge leading eventually to the development of some useful product, process, or service. A second loop in Figure 4.1 is the basic-research loop. The forces here are specific to the science and technology world, and their origin is more obscure than that of applied research. However, it can be said that basic research comes also to fulfill humanity needs, and, at the end, results of basic research arrive at the society-economy node (note possible combinations of routes in Figure 4.1). Note that no matter where research originated, its results enter a common pool of knowledge and techniques. We now turn to changes occurring within that pool.

CYCLIC PATTERNS IN TECHNOLOGY

We draw attention here to the work of Mensch (1979), which defined and studied six stages in the transfer of knowledge:

1. Discovery or development of a new theory (perception)
2. Observation of a possible practical application (discovery, basic invention)
3. Proof of the technical practicability of the idea (feasibility)
4. Beginning of market-oriented experiments with the idea (development)
5. Decision to implement the new technology (decision)
6. Production beginning with the new process or the new type of product being introduced in the market (basic innovation)

Mensch analyzed the relevant data of the last two hundred years, dating the stages of basic innovations during that period. Results are given in Table 4.1.

One of the more interesting results was that throughout history innovations seemed to appear in clusters. The clustering coincided with the fact that frequency of discoveries, as well as speed of knowledge transfer, varied in a set pattern (see Figure 4.2). Each cluster lasted twenty to thirty years, and the recurrence period was fifty to sixty years. The cyclic pattern of innovations was found to be highly correlated with phases of the long economic waves, known as Kondratiev cycles (Freeman, 1984). In particular, the economy recovery phase was correlated with high frequency of basic innovation, while low frequency was correlated with a recession phase.

We refer now to the well-known technology life cycle. Such a cycle begins with the emergence of a new technology, based on a cluster of innovations in new products and new processes. Obviously, a period of high frequency of basic innovations is also a period for emergence of new basic

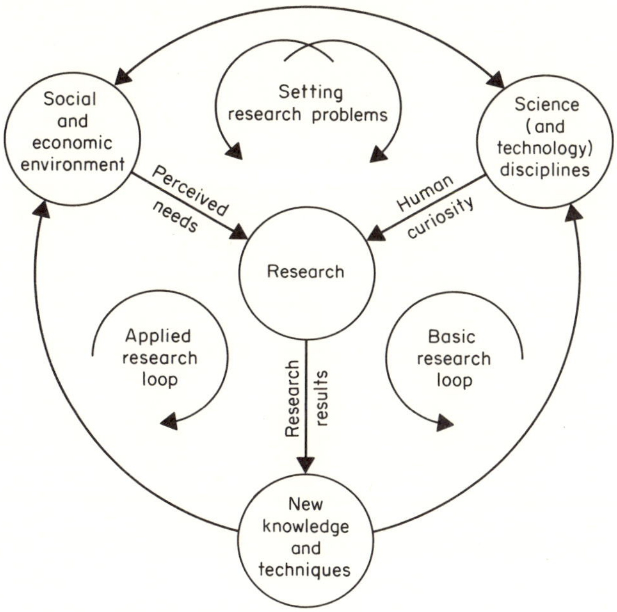

Figure 4.1. Closing research loops

technologies; hence, a wave of new technologies, synchronized with the economic long wave (see Wilkinson 1983).

Accumulation of new knowledge affects the structure of disciplines in several ways. Changes may occur in the content of a discipline and in its definition. Even new disciplines may eventually emerge. Changes in disciplines do occur at a very slow pace. Are those changes correlated with phases of the long waves in economy and technology? If this is the case,

Table 4.1. Frequency distributions of events in the transfer of knowledge

Hurdle in transfer of knowledge	Empirical distribution (μ/σ)			Estimated distribution (μ/σ)
Stage 1	1775/41	1825/39		1935/32
Stage 2			1904/20	1959/17
Stage 3		1826/16	1922/11	1971/10
Stage 4			1928/10	1979/7
Stage 5				1985/5
Stage 6	1825/18	1881/11	1935/8	1989/5

μ = year in which half of all events had taken place

σ = standard deviation in years

Source: From Mensch 1979.

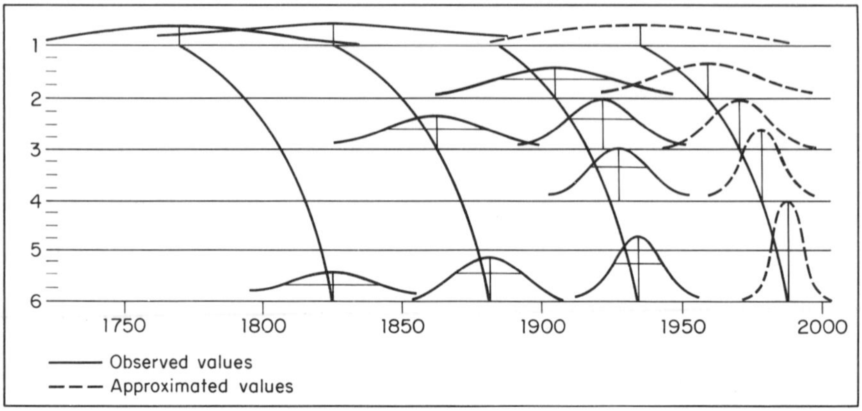

Legend: 1. New theories 2. Basic inventions 3. Technical feasibility 4. Beginning of development 5. Innovation decisions 6. Basic innovations

Source: From Mensch 1979.

Figure 4.2. Composite view of the frequencies of events in the transfer of knowledge

then the cluster of innovations evident in the 1970s and 1980s is to be accompanied by evolutions of discipline areas, by an emergence of new disciplines, and also by a high awareness of interdisciplinary research.

FROM DISCIPLINES TO INTELLECTUAL SKILLS

There is no one satisfactory definition of what a discipline is. Encountering this problem, Porter and Rossini have suggested the notion of intellectual skills needed for research, and they developed the STRAP framework for problem-focused research (Porter and Rossini 1984). They have distinguished between two types of skills: substantive knowledge area (S) and technique (T). Within each type of skill, two levels were defined. For a knowledge area, there is the comprehensive frontier professional skill (S) and, at a lower level, the journeyman, textbook skill (s). For a technique, there is the expert skill (T) and, at a lower level, the technician skill (t). Using the Porter-Rossini notion, we can chart research areas in an S-T plane, as in Figure 4.3. Each point in the chart represents a knowledge-technique pair—a substantive knowledge area and a technique for processing knowledge of this area.

An established research area comprises usually a fixed set of knowledge and technique skills, defined as a discipline. But the same skills, in other combinations, may be used in other disciplines. However, each pair of two knowledge-technique skills belongs to one and only one discipline. Now problem-focused research also needs a set of knowledge and technique skills, but this set is not necessarily contained within the boundaries of a single discipline.

Figure 4.3 charts an example of a research that exploits a set of knowledge-technique skills, applied usually to several different disciplines. The STRAP framework provides for such a case the notion of range (R). In our chart, R is measured by the number of borders crossed within the defined interdisciplinary research area. Note that research may also cross the boundaries of grand disciplinary categories. The range measure should give a higher weight to this type of crossing than to a simple border crossing.

FOCUS ON PROFESSIONAL AND EXPERT SKILLS

The descriptions given above are neat and nice as long as the borders in our chart are well defined. But here we have an inherent difficulty. Research activity not only uses knowledge and techniques, but it also generates new knowledge and invents new techniques. At this point we can make use of the notion of the evolution of disciplines, developed previously.

To be efficient, interdisciplinary research has to distinguish between the

Figure 4.3. A knowledge-technique skills chart

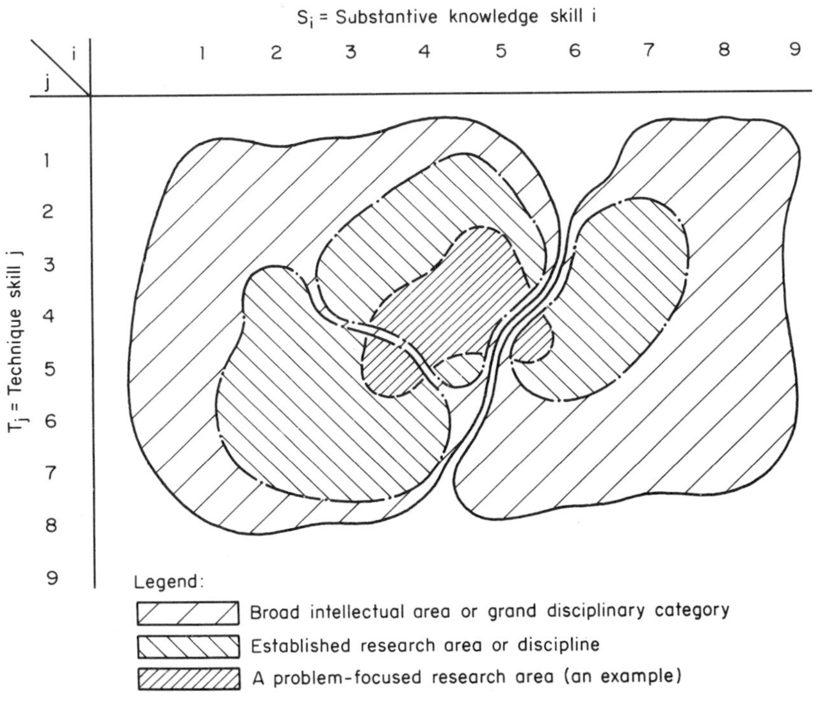

active and passive roles of skills borrowed from the different disciplines. Skills typical of a mature and stable discipline are reckoned to be well established. If needed, they are used as a support activity, not research (e.g., statistical analysis). Usually, such support can be provided by a textbook skill level (s) or technical skill level (t). On the other hand, skills typical of an ascending discipline may still be in their evolutionary mode. Each research project, especially an interdisciplinary research project with its border problems, may introduce changes into the skills. Thus, research in such a case has to regard the relevant knowledge and techniques as part of the problem to be investigated. Professional and expert skills (S and T) have to be incorporated within the core of the research group.

Note that the knowledge-technique skills charts (Figure 4.3) may be used also to map technologies. Applying our nomenclature, technology is defined as a set of techniques and knowledge needed to render a certain product or service. Each technology is thus represented by an area in the knowledge-technique chart, not necessarily limited to any single discipline. Mature technologies may rely on textbook and technician skills (s and t), while professional and expert skills (S and T) are needed for advancing technologies.

An applied research project, with a certain end product as its aim, is very often used as a tool for advancing technologies toward this product. Thus, applied research, though defined in the domain of a single technology application, tends to become a true interdisciplinary research project, and helps in advancing new disciplines.

SUMMARY AND DISCUSSION

This paper has described several environmental parameters that may be seen as preconditions to research at large and to interdisciplinary research in particular. We have tried to show the possibility of a recurrent and cyclic pattern of those parameters, and they are summarized in Table 4.2. Note that a typical life cycle may be of the order of fifty to sixty years. No attempt has been made to establish cause-effect relations among the parameters or to define phase differences between them. However, following our discussion above, it seems that all the parameters of Table 4.2 are interrelated and influence each other. The last entry in Table 4.2 is a result of speculating about cyclic changes in education, changes that may fit the cyclic pattern of the other parameters in the table. That entry was brought as an example to other relevant parameters that could be studied in the context of the model suggested in this paper.

Obviously, more work has to be done before attaining a thorough understanding of the model. Main research questions must refer to links, through which each parameter influences the other ones. Sample questions:

- Do indicators to society interest (e.g., public research grants) support the model suggested here?

Table 4.2. Possibly related cyclic patterns

Parameter \ Mode	Emergence	Maturity
Economy trend	End of depression, recovery phase	End of prosperity, recession phase
Prevailing disciplines	New, evolving disciplines	Time-honored disciplines
Dominant technologies	High technologies	Established technologies
Frequency of innovations	High	Low
Knowledge transfer speed	Fast	Slow
Research focal point	Extending knowledge areas	Profound insight
Research main attitudes	Interdisciplinary	Monodisciplinary
Interdisciplinary research skills needed	Expert and professional skills	Textbook and technician skills
(Speculated) Educational background needed	Broad, philosophical	Deep, narrow expertise

- What attributes precipitate knowledge area growth until it is recognized as an established discipline? How should research problems be posed so as to maximize their effects on that process?
- How did the main thrusts of interdisciplinary research change over time? What governs the setting of research problems?
- How do intellectual environment and availability of knowledge and skills influence the course of research?
- What is the attitude of professionals in mature disciplines toward participation in true interdisciplinary research? Is the attitude of those in evolving disciplines different?
- How does career path influence participation in interdisciplinary research? Is age a factor in the decision to participate?

Studying life-cycle modes described above may help to match research with predicted preconditions. But furthermore, the revealed long-wave patterns may provide an interesting historical perspective on dominant phenomena of our times.

REFERENCES

Freeman, C. 1984. *Long waves in the world economy*. London: France Pinter.
Mensch, G. 1979. *Stalemate in technology*. Cambridge, Mass.: Ballinger.

Porter, A. L., and F. A. Rossini. 1984. Interdisciplinary research redefined: Multi-skill, problem-focused research in the STRAP framework. *R&D Management* 14(2).

Wilkinson, A. 1983. Technology: An increasingly dominant factor in corporate strategy. *R&D Management* 13(4).

II
INTERDISCIPLINARY RESEARCH IN NORTH AMERICA

Interdisciplinary research is long-standing and widely practiced in North America. As indicated in the papers in this section, interdisciplinary research is now common in federal agencies, state governments, industry, and universities. Within the United States, a semblance of the interdisciplinary research approach began in 1862 when Congress passed the Organic Act creating a federal agricultural research organization and the Morrill Act which created the land-grant colleges of agriculture, thus linking the U.S. Department of Agriculture with the academic community in a broad program of agricultural research and education. In 1887, this federal-university cooperative research linkage was expanded by passage of the Hatch Act, creating state agricultural experiment stations supported by formula funding earmarked for each state. The goal was to bring the research efforts of federal, state, and university scientists together to improve crop production and protection systems. Those efforts continue today and have grown increasingly interdisciplinary as science, technology, and economic competitiveness have advanced.

The growing prevalence of interdisciplinary research is not limited to agriculture; it extends to virtually all scientific fields. The explosion of new knowledge, the complexity of societal programs, and the drive to convert scientific advances into technological advantage in the world marketplace have spawned or expanded the need to apply the interdisciplinary approach. Many of the motivating factors and the key issues are discussed in depth in the papers in this section.

5

Developing a Plant Health-Care Initiative in U.S. Agriculture

JOHN M. BARNES

Against the background of strong discipline sciences and strong science departments in the land-grant universities, state and federal scientists initiated dialogue on issues facing U.S. crop production and protection systems. Federal funding provided support for the initial cross-disciplinary workshop, but a national, multidisciplinary professional science consortium was a crucial focal point for organizing the meeting. Initially, there was apparent consensus supporting a proposal for a national plant health-care system. Recently, however, unanimity eroded as perceptions of loss of vested interest and peer discipline status emerged. Nevertheless, a large majority of discipline science leaders feel an urgency to resolve differences, marshalling talents and resources to develop a more holistic, effective system. Predictability of outcome remains elusive. Based upon this experience, a process evaluation paradigm is presented.

BACKGROUND

In the 124 years since Congress passed the Organic Act of 1862 creating a federal agricultural research organization in the U.S. Department of Agriculture and the Second Morrill Act of 1862, which created the land-grant colleges of agriculture, the agricultural research and education base of the United States has continued to be a global leader. In 1887, the Hatch Act created state agricultural experiment stations supported by formula funding earmarked for each state. This funding approach has provided long-term, stable support for state agricultural research, while leveraging funds from other sources and providing seed money for research projects by new faculty. These three pieces of legislation have fostered development of strong discipline science in universities and federal organizations. Discipline strength has been a keystone for the generation and application of basic knowledge.

Today, Western agricultural enterprises have moved into a complex, high-technology arena. The massive accrual of new knowledge is providing the base for technological achievements undreamed of in 1862. Traditional discipline sciences in the United States are now largely composed of subdiscipline specialty fields. Because of past contributions of strong science disciplines to advancement of U.S. agriculture, there has been little pressure to change the basic discipline department organization at the land-grant universities. Research programs in these universities have maintained focus on mission-oriented projects to improve quality of life for each state's clientele. Today these institutions have also developed programs of national and international scope.

It is ironic that along with the promise of even greater technological marvels, the United States is faced with a depressed agricultural economy, declining undergraduate enrollments in colleges of agriculture, escalating costs of training graduate students, and increasing costs to conduct research. There is a pervasive view that we cannot remain organized as at present, nor with unchanging concepts of anticipated crop-management system needs in achieving sustainable productivity with optimized profitability.

THE PROBLEM

More than ten years ago, U.S. science leaders recognized the increasing complexity in managing cropping systems and proposed a national research and action program known as integrated pest management (IPM). The concept recognized the need for increased cross-discipline collaboration in designing and implementing research efforts to provide the basic information needed to mobilize pest-management systems. As the program evolved, economists, systems scientists, and production discipline (e.g., agronomy, horticulture, plant breeding) scientists became involved.

Proposals have been made to broaden the scope of the program, essentially by renaming it (e.g., *integrated crop management, sustained-yield agroecosystems*). However, the *IPM* acronym has survived. There still is concern in some parts of the agricultural research community that *IPM* does not reflect the nonpest components of production-system management, particularly because of significant involvement of a broadened spectrum of disciplines and the importance of a more holistic framework in which to address future scenarios.

THE PROCESS

In September 1985, the Cooperative State Research Service (CSRS), USDA, supported a workshop entitled "Interdisciplinary Issues in Plant Protection." We encouraged an interdisciplinary science organization—the Intersociety Consortium for Plant Protection (ISCPP)—to organize the workshop and to include Agronomy Society of America and Soil Science Society of America representatives. Because of the diverse backgrounds of prospective participants, no formal agenda was developed, but reference material suggested by these people was circulated prior to the meeting to help increase the level of shared perspectives on relevant issues.

It is important to note that CSRS emphasized process; it was imperative not to proceed too rapidly, thus giving these science leaders time to ponder, debate, and digest the respective subject matter, issues, and terminology being shared. Nevertheless, two particularly eloquent, strong leaders convinced the gathering to write a proposal for a national plant health system. A proposal outline was prepared during the workshop, and one scientist agreed to write a first-draft proposal from the outline. Although my CSRS colleague and I were (and remain) concerned that the issues would be too tightly bound by such a document at that stage, we did not intervene. Our credibility rested on our allegiance to support consensus development.

The first-draft proposal was circulated to workshop participants for editing and general reaction. Many helpful suggestions were made and incorporated in the final draft. This proposal was sent to the executive committee of the intersociety consortium.

CURRENT STATUS

Recently, some erosion has occurred in the consensus that initially supported the concept of a national plant health system. As the proposal was shared among additional leaders of the involved disciplines, perspectives of alarm, particularly regarding implementations for curriculum changes leading to a Doctor of Plant Health degree, surfaced within one professional society. Some discipline representatives sense that conflict has also emerged over the adequacy of the IPM initiative to meet future needs and that the Doctor of Plant Health implies primacy of a particular discipline over peer disciplines in the area of education.

Now hindsight and the CSRS counsel not to proceed too rapidly echo within the system. With such major conceptual changes as embodied in the proposal, it appears that superlative labor will be required to allay current sensitivities and to restore mutual credibility and a sense of shared benefits. The proposal is in abeyance; it has, in my opinion, forced a closed-ended, presumed-product situation in which there is little room for constructive dialogue and rapprochement.

ASSESSMENT

The history of developing agricultural research, education, and extensions information initiatives is marked by collaboration within a dispersed network of federal, state, and (sometimes) industry science leaders. The anticipated results are usually achieved, and this organizational philosophy is usually opposed to institute structures. Thus, permanence, efficiency in implementation, and focus for support are sometimes sacrificed in the network structure. But when consensus is achieved in science networks, it is well-conceived and, with time, is proven correct.

In the academic setting, leaders can only serve as part-time planners. They are willing to serve under these conditions while maintaining currency in their respective disciplines. On this basis, the ISCPP, interacting with the discipline science societies, selected senior, high-ranking scientists to participate in the initial workshop. Thus, certain strong leaders have taken positions that are in conflict.

Perhaps this situation is a bellwether for major changes in the way land-grant universities are organized. Future growth (or even survival) may depend on institutional flexibility to better accommodate problem-centered initiatives. Resolute decisions to focus human talent and other resources have been hampered by territorialism and sensitivities that flourished in the department-centered universities. This trait spills over into the discipline science associations. Perhaps the stage is set for the appearance of the "invisible college" in response to challenges such as the new biotechnology initiative. Many universities have made significant changes in faculty organization to better compete for biotechnology research funding. There may then be an opportunity to study one another's work, leading to "respectful but competitive rivalry" (Klein 1985) apart from classical departments and professional science societies.

The problems that have been discussed are outlined in Table 5.1. The process of seeking cross-discipline dialogue and decision making consisted of three phases. Following workshop dialogue (Phase I) on the interdisci-

Table 5.1. Problems in achieving cross-discipline dialogue and decisions: A paradigm for evaluation

Process		Outcomes
	Interactive Disciplines: a b . . . *n*	
Phase I	Dialogue (workshop)	1. Fully shared benefits 2. Beneficiaries compromise 3. Clear losers 4. Abort (regroup?)
	↓	
Phase II	Consensus on concepts	1. Total support 2. Conflict resolution 3. Majority rule 4. Open-ended (regroup?)
	↓	
Phase III	Product(s)	1. Firm plan 2. Options 3. Weak plan 4. None

plinary issue in plant protection, we are now in Phase II, seeking consensus on a proposal for a plant health-care initiative in U.S. agriculture. In fact, the outcomes for Phase II are in doubt, and the anticipated products (Phase III) are even more ephemeral. For each phase of the process, outcomes are ranked in descending order for quality attributes and can be linked by matching rank order across the three phases. Thus, if during the interdisciplinary dialogue the outcome was that participants perceived "fully shared benefits," "total support" for consensus would have developed, and the product would be a "firm plan." At this point, some participants perceive their discipline to be "clear losers." However, there is also a feeling that consensus should be achieved through "majority rule." But, following through to Phase III, the product would be a "weak plan" and therefore an undesirable outcome. It is intriguing to note that in the case of the lowest quality attribute in Phase II an "abort" outcome would preserve an "open-ended" situation in which certain leaders could regroup later. In my view, the issues and needs are so important that it would be imperative for leaders to agree in an "open-ended" view on consensus if they were to abort dialogue at this time.

Table 5.1 also portrays stark alternatives that I feel should be shown to the workshop participants, to stimulate serious reflection about the quality of the process in which they are involved, using this outline as a paradigm for self-evaluation. I retain trust in these leaders to work out differences in a spirit of renewed commitment to a role in shaping the course of future events rather than merely responding to them.

REFERENCE

Klein, J. T. 1985. The evolution of a body of knowledge. *Knowledge: Creation, Diffusion, Utilization* 7(2):117–42.

6
Interdisciplinary Research in a High-Technology Company

W. T. SACKETT

In reviewing interdisciplinary research in my former company, Honeywell Inc., I will first describe the company, its overall technology strategies, then its central research centers and their business and technology strategy. I will give a few examples of programs to show the types of R&D and then discuss organizations and styles used in carrying out R&D projects. I will then describe some of the approaches we evolved to make interdisciplinary research effective.

BACKGROUND

Honeywell Inc. is a multinational company engaged in manufacturing, sales, and service. Revenue is just under $7 billion. There are five major business areas, about fifty major divisions, four major research centers, several smaller R&D operations overseas, and about ninety thousand people including about fifteen thousand engineers. The major business groupings are industrial and building control systems, control products (components), computers, aerospace and defense, and international.

The divisions of the company have a great deal of autonomy. In past years, they developed their strategies with constraining company principles and dominantly financial corporate guidance. Recent years have seen increasing strategic control at the corporate and business area level, with much emphasis on "cross-corporate collaboration."

COMPANY TECHNOLOGY STRATEGY

The company's technology strategy varies somewhat with business area. On the average, it spends 7 percent of revenue on R&D. Typically, each

The views of Honeywell's organization, strategies, and approaches are my own and have not been reviewed or approved by Honeywell corporate management. Since this paper was written, Honeywell has undergone several major organizational changes.

division will spend about the same percentage of revenue on R&D as the average of its competition—from a low of 2 percent to a high of 15 percent. In addition, customer funding for R&D is very important, particularly to the aerospace and defense business. Almost half the company's total R&D is performed in aerospace and defense, more than 90 percent of it under customer funding. Of the total R&D, roughly 90 percent of the funds are spent in the divisions. The remaining 10 percent is controlled centrally, and about two-thirds of that is spent in the R&D centers.

In past years, only the aerospace and defense business considered technology leadership to be a necessary business strategy; the other businesses either aspired to competence in technology or had a technology-follower stance. Around 1980, the importance of technology became much clearer to top management; investments in technology have increased steadily, and the company has begun to characterize itself as a high-technology company. It has demonstrated its technology leadership by some surprising major contract wins (VHSIC phases zero, one, and two, for example).

CENTRAL RESEARCH DEPARTMENTS

The company's central research centers include the Systems and Research Center, the Physical Sciences Center, the Systems Development Division, and the Solid State Electronics Division. I was associated with the first three, for twenty years with the first, starting as research supervisor, becoming research director, and then center director. After that I became vice-president of the Corporate Technology Center, which included the Physical Sciences Center and Computer Sciences Center. The latter is now a part of the Systems Development Division.

Central Research Center Strategies

The main strategy for research center effectiveness was as follows. First, pick the key technologies that would be important to the part of the company served. Second, develop competence in those technologies by acquiring the best possible people and doing company-funded research at the state of the art, or as near to the state of the art as practical. Finally, translate that competence into business effectiveness by forming teams with divisional engineering to develop products or services that are enhanced by the technology. Forming teams with divisional people so that the products or services were developed jointly, with early commitment of division management, was a necessary condition for business success. The strategy of creating new ventures, independent of existing divisions, to exploit research competence was seldom attempted.

Why the emphasis on technology rather than product development? We had a number of experiences trying to transfer to a division products we thought were brilliantly conceived; usually the efforts were successfully resisted by the division and the transfer failed. The basic reason was that a new product represents large risks to division management—a need for investment of anywhere from five hundred thousand to twenty million dollars. If they haven't had their engineers working for you, they don't know how to assess the risks. Moreover, research people seldom understand the realities of design for manufacture, so division conservatism is usually justified.

Leveraging

All of the research centers use government contracts to leverage instruments of company funds. Besides allowing us to have a larger, more capable operation, there are indirect benefits. Competing for contracts provides a way of measuring ourselves against our competition. The game is competitive, stimulating, and energizing. Contract wins provide short-term rewards for effort.

We became good enough in some of the research sections to attain ratios of up to 10 to 1 of contract to company support, but we gradually learned that if the ratio exceeded 3 to 1, the researchers were too busy with contracts to have time for their fundamental business of helping the divisions to exploit advanced technology.

Complexities of These Research Strategies

Many of our major interdisciplinary research projects involved several divisions as well as several disciplines. This was additionally complicated by geography, since it seemed that at least one member of the team would be several thousand miles away. Different management styles added to the complexity, with many divisions having little sympathy for our concepts of consensus for important decisions.

EXAMPLES OF TECHNOLOGY PROGRAMS

These examples are given to provide a flavor of the type of R&D done in the research centers.

Automatic Control

Honeywell considers itself a leader in control, and in some areas they dominate, such as residential heating and spacecraft control. The Systems and Research Center (SRC) helped our Aerospace Division win the flight controls for the space shuttle by winning a series of control theory development contracts from NASA, then winning specific shuttle control systems studies, and then by joining them in bids to prime contractors for the flight control subcontract. SRC still has one of the premier industrial research groups in automatic control theory and appications.

Laser Gyro

SRC started research in lasers in 1961, shortly after the first laser was announced. Their work on laser gyros began in 1963 and was the most successful from a business perspective of any of the research at SRC. Today, thanks to the inspired technical leadership of Joe Killpatrick, now a Honeywell Fellow, Honeywell dominates the laser navigation field. The laser gyro is the key component in systems responsible for hundreds of millions of revenue for the aerospace and defense business. The gyro itself was a fantastic achievement of interdisciplinary teams involving physics, optics, electronics, mechanical engineering, navigation and guidance, and computer science.

Gallium-Arsenide

Honeywell's Physical Sciences Center (PSC) started research in compound semiconductors in the early 1960s and began experimenting with high-speed gallium-arsenide electronics about 1979. In 1983, PSC teamed with Rockwell, SRC, and Honeywell's Optoelectronics Division to win the first pilot line contract for gallium-arsenide electronics from DARPA. PSC produced the first gallium-arsenide gate arrays available for companies to use in experimental development work.

DOMINANT STYLES OF RESEARCH

In discussing dominant styles of conducting research, I would first recall that all research in the centers was under project control. Projects are usually formally established, with goals, milestones, and budgets for control. Projects that fall entirely within one discipline are typically small. Most of the research is problem- or goal-oriented and requires larger projects that could be characterized as multidisciplinary or interdisciplinary research.

Then, before talking about the various styles of carrying out projects, I should define how I use the terms *interdisciplinary* or *multidisciplinary.* I use the concept that if a project could be completely subdivided and perceived out in unidisciplinary packages, it was multidisciplinary. If, after subdividing out as much as possible, there was still work that required people from different disciplines working together to make progress, it was interdisciplinary. This is not inconsistent with the literature.

The definitions do not, however, characterize well what goes on in large projects. These require continuing team attention to defining the problem and subdividing out pieces for individuals to work on. This is a recurring process as more insight is gained by research on the pieces. From this perspective, the approach to research that is most common in my company is a combination of inter- and multidisciplinary.

There were three dominant styles of carrying out projects, and I characterize them colloquially as we used to speak of them. Of course, mixtures of these styles also occurred.

Ace with Consultants

This terminology is used to describe small interdisciplinary research projects usually performed by a single investigator, organizationally located in a functional section. The ace would seek consulting help when expertise in other areas was needed.

Super Ace, Ace Teams

This terminology describes the traditional approach to large interdisciplinary research projects. The super-ace leader assembled a team of aces from the disciplines necessary to get the work done. The leader partitioned the work and handed out individual assignments. Negotiations took place mostly one-on-one. Reporting assignments were handed in to the super ace, who put them together into the team output. This approach worked well if the super ace was indeed a superior technologist and leader.

We became concerned at one time that our proposal win percentage was not as high as we wanted, so we did an analysis of wins and losses of the previous three years and found many shortcomings. Out of this analysis, under the leadership of Dr. Grant Skelton, came an approach that led to a sharp increase in our win ratios, which we characterized as the "boiler room." The win ratios rose from the 30-percentile neighborhood to the high 70s.

Boiler-Room Teams

The designation *boiler-room* came from the noise that came out of the assigned work room during some of our rather loud attempts to reach consensus decisions. Our boiler-room proposal efforts started us on the path to true teamwork in research. Typically, a proposal leader was in charge, but every key issue in the proposal was worked through by the team. Before individual work assignments were made, everyone agreed on the key elements of the proposal and the selling message. Perhaps a better designation would be *consensus teams*, since all major issues were decided by consensus.

MAKING IT WORK EFFECTIVELY

No matter how effectively individual research projects are executed in an industrial research center setting, if the strategies don't lead to technology strengths that match company needs, the center fails. That truth is made no less obnoxious by the fact that it takes some years to develop technology capability, and if the right guesses weren't made five to ten years ago, the research center may be irrelevant today. Moreover, corporate and divisional long-range plans seldom extend beyond three years.

So a vital issue for research management is picking the key disciplines in which to develop competence. This is the dilemma of strategic linking of technology and business strategy. It is accentuated when top management has little grasp of technology and when the technology leaders have little grasp of business. But by proper initiative on the part of research management in acquiring a knowledge of the businesses served and of projecting potential impacts of technology developments, a set of educated guesses can evolve into proper strengths in key disciplines.

Organization

The above discussion of key disciplines assumes that when centers start up they usually start with a functional section organization, with a few closely related disciplines organized into a single section, led by a section leader.

As the center grows in size and competence, increasingly ambitious projects are taken up. In the beginning they are managed under the sectional leader. Later, if successful, they are reported to a program manager who parallels the section leader. This leads naturally to a mixed organization, and then logically to a matrix organization as the center grows and takes on larger and larger projects.

Functional Discipline Sections

Functional discipline sections ranged from a minimum size of four to a maximum of about fifteen. Below four, we tended to combine a section with the section nearest in discipline. As a section succeeded in its research business and grew above ten, we would, if logical, split and nucleate a new section. Typically, two to four sections would report to a manager, and three to four managers to a director. Parallel to the section leaders would be a business administrator, a marketing representative, and one or more secretaries. These people functioned as partners of a section's business enterprise whose mission was to provide advanced technology and new business starts to the divisions they served.

Project Sections

As time went on, a significant number of programs would grow to a size and importance that made it logical to give the program manager the status of a section leader by having him report to a manager. With bigger programs still, the program manager would report at the director level.

This worked fine until the program was finished or transferred to the division. Then there would be a scramble for new resources or to find homes for the people unemployed as the program ended. This led us to matrix management.

Matrix Management

Matrix management provides a matrix overlay of programs on functional sections. Program workers have homes in a section and may be assigned either part-time or full-time to programs. Not all workers in disciplines work on programs. Matrix management is notorious for its difficulty. I saw it fail in one of our research centers. To make it work in SEC, we spent many days on team building between program managers and section managers. We carefully derived ground rules for who was responsible for what in all aspects of our business. We worked out issues of rewards and credits so that each organization received credit for contract bookings and sales that were worked jointly. We addressed the "pass the problem employees" issue by trying to get program managers and section managers in a genuine partnership mode.

The issue of power balance between program management and functional management must be addressed. We gave each discretionary resources and tried to achieve a power balance by adjusting resource magnitudes. Matrix management can be made to work, but it takes more effort than the less complex functional management.

PARTICIPATIVE MANAGEMENT

I believe that the only effective management style for a research center is a participative style. A key element in participation is the way decisions are made—and whether there are ground rules for decision making that the management team understands. After about a year of experimenting with team-style management with little progress, my team adopted the set of ground rules described below and began to progress toward effective functioning. We did a lot of team building and departmental problem solving in the team and evolved to an overlapping, interlinked management structure similar to that described by Rensis Likert (1967).

ALL OTHER STYLES OF MANAGEMENT

The basic problem with authoritarian management of research is the impossible demands of knowledge and judgment it places on the leader. For a small enough department, narrowly focused authoritarian leadership can be as effective as the leader is, but motivation and synergy depend greatly on the charisma and charm of the leader.

The major problems with consultative management are that the information transfer is seldom good enough, and the empowerment of individuals that happens in well-functioning teams just doesn't occur.

Democratic management is not a favored style in industry. Decisions are not made by voting unless the stakes are low. Councils are advisory to management rather than decision bodies.

Leadership and responsibility are key ingredients of successful research management. We tried an experiment with a leaderless team for six months when one of our managers was on temporary assignment with a division. Although things didn't go completely to pot, the team expressed discomfort, and outsiders who had to deal with the leaderless team were irritated by the difficulties they encountered.

GROUND RULES FOR DECISION MAKING

As indicated before, the approach to decision making has the most impact on team functioning. If the leader holds the important decisions as his or hers by right, no amount of team building or consultation will energize the team. On the other hand, if the important decisions of the team are consensus decisions, the team leader can participate as a team member in arriving at a consensus, and if the team members are reasonably empowered, the leader's position will not unduly influence the outcome.

If consensus cannot be reached in reasonable time, the team leader should decide whether to make a default decision or defer the decision for more information or thought. All decisions that the team members must deal with cannot be consensus—there simply isn't time. That's why it's so important to formulate decision-making ground rules so that the team members are neither paralyzed nor continually surprised.

Figure 6.1 shows the decision model my management team devised after a lot of discussion. We arrived at five categories of decisions. Category A covered decisions that the team leader decided would not be shared with the team. Category B was for decisions the team leader would normally make in day-to-day operations but with notification to the team, so that if

Figure 6.1. Decision model

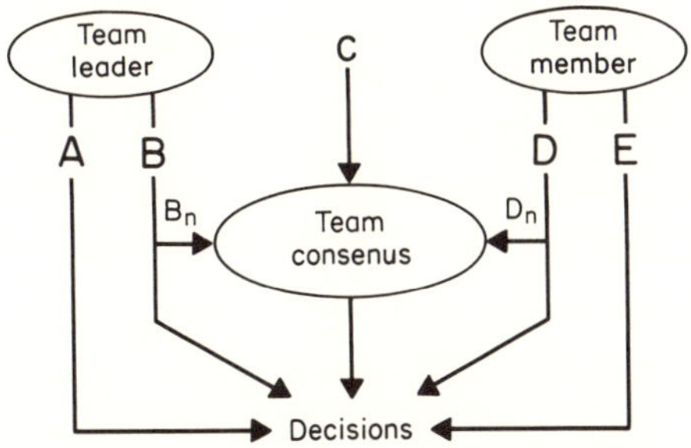

any team member so wished, the decision could be brought in to the team for reconsideration and consensus. Category C covered important issues agreed in advance to belong to the team for consensus decision making. Category D described decisions that any team member could make for the team with notification and reconsideration by the team if any other team member so desired. Category E covered decisions that were in the purview of the individual team member, his or her bailiwick. Table 6.1 gives examples of decisions in the various categories.

Clearing the air about how the boss and his or her team would handle decisions was a major breakthrough in the team's evolution toward effectiveness. Before that, the expectations of team members in this area were not clear, and the level of trust was not adequate. I believe the details of the model are much less important than dealing with the issue of how decisions are to be handled. If the team leader avoids this issue and is arbitrary in his or her choice of decisions to share, the team will feel manipulated and will not reach their potential in effectiveness.

For this particular decision-making approach to work well, the team members need to understand how each will react to various decisions in order to effectively make decisions for the team. It usually requires a significant amount of team building to reach this level of understanding.

Effective versus Ineffective Teams

There is an enormous difference between effective and ineffective teams. That fact is demonstrated so graphically in sports events that it should be evident to all. For some reason the analogy for teams in R&D is not con-

Table 6.1. Sample decisions

Category A:	Decisions made by team leader • Team member appraisal • Team member salary
Category B:	Decisions made by team leader with notification to team • Operating decisions • Minor resource allocation
Category C:	Decisions made by team consensus • Major resource allocation • Organizational policies • Structural changes • Changes to team membership
Category D:	Decisions made by any team member with notification to team • Minor resource allocation
Category E:	Decisions made by team member • Operating decisions in member's own bailiwick

nected well enough for the value of proper investments in team building to be more commonly accepted.

Some of the less effective teams I've encountered display aggression rather than open disagreement. They typically cut one another off, interrupt, listen selectively, and play games. I've seen others display low energy, pull in different directions, and be unable to focus on the task. I've seen still other ineffective teams get stuck in their development at a stage where their social relations are excellent, where they are very comfortable with one another. However, they seem more interested in the social exchange than in the task and are not very productive. But they are apt to think of themselves as a great team because they get along so well.

On effective teams I've encountered, members focus well on the task at hand, display lots of energy, listen actively, communicate relevant data and concepts, and confront differences openly and usually without hostility. They use conflict to energize creativity, that is, to produce creative alternatives, and to seek better solutions. Quiet members of the team are drawn into the issues. In short, members characteristically use empowering behaviors and avoid disempowering behaviors.

TEAM BUILDING

Since teams are so important to interdisciplinary research, some discussion of team building is in order. I will not attempt a detailed description of how to do team building, but rather will comment on some elements I believe are important. What I have to say is based on my own experience with team building—which, though extensive, hasn't led me to an understanding of how to do it effectively and reliably regardless of the team makeup. It seems to be different for each team, and that difference isn't accounted for by the quality of the members.

What do I mean by team building versus team training? You can gain a lot of benefit by training for good interpersonal interaction and active listening by team members, but for a group to become an effective team, the members must define and adopt a set of common goals for the team—what Peters and Waterman (1982) call superordinate goals. The members must deal with the conflict between their personal goals and the team goals. It isn't rational to expect complete commitment to team goals, yet the members of an effective team must know what they can count on from one another.

I believe there are some necessary conditions for building an effective team. First, the members must be competent to function in the arena of the business. No amount of team building will compensate for incompetence. Second, there must be common goals that the team members all endorse and commit to. Third, there must be a reasonable power balance on the team—that is, the individual members must be reasonably empowered. If the leader is domineering and the other members submissive, or even if any member of the team is disproportionately powerful, team building is difficult. Fourth, the team members must be willing to invest the time and energy to establish the trust and appropriately lower the guards that individuals have been conditioned to in most business environments.

Time is one of the huge barriers to team building. Usually, team building requires meeting away from the work setting. Professionals tend to resent time spent in team building, especially if their work keeps piling up back at the shop. Off site team building tends to grow in effectiveness with length of time (at least up to a week, the longest of my experience). Yet it seems nearly impossible to get more than two days at a time in business organizations. This is why, in industry, team building is done around work issues, such as strategic planning. The divided focus of such a session can be counterproductive if insufficient time is given to interpersonal issues and team process. Yet the presence of the work issue is reassuring to some of the team members in that their efforts are at least partially valid.

Effective team building requires the assistance of a skilled professional consultant who can focus on process and intervene when behavior becomes inappropriate. When the time costs of the team members are considered, the investment in a good consultant makes good sense, no matter how skilled individuals on the team may be in process consulting. The detachment and advice of the consultant can be invaluable.

TECHNOLOGY TRANSFER

The crucial output for an industrial research center is technology transfer. If the divisions served by the center don't feel the output in their products or services, the center will not prosper. Honeywell eliminated an applied research department after about six or seven years when divisional management complained that the center's costs weren't justified by their output to them. Since the corporation's revenue and profits all come from the divisions, if you don't influence that profit stream in some positive way, you are just not relevant to them.

Reports, Patents, Publications

These normal outputs of research are necessary but far from sufficient for industrial research. In fact, depending on them to serve the customer base can even be negative, as one of our research sections learned. After receiving a series of ridiculously hard-to-read reports, the divisions hired a consultant to read and evaluate the reports. Fortunately, the consultant was positive about the long-range value of the work described. (If the section hadn't distributed them so widely with statements of their importance, their customer relations would have been better!)

Consulting and Assistance

Consulting as a form of technology transfer mainly provides a chance to build customer relations with quick turnaround responses to requests from the division for short-term help. *Assistance* is terminology we used to describe a form of body-shop help where the division was short of engineers. We always tried to respond to these requests, because sometimes we had to go to the divisions to seek work for our people when anticipated contracts did not come in. Assistance helps in technology transfer mainly in that it helps the assigned researchers to become acquainted with the division's people and problems.

People Transfers

People transfers are regarded by some as the best way to transfer technology. We found people transfer to be a preferred method when you could make it happen. However, it was often difficult to make happen. People were reluctant to transfer from the research center, especially when the move was outside the region. Hence, it was not a reliable method. On the whole, people transfers are not the answer to technology transfer. On the other hand, we maintained an open door for all of our divisions and allowed them to freely approach our people with offers for transfer. We would then provide counsel and sometimes counteroffers but allow the people to decide whether or not to accept the transfer offer. Building up an alumni community in the divisions was very helpful to customer relations.

Joint Projects

The fundamental approach to technology transfer that worked best for us was establishing joint product or service development programs with the divisions to infuse our technology. This required a lot of interaction and salesmanship from our research managers to their counterpart managers in the divisions in order to help them see how our technology could improve their products. The interaction was motivated by survival, since one of the strong criteria for investments in their technology was the interest and support expressed by divisional management.

Often, starting a joint project was facilitated through the funding that came from having a contract that permitted or required working together. When no contract was available, it sometimes was necessary to entice the division by subsidizing the project to get it going. A frequent arrangement was for the center and the division to contribute funds equally until it became clear that the joint project would pay off for the division, at which point their share of the funding would increase.

CONCLUSION

Interdisciplinary research in an industrial setting can be a rewarding experience, both for the company and for the research people. Making it successful requires attention to missions, strategy, goal setting, and planning. It requires significant attention to training and developing leadership and management skills, team building, developing interpersonal skills, and encouraging continuing personal and professional growth of the people. Time, energy, and money must be invested to develop these environmental conditions for success. Most of the techniques industry has learned to deploy in creating this climate for R&D success were developed in academia. My question is, why aren't these techniques used more often in academia?

REFERENCES

Likert, R. 1967. *The human organization: Its management and value.* New York: McGraw-Hill.

Peters, T. J., and R. H. Waterman, Jr. 1982. *In search of excellence: Lessons from America's best-run companies.* New York: Harper and Row.

7

A Prognosticative Approach to Conflict Management in University Interdisciplinary Research

ALOK K. CHAKRABARTI
RICHARD W. SCHNEIDER

Interdisciplinary research has become increasingly prevalent for multiple reasons. As federal funds for university-based research become less available, universities seek other sources, such as private industry, for their support. Moreover, there are a few federal programs that either encourage or mandate supplemental funding from private sources. These sources generally fund mission-oriented or problem-focused research rather than discipline-bound programs. Many of the federal programs are also mission-oriented and interdisciplinary in nature.

Funding prospects are not the only motivation. Interdisciplinary research provides a potential for refinement and advancement of a discipline by challenging the conceptual framework, methodological approaches, and analytical tools of a specific discipline (Russell 1982). This provides an excellent opportunity for personal development and growth of the researchers as well as a training opportunity for the novice members of the team.

Many scientists in universities as well as in industry perceive new scientific and technical challenges that need interdisciplinary approaches as a result of the development of other allied technology. For example, the recent advancements in electronics have provided new challenges and opportunities to chemical and biotechnical research.

As interdisciplinary research grows in university campuses, university

This work was partially supported by a grant from the Division of Science Resources Studies, National Science Foundation, to the Center for Research on Technology and Strategy, Drexel University. The opinions expressed are those of the authors and do not reflect the views of the National Science Foundation.

administration must be more careful in managing this type of research. Potential for conflicts in interdisciplinary research is quite high, and one must develop mechanisms for anticipating and resolving those conflicts. We have provided a theoretical framework for conflict and for the management of such conflicts.

EPISTEMOLOGICAL ISSUES

Distinction between interdisciplinary and cross-disciplinary research is important in order to understand the inherent conflicts. In both instances, people from different disciplines participate in a project, but in interdisciplinary research an integrated effort is required.

Interdisciplinary research has the following eight characteristics (Birnbaum 1981):

1. Different bodies of knowledge are represented in the group.
2. Different approaches to problem solving are used.
3. Different roles are assumed by the members in problem solving.
4. Group works on a common problem.
5. Group shares responsibility for the final outcome.
6. Group shares common facility.
7. Nature of the problem determines group membership.
8. Group members are interdependent on each other.

From an epistemological point of view, interdisciplinary research has potential for conflict embedded in various ways. Any problem-solving activity has four interactive elements: (1) identification of reality and the problem, (2) conceptualization of the model, (3) development of the scientific model (descriptive or predictive), and (4) development of the solution (Mitroff et al. 1974).

Disciplines provide a paradigm for a researcher to go through all these elements (Kuhn 1970). The paradigm provides a guideline to define the problem and to develop a conceptual model. The paradigm also provides a research method and, finally and most important, the standards for acceptance of the research output.

Consider the problem of why recent Asian immigrant school-children have done better than others (Butterfield 1986). Sociologists have focused on the family structure and environment, psychologists focused on IQ and motivation, and a pediatrician used neonatal behavior assessment to predict the differences in learning ability among children of different ethnic backgrounds. This example is used to highlight the importance of the disciplinary background of the researcher in the definition of the problem itself and consequent development of the conceptual model. Research methods of the different disciplines vary a great deal. Mediating the differences among the researchers from different disciplines is important in successful interdisciplinary research.

In cross-disciplinary research, this problem is less acute. Here the researchers from different disciplines work on discrete parts of the problems. Their output is judged by the standards of their individual disciplines, unlike interdisciplinary research output, which, as an integrated one, must be evaluated by a different standard which is not clear in many instances.

INTERDISCIPLINARY RESEARCH: CONTINGENCIES FOR SUCCESS

Birnbaum (1981) investigated the contingencies for successful interdisciplinary research. According to him, interdisciplinary research is more successful under the following problem situation: the problem is complex with many interrelationships, difficult to define, and without an existing discipline to cover it; there is no clearly identifiable client for the research output; and initiating and implementing stages are better suited for interdisciplinary types of research.

Birnbaum's study involved interdisciplinary research in academic settings. He advocated only selective use of integrated interdisciplinary research.

Problems of interdisciplinary research in universities are embedded on the basis of complex territorial or turf struggles which include both organizational and cognitive components (Rip 1985). In industry, the territorial struggle is often an organizational one; in universities, the turf is both institutional and cognitive. Birnbaum's suggestion that loosely coupled multidisciplinary research seems to be more effective in the university setting is a sensible one, because it avoids the turf battle.

INTERGROUP CONFLICT: BEHAVIORAL ANALYSIS OF CONFLICT CAUSES

There are four types of conflict in technical organizations based on the basic issues and parties concerned (Evan 1965). Technical conflicts among peers relate to technical goals, milestones, means, and interpretation of data. Technical conflict between supervisor and subordinate relates to project administration. Interpersonal conflict between peers centers on personal trust, likes, and apprehensions. Power and authority clashes are manifested in interpersonal conflicts between supervisor and subordinates. Interdisciplinary research teams lend themselves very easily to all four types of conflicts.

Mutual task dependency—defined as the extent to which two persons are dependent on each other for information, compliance, and other coordinative acts for performance of their respective tasks—is a major source of conflict in groups (Schmidt and Kochan 1972; Thompson 1967; Walton and Dutton 1969). Task-related asymmetry between group members is also a major factor in conflict (Dalton 1959; Lawrence and Lorsch 1967; Walton and Dutton 1969). Asymmetry may occur as a result of unequal power balance between different organizational subunits, increased level of dependency on other units, unequal prestige, or different incentives to cooperate in achieving common goals. Seiler (1963) reported interference, blocking, and retaliation practiced by engineering personnel against research personnel.

ORGANIZATIONAL CONTEXT FOR CONFLICT

Walton, Dutton, and Cafferty (1969) identified four types of organizational contexts leading to conflicts:

(1) Suboptimizing incentives because of supervisory failure to emphasize and reward cooperation and conflict of interest in goals and objectives, rewards, and inducements are offered to members to pursue suboptimal or proximal goals. In the university setting, the doctrine of "publish or perish" severely discourages talented faculty from providing meaningful cooperation in projects that may not lead to publication in prestigious journals. On the other hand, those who get into interdisciplinary types of research are sometimes denied tenure and promotion because the quality of their work becomes suspect as it has not been published in journals recognized by the members of the specific discipline representing the faculty member's academic department.

(2) Jurisdictional ambiguity related to the right to initiate work, to carry out activities, to allocate resources, and to exercise control over different departments creates conflicts. Problems of jurisdictional ambiguity are enhanced in universities where multiple organizational units are involved in similar areas. Computer science in many universities is in the domain of a number of academic departments, such as electrical engineering, mathematics, computer sciences, computer engineering, library science, psychology, or linguistics, as well as business administration. Each department will have its own focus and paradigm to approach problems related to computers. Development of interdisciplinary programs and research is not a trivial problem involving the different organizational subunits.

(3) Communication barriers between different groups develop because of various factors, as follows:

- Physical space barriers (example: round building with alcoves on perimeter)
- Time barriers
- Mutual ignorance of each other's needs
- Lack of interpersonal needs

Thompson (1985) presented a shared a priori model based on Weaver's mathematical model for communication to understand communication problems in interdisciplinary research. To improve or solve communication problems, one ought to improve communication at all three levels—syntactic, semantic, and pragmatic.

(4) Task conditions such as budget constraints, responsibility, and underutilization of personnel create conflict in projects involving different organizational units. Supervisory and management practices sometimes also aggravate conflicts.

Indicators for Interunit Conflict

Identifying conflict is not a difficult task, and management should be able to recognize the signs of different types of conflict through any one of the following indicators:

- *Interference.* Does one department show lack of consideration for another? Do members of one department or unit interfere with another? Do members of one department refuse to yield assistance to another?
- *Overstatement.* Does one unit try to exaggerate its needs in order to influence another unit? Does one unit often show signs of crisis although in reality there may not be any crisis?
- *Annoyance.* Does one unit show adverse feelings or dislike for another?
- *Distrust.* Is there a lack of trust between departments?

MANAGING CONFLICTS

While one cannot expect to eliminate conflict in organizational situations, management must be ready to deal with them in a constructive manner. Russell (1982) has categorized the administrative issues in three dimensions: people, disciplinary, and administration, each containing a number of issues. These dimensions are not necessarily orthogonal. As a matter of fact, they are highly interactive. Accountability for funds and intellectual property are issues in the administrative dimensions that may have significant impact on people-related issues such as rewards or problem focus. Disciplinary issues such as peer approval or maintenance of standards cannot be ignored; on the contrary, they must be taken into account in the evaluation and control systems by the management.

According to Walton and Dutton (1969), response patterns of higher-level executives affect the contextual conditions for conflict while management of interface between organizational subunits affect the immediate causes of conflict. Thus, the role of managers at different levels of organizational hierarchy differs in management of conflict. Higher-level executives ought to set the contextual conditions and direction for operational-level executives to successfully manage the organization.

CASE EXAMPLES

Control Data Corporation has developed Control Data Engineering Center Network as a means for cooperative research with a number of universities in the United States (Krueger and Hexter 1986). The basic tenets of the paradigm followed in this model for cooperative research are as follows:

1. Program-oriented, focused research is to be carried out at specific university research centers.
2. Structure for accountability of resources and activities is provided.
3. Efficient information transfer between participating universities through electronic communication is arranged.
4. Provision for encouraging proactive technology transfer and cooperation is made.
5. Research cost is shared by different sources of funds.
6. Research support is provided from industry through a consortium.

Success of such cooperative research depends on several factors. First, industry will have to forsake some proprietary interests to facilitate sharing of information with universities. Rearrangement of priorities is also necessary for government to support cooperative research. Universities will also have to change the individual investigator model to make cooperative research efforts a success (Kreuger and Hexter 1986).

The National Science Foundation has sponsored a number of university-industry cooperative research centers in several fields. The following centers have been in existence for several years: Welding Research Center at Ohio State University, Polymer Research Center at University of Massachusetts, Applied Polymer Research Center at Case Western Reserve University, Interactive Computer Graphics Center at Rensselaer Polytechnic Institute, Center for Signal Processing at North Carolina State University, Ceramics Research Center at Rutgers University, Building Materials Research Center at Iowa State University, Robotics Research Center at University of Rhode Island.

Some of the centers have been quite successful in terms of organizational growth. The history of these centers shows that one of the keys to success is involvement of top management in the university to set the contextual conditions. For example, in RPI's case, several administrators told Chakrabarti that success of the center was a high priority and that rewards of the participating faculty were dependent on their contribution to the center's success. Administratively, the center's organization was kept simple by having the director report to the dean of engineering. Higher levels of administrators including several trustees of the university were involved in fund-raising activities. In other words, the center was given new sources of money instead of sharing resources with other academic departments. The center was involved in curriculum in computer graphics which was not in the domain of any other academic department; thus, jurisdictional ambiguity was minimized.

Project selection at the center was carried out by the director on the advice of the participating industry members on an informal basis. Contact with industry was maintained informally through multiple channels. Graduate students at the center worked during the summer with the industrial clients. This helped effect transfer of information between the center and its industrial associates.

Other centers developed different mechanisms for interface with industry. For example, the Welding Research Institute at Ohio State University used a much more formal approach to project selection. The same was true for the Polymer Center at the University of Massachusetts, where several prestigious professors were involved. A proper system for resource allocation was necessary to mediate the differences instead of the informal approach used in a private university such as RPI.

Importance of top management support is evidenced in the case of the Robotics Institute at the University of Rhode Island. Rapid turnover of senior administrators within the university created a number of difficulties for the center.

CONCLUSION

Interdisciplinary research has become increasingly important in universities as they become more involved in problem-focused, cooperative research. Federal agencies such as the National Science Foundation have helped establish several cooperative research centers in universities. In this paper we have outlined some of the contingencies for conflict in interdisciplinary research and what one may expect to find in such research centers. Success of the centers depends on efficient management of these conflicts. Universities face the critical issue of ensuring enrichment of the faculty's research agenda without subordinating it to the goals of the sponsor (National Science Board 1982). Maintenance of academic freedom is at the heart of a university's ability to make real contributions to society. A number of universities have developed some models for resolving conflicts that can be successfully applied in other cases of interdisciplinary research.

REFERENCES

Birnbaum, Philip H. 1981. Contingencies for interdisciplinary research: Matching research questions with research organization. *Management Science* 27(11).

Butterfield, 1986. Why Asians are going to the head of the class. *New York Times Educational Supplement,* August 3.

Dalton, M., 1959. *Men who manage.* New York: Wiley.

Evan, W. M., 1965. Conflict and performance in R&D organizations: Some preliminary findings. *Industrial Management Review,* 7(1):37–36.

Krueger, E. R., and R. M. Hexter. 1986. Perspectives on a new paradigm for cooperative research. *IEEE Transactions on Engineering Management,* E-29(2).

Kuhn, Thomas S., 1970. *The structure of scientific revolutions,* 2d ed. Chicago: University of Chicago Press.

Lawrence, Paul R., and Jay W. Lorsch. 1967. *Organizations and environment: Managing differentiation and integration.* Homewood, Ill.: Irwin.

Mitroff, Ian I., Frederick Betz, Luis R. Pondy, and Francisco Sagasti. 1974. On managing science in the systems age: Two schemas for the study of science as a whole systems phenomenon. *Interfaces* 4:46–58.

National Science Board. 1982. *University-industry research relationships: Myths, realities and potentials.* Washington, D.C.: National Science Foundation.

Rip, Arie. 1985. Interdisciplinary without disciplines? A view from the sociology of science. In B. W. Mar, W. T. Newell, and B. O. Saxberg, eds., *Managing high technology: An interdisciplinary perspective.* Amsterdam: Elsevier Science.

Russell, Martha G., ed. *Enabling interdisciplinary research: Perspectives from agriculture, forestry, and home economics.* University of Minnesota, Misc. Publications 19.

Schmidt, S. M., and T. A. Kochan. 1972. Conflict: Towards conceptual clarity. *Administrative Science Quarterly.* 17:359–70.

Seiler, J. A. 1963. Diagnosing interdepartmental conflicts. *Harvard Business Review,* 41:121–32.

Thompson, Charles W. N. 1985. The shared a priori model as a framework in examining interdisciplinary process. In B. W. Mar, W. T. Newell, and B. O. Saxberg, eds., *Managing high technology: An interdisciplinary perspective.* Amsterdam: Elsevier Science.

Thompson, J. D. 1967. *Organizations in action.* New York: McGraw-Hill.

Walton, R. E., and J. M. Dutton. 1969. The management of interdepartmental conflict: A model and review. *Administrative Science Quarterly.* 14:522–42.

Walton, R. E., J. M. Dutton, and T. P. Cafferty. 1969. Organizational context and interdepartmental conflict. *Administrative Science Quarterly.* 14:73–84.

8

The Impact of Interdisciplinary Activities on Departmental Disciplines

MARTHA GARRETT RUSSELL

This paper describes the production economy of academic research and the interdependency of graduate education and research. It describes the influence of interdisciplinary research activities on academic research in the departmental/disciplinary environment. Examples supporting this premise are drawn from the Microelectronic and Information Sciences Center at the University of Minnesota.

THE ACADEMIC RESEARCH ENVIRONMENT

Two characteristics distinguish educational institutions from other research organizations: their mission to discover talent and their responsibility to develop that talent through educational activities. Discovering talent, instruction, and research are the three types of production activities of the education industry (Schultz 1986).

Research, instruction, and recruitment are all highly labor-intensive and very costly. Faculty scientists are the critical resource in all of these activities. Faculty scientists, in turn, need funds to pay for research assistants and to procure equipment and supplies with which to conduct their research. These funds are acquired through the initiative, productivity, and prestige of faculty scientists and the students they educate and through the commitment of the academic institution to the disciplines represented by these faculty members.

These are the inputs for research—faculty time, research support, and graduate students. These inputs are used by faculty scientists to conduct research within the context of a given production environment. I have previously identified this production environment for higher education as an integration of several components: the graduate and undergraduate education programs of the department, the research instrumentalities that comprise the field of inquiry, and the prestige of both the department and the institution (Russell 1983a). The outputs of this production process include new knowledge and new scientists. The production environment is reflected in that process, and it influences the ways in which research inputs are translated into research outputs in departments. (See Figure 8.1)

THE INTERDEPENDENCY OF GRADUATE EDUCATION AND RESEARCH

Because of the interrelatedness of the educational and research production functions of higher educational institutions, their products—new scientists and new knowledge—are interdependent. New scientists and new knowledge are the joint products of academic research. In a recent analysis of factors influencing research productivity in academic departments, I found that the single most important indicator of either product was the number of graduate-level courses taught by a faculty member (Russell 1983a).

This relationship can be understood in light of the lock-step of graduate education and research. Faculty members and graduate students identify mutual research interests though top-level graduate courses. The content of these courses consists primarily of state-of-the-art research issues and methodologies. Through these courses, faculty members recruit graduate students to work with them, and graduate students acquire the prerequisite knowledge to contribute to research activities. Most graduate students are supported by research assistantships under their faculty advisors during their dissertation study. Graduate students working on research projects provide an affordable source of manpower to complement faculty research time; they also provide intellectual stimulus.

DEPARTMENTAL ECONOMY

Typically, university departments organize their instructional activities so that the revenues generated from undergraduate education provide at least

Figure 8.1. Departmental production economy

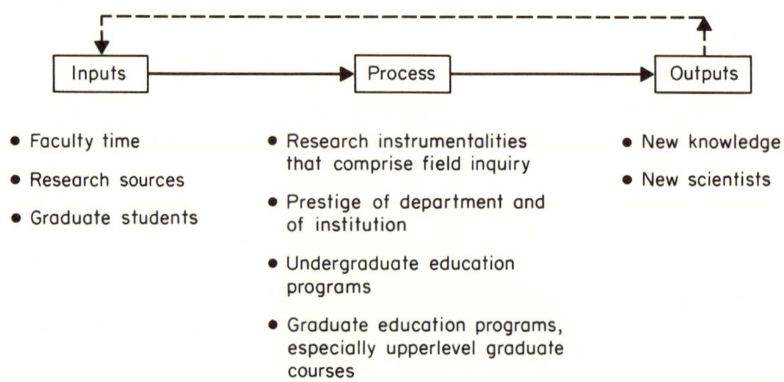

a portion of the resources needed to sustain the expense of faculty time for research and smaller seminar classes for graduate students (James and Neuberger 1981). Prestigious departments in research universities establish a balance between undergraduate and graduate programs. Responsibilities are administered so that undergraduate instruction provides funds from central university budgets sufficient to sustain the margin of faculty time necessary to obtain funds for research programs and maintain a graduate education and research program. The role of the department head is strategic in providing leadership and management in such administration (Sauer 1982).

Typically also, graduate students complete degree requirements in the course of carrying out research programs under the guidance of their faculty advisors. The substance of the degree is based on the research expertise of the faculty. The prestige of the degree is developed and maintained by the esteem in which academic peers hold the discipline and with which the expertise is exercised. The structure of the graduate degree program—the time required to complete the Ph.D. degree, sequence and content of coursework, teaching and research activities of students and faculty, and the attrition rates at certain critical approval stages—establishes the production environment for research.

These internal elements—substance, prestige, and structure—are, in turn, influenced by the academic labor market and by the demand for new knowledge in that particular field (Breneman 1978). All of these factors are departmentally based, and in many cases they are discipline-oriented. The graduate program is an especially important component of this environment for research. Disciplinary research establishes the nature and the prestige of the graduate program, a fundamental component of the resource foundation upon which university research is based. Inputs, processes, and outputs of academic productivity are defined by departments. Departments, in turn, are defined by their disciplinary references. (See Figure 8.2.)

THE INTERDISCIPLINARY INFLUENCE

Interdisciplinary research (IDR) activities affect these sets of relationships in several ways. Interdisciplinary research differs from disciplinary research in objectives, in boundaries of the problem domain, and in the structure of the process. By nature of these differences and the resultant changes in inputs and processes, interdisciplinary research involvements influence the departmental production economy and the outputs generated. (See Figure 8.3.)

The objectives of interdisciplinary research are centered on either defining a problem or solving it. This is somewhat different from the objectives of departmental research. Departmental objectives center around raising the scholarly prestige of the department in relation to peer departments

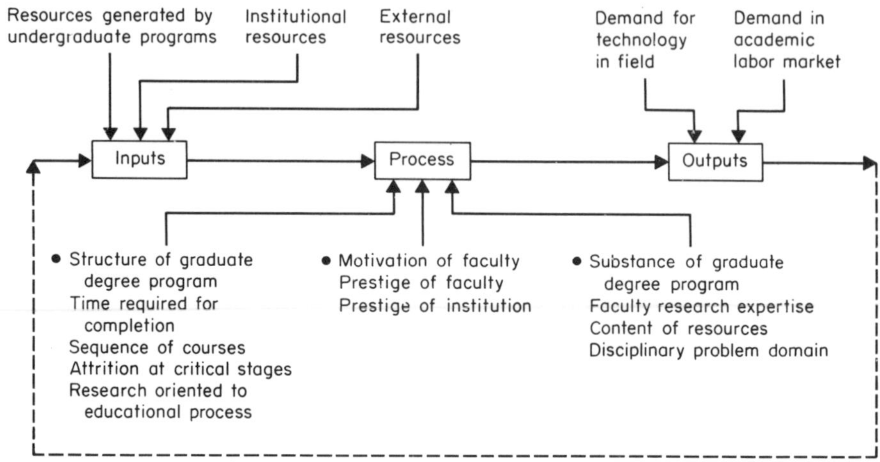

Figure 8.2. Disciplinary influences on the departmental production process

and generating increased revenues for research programs in the department. Vasconcellos's observations concerning conflict between line and staff management of interdisciplinary teams in government research organizations are relevant to academic organizations as well. The objectives of departmental research are different from those of interdisciplinary research. Lack of agreement about the priorities among the various objectives has been identified as the main reason for conflict among research managers (Vasconcellos 1986).

Figure 8.3. Interdisciplinary influences on the departmental production process

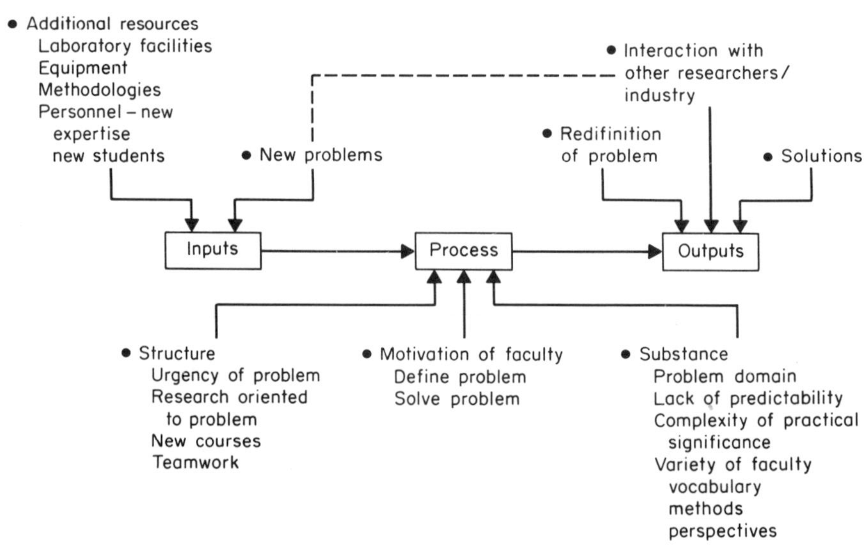

The incentives and evaluation for interdisciplinary research also differ from departmental programs (Russell 1983b). IDR researchers are motivated to work on problems of practical significance. Whether it is defining the problem or solving it, interdisciplinary researchers are motivated by their interest in the problem and their eagerness to work with colleagues. They define their success in interdisciplinary research teams in terms of the problem's solution or its redefinition (Russell and Sauer 1983). The problem is their objective. Because of this, the results of interdisciplinary research differ from departmental research in both type and quantity of outputs (Birnbaum 1983). Interdisciplinary research tends to generate fewer Ph.D. degrees and fewer peer-reviewed publications. These are the fundamental products of the disciplinary research that departments encourage.

It has been observed that interdisciplinary problems differ from disciplinary problems in terms of domain, definition, and urgency (Klein 1985). To be addressed within a disciplinary context, problems must fall within a set of domain parameters that identify the issues and concerns considered relevant for the disciplinary paradigm. These parameters help define the problem in clear, unambiguous terms. Frequently the problems addressed by interdisciplinary research are those that do not fall conveniently within disciplinary paradigms. They tend to be ill defined and unpredictable because of their complexity and their novelty.

This lack of predictability is compounded by the sense of urgency that frequently characterizes interdisciplinary research. Problems that are both unpredictable and urgent tend to require highly coordinated research management in an environment in which competition and innovation are valued (Pearson, Payne, and Gunz 1979). Clearly, the influence of these problems on an environment geared toward collaborative, educational experiences is partially detrimental to the smooth-running, productive economy of academic departments.

THE IMPACT ON DISCIPLINES

When researchers from different disciplines work together, they bring new concepts, vocabulary, methods, and perspectives, which they share with each other to varying extents. Through their cooperation, additional resources are available—laboratory facilities, equipment, methodologies, and personnel. The availability and the mix of these resources have an impact on the researchers, as well as on the research.

The most powerful and lasting impacts that can be made in the disciplinary environment of university departments are made through the addition of new expertise, new courses, and the quality of students. Interdisciplinary activities can influence the initiation and the implementation of all three types of impacts. In addition, the interdisciplinary research process requires teamwork rather than individual activity and follows the time lines of the problem, rather than those of the degree-based production economy in departments.

AN EXAMPLE OF SYNERGISTIC IMPACTS

The scientific mission of the Microelectronic and Information Sciences Center at the University of Minnesota spans a wide scope of studies, including characterization and analysis of traditional and new materials and processes used for integrated circuits, design and simulation of integrated circuits and tools for integrated circuit design and fabrication, techniques for fabrication, algorithms for computation, and applications in system configuration, expert systems, and robotics.

The methodologies for such studies have their roots in the scientific disciplines of mathematics, physics, chemistry, and other materials sciences, as well as in chemical engineering, electrical engineering, and computer engineering. The departmental homes of faculty and students participating in the MEIS Center's programs have been physics, chemistry, electrical engineering, computer science, chemical engineering and materials science, management of information science, and psychology. (See Table 8.1.)

Over a five-year period, three generations of team projects were funded. Descriptions of the departmental mix and outcomes of each are described in Table 8.2. Because it is not possible to describe in detail the impacts of each project, several outputs of one generation of projects which have then become inputs to the next generation of projects have been selected to exemplify the impacts of interdisciplinary activities in departments. These outputs include the addition of new faculty, collaboration, competition, the acquisition of new equipment, the establishment of new curricula, and the education of new scientists.

Addition of New Faculty

Interdisciplinary activities influence the configuration of departmental expertise by justifying the addition of new faculty scientists to the academic community. When interdisciplinary research teams assemble to develop an approach to a new problem, they sometimes identify the need to add to their team an expert who was not part of the original team. If this expert is not available from existing departmental faculties, new scientists may be brought in for the project. Adjunct faculty, visiting faculty, postdoctoral assistants, and new permanent faculty make differing and sometimes unexpected types of contributions. The impacts made by such persons in introducing their expertise to others become the legacy of the interdisciplinary influence.

The impact of interdisciplinary influences on expertise is delivered primarily to the faculty researchers who participate in interdisciplinary activities. Depending on the centrality of the interdisciplinary activities to their

Table 8.1. Departmental composition of MEIS team projects (number of participating faculty members)

	First round '82–83 Processor array concepts for engineering	Design automation software engineering	High-performance integrated circuits	Ultra-small electronics research	Second-round '84–85 artificially structured materials for micro-electronics	3-Dimensional integrated circuits	III–V Compound semiconductor high-speed devices	Intelligent systems	Third round '86–87 Software engineering for expert systems	III–IV High-speed devices	Parallelism	CAD for VLSI	Fourth round '88–89 NSF ERC for interfacial engineering	Semiconductor engineering	GaAs devices
Chemical Engineering and Materials Science				2	2		3			1			8	2	2
Chemistry				3	4								16		
Computer Science	1	11						2	2		8	2			
Electrical Engineering	5		10	1		7	1	1		2		2	3	3	8
Management and Information Sciences								1	1						
Mechanical Engineering														5	
Physics				6	4					1					1
Psychology								1							
TOTAL	6	11	10	12	10	7	4	5	3	4	8	4	27	10	11

Table 8.2. Interdisciplinary influences on departments

	First round '82–83 Processor array concepts for engineering	Design automation software engineering	High-performance integrated circuits	Ultra-small electronics research	Second round '84–85 Artificially structured materials for micro-electronics	3-Dimensional integrated circuits	III–V Compound semiconductor high-speed devices	Intelligent systems	Third round '86–87 Software engineering for expert systems	III–V High-speed devices	Parallelism	CAD for VLSI	Fourth round '88–89 NSF ERC for interfacial engineering	Semiconductor engineering	GaAs devices
Process															
Curricula															
New seminars	x				x	x		x	x		x	x	x	x	x
New courses	x		x			x	x	x				x		x	
Operation															
Submitted group proposals		x		x		x		x					x	x	x
Received group proposals		x											x	x	
Investments in group lab facilities		x				x		x			x			x	
Composition															
Submitted individual proposals	x	x	x	x	x	x	x	x		x	x				x
Received individual proposals		x	x	x	x	x	x	x	x	x	x				x
Divided equipment resources								x				x			
Outputs															
New Scientists															
M.S. degrees	x	x	x	x	x	x	x	x	x	x	x	x			
Ph.D. degrees	x	x	x	x	x	x	x	x	x	x	x				
New Knowledge															
Publications	x	x	x	x	x	x	x	x	x	x	x	x			
Team-coauthored publications							x	x	x	x		x			
Outputs/inputs															
Interaction with industry	Mod	Lo	Lo	Lo	Mod	Lo	Mod	Hi	Hi	Mod	Mod	Mod	Mod	Hi	Mod
Added faculty					x	x	x	x		x	x			x	x
Added equipment	x			x	x	x	x	x		x	x				x
Redefined problem/team		x	x	x	x		x	x		x					
New project name	Parallelism		3-Dimensional integrated circuits	Artificially structured materials for microelectronics	NSF ERC for interfacial phenomena		III–V High-speed devices	Software engineering for expert systems		GaAs devices					

continuing intellectual interests and on the duration of the involvement, researchers' intellectual approaches, experimental skills, and understanding of phenomena may be forever enlarged or altered. They are continuing members of a faculty and participants in one or more scientific communities, and such changes in expertise accrue to the department or to the discipline.

By identifying additional expertise needed to fully synergize the team projects, MEIS teams succeeded in targeting new faculty positions for the needed specialists. Several of the second- and third-generation teams succeeded in securing the new experts. These new faculty members were, of course, brought into one of the existing departments. However, all groups encountered problems in effectively integrating the new experts into full status as team members. Essentially, these were problems of status concordance (Gillespie and Birnbaum 1980) and resource distribution, in which the new expert threatened the existing team by either perceived status differences, attempts to assume leadership of the project, or reducing the financial resources previously available to team members.

Cooperation

Cooperative activity was generated by several teams, usually to acquire additional resources. During the first round of program development, the MEIS Center awarded seed monies to four groups of faculty members. Two of these groups were interdepartmental. The center's charge to the groups was to develop a team project and submit proposals for funding. Three of the four teams submitted group proposals. In addition, many individual proposals were submitted. None of the group proposals was awarded on first submission; however, one was awarded on a subsequent submission, with modifications in project membership.

The remaining two teams reconfigured themselves slightly and were funded as second-generation projects by the MEIS Center. In the second round, two of the four teams submitted group proposals to external agencies, and all teams submitted individual proposals. Individual but not group proposals were awarded. Subsequently, two of the teams redefined their mission and modified their project membership.

In the third round, one of the redefined teams submitted and received a group award from a corporate sponsor. Another team redefined its focus and membership for a third time. During the fourth round, one project, established without startup funding from MEIS, submitted and received a group project. Another team, which had redefined itself and its objectives, received new startup funding from the dean's office, submitted and received an award to establish a center in its own right.

Out of fourteen projects receiving MEIS funds to establish team projects that would be self-winding and able to generate research support on their own, three were successful. Those three groups have two striking similarities. First, each of these teams identified an individual with the ability to articulate the capabilities and objectives of the team. Each team entrusted that individual with the privilege of influencing the way they worked together as a team. These individuals became the team leaders and were able to successfully represent the team effort to attract potential funding sources. Second, each team was able to agree on a definition of the problem to be studied. This consensus is an essential precondition for successful interdisciplinary research (Schuller 1986; Klein and Porter 1986).

Competition

Interdisciplinary teams are more likely to flourish in institutional environments in which policies do exist to facilitate departmental sharing of generated resources and to conveniently permit departmental cross-charging for the time of faculty members and graduate students and for the use of equipment (Currie 1976). Competition for resources became an issue along two significant dimensions: first, departmental to overhead returns from proposals awarded externally, and, second, support and maintenance for departmental laboratories.

Institutional policies on departmental sharing in overhead returns from externally sponsored research influenced the interdisciplinary environment. Since institutional policy supported the distribution of overhead returns along departmental lines, group proposals were submitted departmentally—with one exception, in which case the proposal carried no overhead because its activities were strictly educational. This resulted in a fractionated approach to developing project objectives. Individual proposals predominated and, in fact, were highly successful. Both these and the successfully submitted group proposals identified a primary departmental affiliation. More than $15 million in external research support was received from 1982–83 through 1987–88. This external support generated significant overhead funds. The failure of the MEIS Center to claim a share of these funds virtually prohibited the construction of a renewal mechanism for startup funds. Because of this, the contributions that established the MEIS Center and the discrete allocations to the center from the State of Minnesota became the limit of the funds available for the center.

Competition for resources was also problematic in the preparation of successful group proposals. That the successful group proposals were developed only after several generations of unsuccessful submissions indicates that some collective learning was necessary and did occur regarding collaboration on objectives and cooperation on issues of departmental administration (Russell 1985).

Acquisition of New Equipment and Facilities

Team project funds were used to purchase equipment, both for individual research laboratories and for group laboratories. No downstream conflicts arose from the equipment for individual labs. However, this was not the case for group labs.

Two departmental laboratories found the investment of resources in the laboratories to create problems as well as solving them. The MEIS Center sponsored significant renovation and remodeling in one laboratory, and some resources were also awarded by MEIS for operation of the laboratory. Because of unanticipated financial shortfalls in the departments, however, operational funds were used as substitutions rather than complements to departmental resources, and that laboratory subsequently was reduced to existence on temporary funds.

At the same time, some companies that had previously supported that laboratory through an industrial affiliates program declined to continue their support. Some companies indicated that their contributions had been redirected through the MEIS Center; others cited different reasons. The result was that the operation of the laboratory became seriously underfunded, and the department blamed this on the influence of the MEIS Center. Laboratory service and supplies suffered enormously, and users from other departments became discouraged from using the laboratory facilities, resulting in a fragmentation of collaborative activities in the laboratory.

Another laboratory was, for the most part, created through the acquisition of research equipment purchased with MEIS team funding. This equipment, once purchased, was located in departmental space and considered a departmental resource. However, while the MEIS funds did purchase the equipment, sufficient departmental resources were not set aside for the maintenance and operation of the equipment, once onsite.

Again, the MEIS Center agreed to provide some interim operating support until the department could cover the costs. Had the leadership of the team continued to reside with a faculty member in that department, this remedy would probably have been sufficient. However, a new team leader emerged, one whose department home was in a different collegiate unit. Questions of equipment ownership and responsibility for maintenance became major issues. Eventually, a division of the equipment was accomplished, with each department agreeing to assume responsibility for the maintenance of its own equipment. The team collaboration fractured, although one segment continued some interdepartmental interaction.

Maintaining and operating equipment becomes an interdepartmental issue for interdisciplinary research administration (Russell 1985). This issue may be more problematic if it arises after the fact than if it is considered in the planning stage.

Establishment of New Curricula

In three projects, new courses were added to departmental curricula as a result of the MEIS-funded projects. In each case, the evidence of need for change was catalyzed by a new expression of inquiry demonstrated in the team projects. These new curricula have generated graduate student enrollments which have, in turn, stimulated two resources: a supply of research assistants for the sponsored projects and several avenues for participating faculty to discuss research in progress. For the most part, the new curricula were departmentally based. Two exceptions, however, illustrate mechanisms by which the establishment of new curricula can make an impact on more than one department.

In one third-generation project, team members were drawn equally from two departments. As they developed complementary research interests and offered special-topics graduate courses focusing on these interests, those courses became part of the curriculum in their respective departments. Through a series of informal seminars, graduate students from each department met faculty members and students from the other departments. Students' decisions to take elective courses from other faculty members on the team project have cross-fertilized the departments and provided an element of cohesion for the project team.

In another third-generation curriculum-oriented program, three departments have cooperatively developed a specialization option which students may elect in conjunction with a standard degree in one of those departments. An introductory course and a focused laboratory course on the cooperative subject matter will be cross-listed and will be required for students who elect to take the specialization. Although interdepartmental research projects have not been undertaken by this particular group of faculty members, students' interdepartmental activities have been greatly enhanced.

Other new courses, established through new expertise developed in conjunction with MEIS-sponsored research, were added to departmental curricula. These new courses reflect changes in the foundation of knowledge upon which the departmental disciplines are built. They have become a legacy of the research programs conducted by the teams.

New Scientists and New Knowledge

The impact of these interdisciplinary influences is carried forward by the academic fabric; they are also continued by the flow of new scientists. Since its initiation in 1982–83, the MEIS doctoral fellowship program has brought nearly one hundred students to study in the fields of microelectronics and information sciences. Additional graduate students and postdoctoral fellows have been employed as research assistants with MEIS support, making a total of almost one hundred and fifty future scientists who have been supported by MEIS.

In addition to these students supported directly by MEIS, more than thirty Ph.D. degrees and more than one hundred M.S. degrees were awarded in the past four years in MEIS areas to other students who had faculty advisors who were brought to the University of Minnesota under MEIS hiring initiatives or had faculty advisors whose teaching and/or research activities were significantly influenced through (1) MEIS funds for research activities which leveraged additional research funds, (2) MEIS investments in laboratory facilities for research and education, and/or (3) new courses or curricula revised through MEIS initiatives.

This leveraging approach has already extended the MEIS influence to almost two hundred additional graduate students in the departments affiliated with the MEIS Center. Because at least five years are required for doctoral degree completion, this impact is just beginning to be visible. Moreover, this capability to identify and educate young people has now become part of the fabric of the university community.

A significant number of papers have been published from the research conducted in conjunction with the MEIS Center. While few of these have been jointly authored between collaborating faculty members, many reflect the faculty–graduate student collaboration that lies at the heart of the production of new scientists and the production of new knowledge. In general, faculty members have tended to continue publishing in the same journals as they did before the interdepartmental influence. However, a number of exceptions to this illustrate the ways in which interdisciplinary collaboration can cross-fertilize the disciplinary archives and in so doing hybridize and invigorate the discipline.

SUMMARY AND CONCLUSION

In summary, the impact of these interdisciplinary/interdepartmental research activities on the production environments of the departments from which faculty were drawn have been significant. (See Figure 8.4.) The changes brought about in the available research expertise have been particularly important. Both by redirecting the research interests of existing faculty and by adding new faculty, a new constellation of research expertise has been created. The capabilities of this expertise have made possible the acquisition of additional research funds, the construction of new and

Figure 8.4. The academic research environment

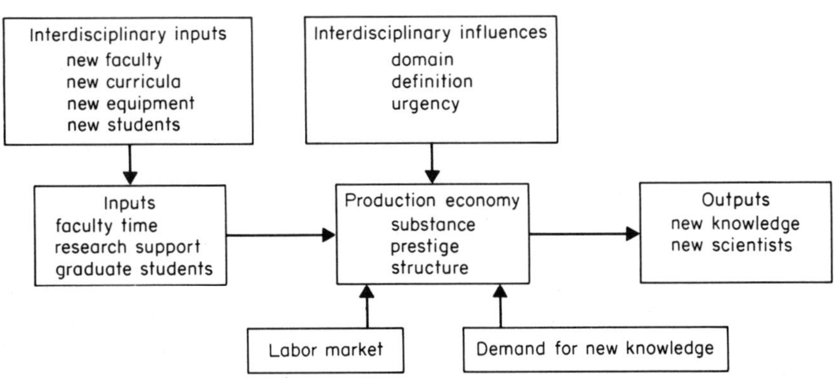

expanded research facilities, and the recruitment of graduate students working on research projects in those facilities. In addition to the projects described above, the MEIS Center also sponsored individual research activities and a full range of technology transfer activities, and these have further enriched the overall capability.

When the MEIS Center began its activities in 1982, sponsored research in fields related to microelectronic and information sciences totaled slightly more than $500,000. About forty faculty members in the Institute of Technology claimed some research interest in these fields; almost all of these faculty members were in the electrical engineering and computer science departments. Courses in the fields of microelectronic and information sciences were limited and offered in these two departments only.

Five years later, more than fifty faculty members are actively conducting research in these areas. These researchers are drawn from several departments and have submitted group proposals to MEIS, as well as to external funding agencies. Through this collaboration, a complement of research interests that are significant to the departmental disciplines and relevant to industry has been developed. In 1985–86 alone, MEIS-related sponsored research totaled more than $4 million. Total external research revenues generated by MEIS-affiliated faculty members were more than $15 million during the five-year period.

Several updated laboratory facilities now offer modernized instrumentation to complement individual faculty labs. The availability of new faculty expertise has made possible the establishment of new courses and new graduate curricula, which in turn has attracted additional graduate students to these programs. Viewed in terms of producing new scientists, this has had a substantial impact. Viewed in terms of new knowledge contributions—through Ph.D. and M.S. theses—this is indeed a significant impact. A review of master's and doctoral thesis topics and faculty publications during these past five years reveals a significantly increased number of publications. Importantly, it also reveals qualitative shifts in the topics studied.

Interestingly, it has been noted that directors of organized research units at universities tend to rank scholarly publication, external fund generation, and professional visibility very high among criteria for evaluating performance (Friedman and Friedman 1986). These tend to be the same criteria that are used by department heads in evaluating performance of faculty members. Differences that lead to conflict between department heads and directors of organized research units may be attributable to conflict over influencing the focus of the research problems. Visibility, prestige, and synergy of the research are critical to both heads and directors. Therefore, the potential exists for cooperation, and the likelihood exists for competition.

Significant changes can occur when departmental faculty members engage in interdepartmental activities. What tends to remain constant, however, are the department homes and the disciplinary communities of the faculty members. Interdisciplinary activities influence departmental programs and their affiliated disciplines. They influence departmental programs in terms of the research interests of faculty members, the funding available for research, research facilities available for research, the structure and content of the graduate degree programs, and the education of new scientists. Interdisciplinary activities influence the disciplines affiliated with these departments through the impacts from the problems studied, through expanded or altered research methodologies, and through changes in the departmental production economy—its inputs, processes, and outputs.

REFERENCES

Birnbaum, P. H. 1983. Predictors of long-term research performance. In S. R. Epton, R. L. Payne, and A. W. Pearson, eds., *Managing interdisciplinary research*. Chichester: John Wiley and Sons.

Breneman, David W. 1978. Effects of recent trends in graduate education on university research capability in physics, chemistry and mathematics. In Bruce R. Smith and Joseph A. Karlesky, eds., *The state of American science: Background papers*. New York: Change Magazine Press, pp. 133–61.

Currie, David M. 1976. Interdisciplinary research and the university reward system. Unpublished Ph.D. dissertation, University of Southern California.

Friedman, Robert S., and Renee C. Friedman. 1986. American science, academic organization, and interdisciplinary research. Presented at the Fourth Interstudy Conference, Minneapolis, August 1986. (Chapter 9 in this volume.)

Gillespie, David F., and Philip H. Birnbaum. 1980. Status concordance, coordination and success in interdisciplinary research teams. *Human Relations* 33:41–56.

James, Estelle, and Egon Neuberger. 1981. The university department as a nonprofit labor cooperative. *Public Choice* 36:585–612.

Klein, Julie T. 1985. The evolution of a body of knowledge. *Knowledge: Creation, Diffusion, Utilization* 7(2):117–42.

Klein, Julie Thompson, and Alan L. Porter. 1986. Preconditions for interdisciplinary research. Presented at the Fourth Interstudy Conference, Minneapolis, August 1986. (Chapter 1 in this volume.)

Pearson, A. W., R. L. Payne, and H. P. Gunz. 1979. Communication, coordination and leadership in interdisciplinary research. In Richard T. Barth and Rudy Steck, eds., *Interdisciplinary research groups: Their management and organization*. Vancouver: International Research Group on Interdisciplinary Programs.

Russell, Martha G. 1983a. Academic research productivity: New knowledge and new scientists in a departmental economy. Unpublished Ph.D. dissertation, University of Minnesota.

———. 1983b. Peer review in interdisciplinary research: Flexibility and responsiveness. In S. R. Epton, R. L. Payne, and A. W. Pearson, eds., *Managing interdisciplinary research*. Chichester: John Wiley and Sons.

———. 1985. Administering interdisciplinary collaboration. In B. W. Mar, W. T. Newell, and B. O. Saxberg, eds., *Managing high technology*. Amsterdam: North Holland, pp. 245–53.

Russell, Martha G., and Richard J. Sauer. 1983. Creating administrative environments for interdisciplinary research. *Journal of the Society of Research Administrators* 14(4):21–31.

Sauer, Richard J. 1982. The role of the department head in interdisciplinary research. In Martha G. Russell, Richard J. Sauer, and John M. Barnes, eds., *Enabling interdisciplinary research: Perspectives from agriculture, forestry, and home economics*. Miscellaneous Publication 19, Agriculture Experiment Station, University of Minnesota.

Schuller, C. Richard. 1986. Three synergistic preconditions for interdisciplinary research: Defined problems, dedicated researchers, supportive environments. Presented at the Fourth Interstudy Conference, Minneapolis, August 1986.

Schultz, Theodore W. 1986. Resources for higher education: An economist's view. *Journal of Political Economy* 76:227–47.

Vasconcellos, Eduardo. 1986. Organization design for interdisciplinary research: Conflicts and performance. Presented at the Fourth Interstudy Conference, Minneapolis, August 1986. (Chapter 12 in this volume.)

9
American Science, Academic Organization, and Interdisciplinary Research

ROBERT S. FRIEDMAN
RENEE C. FRIEDMAN

By inadvertence or design, the scientific enterprise in the United States has always been fragmented, pluralistic, and competitive. The same untidiness, decentralization, and conflict over goals and processes that exist at the macro level are mirrored in the leading research universities. While these institutions do not hold a monopoly over the conduct of basic and applied research, they are perceived as the most fertile environments for creativity and innovation. Wolfle (1972, p.65) offers a compelling rationale:

> The most fundamental and pervasive factor in the universities' growth into the nation's principal research agencies was decentralization. Decentralizing research in many universities instead of centralizing it in a few national research centers guaranteed a dispersed, competitive scientific community. The existence of many universities, all independent of each other and of the federal government, meant that no governmental or other centralized agency could control science, set limits, determine national priorities, or establish orthodoxies. Instead, scientists were free to follow their own system of values, to choose the problems they wanted to investigate, and to reward those among them whose work they regarded most highly.

THE AMERICAN RESEARCH UNIVERSITY

Despite the transformation of the university over the past three centuries, its organizational structure and character still reflect the dominance of the teaching function. The American university is best understood as a collection of fundamentally autonomous units rather than a central authority with departmental subordination. Disciplinary splintering, faculty professionalization, and the ascendency of the research mission have strengthened, not diminished, the role of departments. By virtue of its control over curricular design and degree requirements, areas of research emphasis, professorial appointments, promotion and tenure, and the reward systems, the disciplinary department remains the power center of the university and the single most influential force in shaping the career patterns of faculty (Friedman and Friedman 1985, p.79). Academic departments resemble guilds to which admission depends on a reasonable congruence of the candidate's disciplinary training, values, and methodological orientation with that of the majority (Ikenberry and Friedman 1972, p.15). In return for the scholar's fealty, the department provides citizenship, community, and a political voice. Critics of university organization often assume that the chief impediment of interdisciplinary and multidisciplinary collaboration is the department. Blaming structure ignores the psychosocial needs of academics. The rites of passage nascent scholars undergo during their socialization in order to internalize the values, attitudes, and norms of the peer group to which they aspire argue against personal risk taking. Disciplines or professions furnish us with identity cards, a common tongue, and a set of tools with which we classify and are classified by the larger world (Friedman and Friedman 1982). Moreover, because the university is a political decision-making body in which competing interests vie for scarce resources, the collective will of the department is entrusted to the chairperson, who, as part of the representative process, negotiates on behalf of his or her peers.

Perceived as a zero-sum contest, existing departments and/or colleges frequently form coalitions to block new claimants to the university treasury. How well the department fares in garnering resources depends on several factors, notably student demand, professorial market scarcity, and status. Of the three, status as measured by reputation and position within the disciplinary hierarchy is the trump card.

Within the academic milieu research is valued to the extent that it affects, influences, and is essential for others' work to be successfully accomplished. The most prestigious reputations are held by those who are judged by their peers as most competent in following standard procedures, applying shared skills, and producing significant and relevant work for collective goals (Whitley 1984, p.12). High-paradigm scientific disciplines with the greatest access to external resources and control over the reward structure meted out by society occupy the top rungs of the university status ladder. Pinner's insightful essay (1962, p. 943) explains why society accepts research findings in particular intellectual fields:

> I term "consensual" all those disciplines with respect to which the public at large tends to have no reservations, either as to the competence of the scholars and the truth of their findings or as to the values which inform their work. Correspondingly, I term "dissensual" all disciplines whose value or procedures are widely questioned among the public, either explicitly or implicitly. Mathematics, the natural sciences, and such applied sciences as engineering or veterinary medicine are typically consensual disciplines. Philosophy, the social

> sciences, music, literature, and the fine arts are dissensual. Few people in the community will express doubts about the research findings and teachings of a chemist, nor will they even question his motives and wonder about the values underlying his work. But the findings and teachings of philosophers and economists do not elicit similarly general confidence. The public tends to look for hidden motives, and it easily discounts the teaching and even the data of dissensual disciplines either by directly opposing or by conveniently forgetting and ignoring them.

Disputation and rejection do arise no matter how valid the scientific results of consensual disciplines when the output or outcome is seen as redistributive, as in the case of nuclear waste disposal in the United States (Friedman 1985).

Because the American research universities have become resource-dependent institutions in which little of the real research costs are borne by tuition, endowments, or state aid, societal demand and willingness to fund innovative research are essential. The need to maintain the integrity of the disciplines and to respond to the changing needs and priorities of society has prompted the research universities to establish organizational structures apart from departments. Departments, per se, are ill equipped to engage in collaborative research or tackle problems that transcend disciplinary boundaries. These nondepartmental alternatives, termed organized research units (ORUs), are intended to be complementary to, and not substitutes for, academic departments.

Understandably, these campus parvenus have not met with universal acclaim or acceptance. Like interdisciplinary degree programs, they lack universally agreed-upon intellectual cores and consistent nomenclature across the academic tier. They frequently offer perquisites such as twelve-month contracts and secretarial assistance denied department-bound faculty, thus sparking intraorganizational rivalry and conflict. As noted earlier, academia is a highly individualistic enterprise and not a team sport. Organized research units are often perceived as profiting at the expense of departments and diluting their prestige. However noble their purposes, these newcomers must demonstrate their legitimacy and intellectual credibility to their disciplinary colleagues.

Organized research units come in assorted sizes, shapes, packages, and philosophies. Based on the Becker and Gordon administrative taxonomy (1966), Ikenberry and Friedman (1972, pp.34–39) developed a classification scheme that delineated three ORU models: standard, adaptive, and shadow. A standard institute has sufficient stability in goals and resources to develop a full managerial hierarchy and a permanent professional staff to invest in potentially expensive equipment essential to its tasks and to justify a reasonably permanent allocation of space. In such units staff members usually establish their primary ties and maintain their principal career identification. Adaptive ORUs undergo a continuous process of redefining their goals, initiating and terminating projects, securing and releasing staff, in short adapting to a persistent instability. Shadow institutes have no staff, no allotted space, and no independent budget. The obvious advantage of adaptive and shadow ORUs is their flexibility and response to change. Temporary appointments enable staff recruitment suitable to the task, whereas permanent staff restrict or modify the assignment to fit their competencies. Adaptive ORUs require few alterations in the administrative structure and engender little hostility over dual citizenship. Adaptive ORUs are similar to matrix organizations in that the agency (university) is organized along the traditional functional lines (departments), and these still determine the individual's career development. The tasks undertaken require heterogeneous work groups gathered on an ad hoc basis (Friedman and Friedman 1982, p.141).

DISCIPLINARY VERSUS INTERDISCIPLINARY

The most widely heralded purpose for which these varying structures were developed—engagement in multidisciplinary and interdisciplinary research—is a major source of conflict. *Multidisciplinary* can be described as a loose confederation of individual scholars from different disciplines who share common facilities, common research approaches, and a common environment. The faculty tend to work independently on separate aspects of a larger problem, ceding few of their rights and privileges beyond agreeing to the selection of a team spokesperson (principal investigator). In contrast, *interdisciplinary* involves an interactive joint effort to reach a solution, an elaborate division of labor, and a hierarchy of command whereby the project director has the legitimate authority to provide direction and oversee the research from inception to completion. A standard institute engaged in interdisciplinary research deviates most radically from departmental tradition and style and widens the breach between ORUs and departments. Table 9.1 juxtaposes the values, structures, and processes ascribed to each organization.

Presiding over a society of equals who speak a common language and share a similar approach is different from leading an aggregation of cohorts from disparate intellectual backgrounds who are charting new territory. Weinberg (1970, p.1070) captured the essence of the problem when he wrote, "[University] and the social ethos of the institute: the one is individual and democratic, the other collective and hierarchical." So long as faculty members reside within the confines of the department, they may pursue the research questions of greatest interest to them and ignore the needs or schedules of others. Peer applause and approval motivate the scholarship. The intent is to enhance the stature of the discipline and further the reputation of the individual researcher. How to solve a problem, how not to solve a problem, or how to adapt the problem for eventual solution are all potentially rewardable outcomes. Interdisciplinary research abrogates these personal freedoms. In a metaphorical sense, regional government, with all the constraints imposed by multiple taskmasters and in-

Table 9.1. Comparisons between disciplinary departments and interdisciplinary organizations with respect to values, structures, and processes

Disciplinary departments	Interdisciplinary organizations
Emphasis on individual	Emphasis on team
Discipline orientation	Task orientation
Peer approval	Societal approval
Independence in methodological approach	Group-determined methodological approach
Reward structure in place	Reward structure nebulous
Collegial decision making	Hierarchical decision making
Single jurisdiction	Multiple jurisdiction
Equality of status regardless of rank	Inequality—some individuals more equal than others
Internally generated research ideas	Externally generated problems
Personal competency	Continuum of competence
Outcome or output unpredictable	Output or outcome specificity
Timeless	Time-bound
Peer evaluation	Uncertain or unknown evaluation
Single authorship	Multiple authorship

terest groups, replaces local government. The team is at center stage rather than the individual, and the decision-making authority rests at the top of the pyramid. Verb differences connote role expectations: chairpersons chair while directors direct. Utilitarian, problem-focused, set apart from formal instruction, and accountable to a sponsor, interdisciplinary ORUs particularly stand in marked contrast to academic departments (Friedman and Friedman 1982; Ikenberry and Friedman 1972). Moreover, the problems tend to be externally generated, making ORUs vulnerable to the charge of clientelism. Accepting, evaluating, and rewarding the findings are determined by users, not peers. Indeed, who are the peers? Being of, rather than at, the university requires recognition of, accommodation to, and acceptance of academic standards of conduct and mores. Interdisciplinary ORUs must aim high with respect to location and leadership. Universitywide units under the aegis of the vice-president for research or a similar high-ranking official can draw from the entire professorial spectrum, whereas locus within a college, particularly one of lower status, will dissuade prestigious faculty from participation. Choice of the leader matters greatly. The ORU director must possess scholarly credentials and have a reputation commensurate with that of the ranking members of the departments from which the organization hopes to recruit. Effectiveness in interpersonal relations is secondary to entrepreneurial skills and professional recognition. In the world in which the director matriculates, the rest of the team players matter very little. The emphasis on reputation in the leadership selection process does not signify that handling people, networking, and communications are trivial pursuits, nor is it a given that prominent, successful grant getters are also skilled managers. In the absence of this talent, faculty should insist on the appointment of a second-in-command who does possess these traits. Fostering employee and staff morale is essential in hierarchical organizations.

Playing by the rules also means that interdisciplinary ORUs in research universities that expect significant scholarly productivity are ill advised to undertake major projects that demean institutional prestige. Similarly, such units must not abandon basic academic commitments in dealing with sponsors. These include the linking of research to the educational mission and the expectation that research findings be part of the public domain. Writing sponsored research reports or publishing in nonrefereed house organs are important but insufficient activities. Peer communication, Merton's (1957, p. 557) concept of communality (the free sharing of one's discoveries with others), still holds sway. Doing applied research does not automatically relegate the organization to second-class status. In the hands of gifted researchers, it is possible to satisfy the needs of sponsors and peers (Friedman and Friedman 1982, pp.29–30).

Sharing the wealth with respect to equipment, personnel, and summer employment mitigates the inevitable jealousy between affiliated and unaffiliated faculty. Good citizenship helps. ORU faculty should not be exempted from advising students, chairing or sitting on dissertation committees, performing ambassadorial duties, and participating in department, college, or university governance. Directors must give adequate credit for work performed by junior faculty and list the departmental affiliation of ORU faculty in publications. Directors should keep open the lines of communication with department chairpersons about hiring, promotion recommendation, and salary adjustments. The institute-department relationship is, at best, tenuous and difficult. Yet the tension may have the salubrious effect Coser (1956, p.95) postulates:

> Conflict with another group leads to the mobilization of the energies of group members and hence to increased cohesion of the group. Whether increased centralization accompanies this increase in cohesion depends upon both the character of the conflict and the type of group. Centralization will be more likely to occur in the event of warlike conflict and in differentiated structures requiring division of labor. By the same token, consensus should not be purchased at the price of scholarship.

Interdisciplinary ORUs probably perform best when the cognitive distances between disciplines are short and the broader organizational cultures are similar. Unfortunately, real-world problems are not bound by discipline or college. A public policy issue such as the graying of America requires expertise from psychologists, sociologists, economists, biologists, physicians, and lawyers. In addition to disciplinary differences, the matter of college looms large. A medical school, in contrast to the discipline-based core university, tends not to observe the same conventions, distribute power as widely, or accept Ph.D.'s as equals. Technicians do the work normally assigned to graduate students, the chairmen's power in departments of medicine and surgery is near absolute, and many physicians assume that their clinical ability extends to research. Splitting the organization into functional, nearly autonomous components which report separately to a suprahead makes sense when the gap between intellectual fields cannot be bridged or the behavioral norms, rather than problem resolution, become the focus of the conflict.

Ironically, many of the same features that make the integration of research between the university and medical school difficult also enable the medical school to serve as an interdisciplinary role model. Despite its size and resources, the medical school is a single jurisdiction with few administrative layers. Joint appointments, salaried and courtesy, are commonplace. The complex division of labor and authoritarian structures that vex the core university are standard operating procedures in the medical school. While biochemists may not be held in the same esteem as surgeons, the comparatively higher salaries basic scientists earn in medical schools partially compensate for their lesser status. Moreover, from an interdisciplinary standpoint, medical training, regardless of specialty, is holistic. This preconditioning and emphasis on problem solving explain why an infusion of critical resources rephrases the level of targeted research so quickly and effectively within the medical milieu. The model is not transferable to the university at large but is perhaps adaptable for some types of engineering research. Again, despite the different foci, the methods of inquiry are similar and derive from high-paradigm disciplines. Engineers are socialized, as team players and problem solvers, two necessary foundations for interdisciplinary endeavors.

SUMMARY

Successful interdisciplinary collaboration requires initial and continuing support from three sources: sponsors, university administration, and interested faculty. Interdisciplinary undertakings created by administrative fiat without the real consent of the affected faculty and organizations, required by their sponsors to engage in nonrewarding academic activities, will not survive long (Friedman and Friedman 1982). Further, among the principals, agreement must exist that the problem is intellectually meritorious and solvable. Selection of the appropriate structure—matrix or freestanding—depends on intellectual field subculture and institutional mores.

Paradoxically, the disciplinary department is simultaneously the best friend and the worst enemy of interdisciplinary research organizations. The knowledge explosion, which led to specialization and the proliferation of departments, also fueled the intellectual ferment within departments and shortened the cognitive distances between fields. New theories, emerging technologies, and the reordering of research priorities have reshaped the boundaries and content of disciplines as well as having spawned a variety of organizational configurations.

REFERENCES

Becker, S., and G. Gordon. 1966. An entrepreneurial theory of formal organizations. *Administrative Science Quarterly* 11:315–44.

Coser, L. A. 1956. *The functions of social conflict.* New York: Free Press.

Friedman, R. S. 1985. Political considerations of nuclear waste disposal policy. In S. K. Majundar and E. W. Miller, eds., *Management of radioactive materials and waste: Issues and progress.* Harrisburg: Pennslyvania Academy of Sciences, pp. 203–15.

Friedman, R. S., and R. C. Friedman. 1982. *The role of university organized research units in academic science.* Springfield, Va.: National Technical Information Service, PB82-253394.

———. 1985. Organized research units in academe revisited. In B. W. Mar, W. T. Newell, and B. O. Saxberg, eds., *Managing high technology.* New York: North Holland, pp. 75–91.

Ikenberry, S. O., and R. C. Friedman. 1972. *Beyond academic departments.* San Francisco: Jossey-Bass.

Merton, R. K. 1957. *Social theory and social structures.* Glencoe, Ill.: Free Press.

Pinner, F. 1962. The crisis of the state universities: Analysis and remedies. In N. Sanford, ed., *The American college: A psychological and social interpretation of the higher learning.* New York: Wiley, pp. 940–71.

Weinberg, A. M. 1970. Scientific teams and scientific laboratories. *Daedalus* 10:1056–75.

Whitley, R. 1984. *The intellectual and social organization of the sciences.* Oxford: Clarendon Press.

Wolfle, D. 1972. *The home of science.* New York: McGraw-Hill.

10
Georgia Tech Research Institute: An Interdisciplinary Perspective

DONALD J. GRACE
FREDERICK A. ROSSINI

This paper discusses the history and current status of the Georgia Tech Research Institute (GTRI) with emphasis on cross-organizational and cross-disciplinary interaction. GTRI is a contract research organization which has been an integral part of Georgia Tech for more than fifty years. Functionally oriented, GTRI interacts with the academic units of Georgia Tech, and its researchers participate in the interdisciplinary research centers which utilize elements of GTRI and the academic units. The paper analyzes issues causing potential friction between academic and professional researchers, such as overhead, space, and faculty status. Finally, future plans and prospects for GTRI are presented.

The Georgia Tech Research Institute, formerly known as the Engineering Experiment Station, operates as a full-time nonprofit research organization. Its professional staff of nearly six hundred researchers manages individual projects which currently have an annual value of $65 million. Among other things, it does applied research for the Department of Defense, works in several overseas locations, and manages technical assistance and economic development offices in the state of Georgia. Operationally, it is quite similar to many of the well-known not-for-profit organizations, such as SRI International and Battelle. Yet it is not a separate corporate entity. It reports through the administrative structure of a university and is continually evolving closer ties with its academic colleagues at the Georgia Institute of Technology. We believe this arrangement to be unique among universities.

How it came about during the past seventy years is a story that highlights the potential sources of strength and friction between academic and research organizations. Many of the problems that had to be addressed in its growth toward maturity are currently cited as major barriers to the formation of similar relationships at other universities. By summarizing some key elements of the past, we hope to underscore the role of such a research organization in a university and to exemplify the way it works at Georgia Tech today. Some recent examples of interdisciplinary activity will be outlined later in the paper, followed by an analysis of present status and long-range plans.

THE BEGINNING

The saga really begins in the early 1880s, less than twenty years after the Civil War, when several influential Georgians decided that the state needed a technological institution to complement its already one hundred-year-old University of Georgia, which emphasized agriculture and the liberal arts. As a result, Georgia Tech came into being in 1885. To this day it remains the only engineering college in the state of Georgia.

In the same time frame, the Morrill Acts of 1862 and 1890 created the land-grant universities and led to the evolution of agricultural experiment stations, which continue to this day in providing research, development, and technology transfer throughout the United States. In the years since, federal funding for agricultural experiment stations at all land-grant colleges has been furnished annually and reliably. In the early 1900s, engineering experiment stations began to appear in the United States, the first being established at the University of Illinois in 1903, followed by Iowa State in 1904. They were intended to be analogous to the highly successful agricultural stations, but there was never any federal commitment to provide funds on a regular basis for their operation, so their individual performance depended on obtaining occasional gifts or grants and on award of sponsored contracts.

A significant push to get federal funding for engineering experiment stations was launched in Congress in 1916 as part of the preparedness campaign prior to the United States' entry into World War I. In Georgia, a political battle ensued between Georgia Tech and the University of Georgia over which university should receive these anticipated federal funds. While the University of Georgia was the land-grant college, all of the engineering was at Georgia Tech. Meanwhile, the Georgia legislature established the Engineering Experiment Station (EES) in August of 1919; it was given a legislative charter and placed administratively at Georgia Tech. Still, the clash over possible federal funding remained bitter between the two universities, even as late as 1922. There was little need to squabble over state funding because the first legislative appropriation for EES was not passed until 1934.

In 1929, a group of Georgia Tech professors began discussing formation of an engineering experiment station, unaware that it had already existed for ten years. Five years later, it received an initial budget of five thousand dollars intended "to study engineering problems of commercial, economic, and social interest to Georgia and the South."

The early work of the station was carried out in the basement of the

Shop building. Faculty members worked there part-time in addition to their teaching; there were no full-time researchers at that time. As an adjunct, the Industrial Development Council (IDC) was established in 1938 with the objective of serving as a contractual agency for the station, to administer patents and to help develop its research projects.

After a few years of respectable growth, fiscal years 1939 and 1940 were disastrous in terms of state funding, with the legislature cutting the budget by 40 percent over these years. This, however, prompted EES to be more aggressive in seeking outside-sponsored projects. In those years, the diversity of programs ranged from helicopter research to application of the attic fan in southern homes. Station research was concentrated essentially on Georgia and southeastern regional economic development. Even during the early years of World War II, EES had no significant war-related activity. By 1943, the accelerated pace of the war began to have an impact. The station budget for 1944, for the first time, had more than half of its total funding coming from outside sources rather than the state legislature. This trend was never subsequently reversed. In 1944, there were seventeen full-time and nearly one hundred part-time staff members conducting thirty different projects. By 1945, the EES budget was almost $240,000. This amount was trivial compared to MIT, which had more than $100 million of federal defense funding during the same year, but a key interaction had begun which became a major factor in the subsequent growth and nature of EES and continues to be vital even today. The Department of Defense represents 70 percent of the station's current sponsored funding.

By 1948, Georgia Tech ranked fourth in size in a group of 143 engineering colleges in the United States. Its enrollment had doubled since 1945, extension work had increased tenfold, and EES research had increased fivefold in the same three years.

Meanwhile, the Industrial Development Council had become relatively dormant and a new organization to be called the Georgia Tech Research Institute was founded in 1946. Among other functions, this entity is a separately chartered nonprofit corporation registered in Georgia. It has an independent board of directors, including the president of Georgia Tech, with most of the remaining members required to be Georgia Tech staff members or alumni. (To add to the readers' confusion, it was decided in 1984 to change the name of the Engineering Experiment Station. It was agreed that the most appropriate name would be the Georgia Tech Research Institute. To accomplish this, the nonprofit corporation, GTRI, had to change *its* name to the Georgia Tech Research Corporation, GTRC.)

As administrator of all external contracts, GTRI/GTRC can accrue and redistribute funds, as well as carry over projects from one fiscal year to another (the state of Georgia works on a zero-based budget which does not permit this). Operationally, it now handles all of Georgia Tech's research contracts, for both the academic units and EES. Such flexibility is almost mandatory in state universities where significant amounts of sponsored research are done.

During the first full year of operation under the newly formed GTRI, EES had its busiest year in history, with an operating budget of almost half a million dollars, 87 percent of it coming from external contracts. There were fifty-six full-time researchers and ninety-five part-time researchers. Within the mix of contracts, there was an increasing amount of government-classified work.

A 1948 study conducted by the Association of Land Grant Colleges and Universities listed the dollar value of research at EES, as compared with other engineering experiment stations, second in the nation and first in the South, ranking it behind only Purdue. As the size and visibility of the station's program grew, so did its autonomy. Inevitably, friction with faculty members not intimately involved in its projects also increased. There was an attitude in some quarters that the station was becoming the "tail that wagged the dog." Still another kind of problem arose when the director of GTRI became president of Scientific Associates, a direct spinoff from the station which was incorporated in 1951. This firm later evolved into Scientific Atlanta, a multi-million-dollar Atlanta-based company for which Georgia Tech now claims a prideful parentage. At that time, though, the Georgia Tech administration viewed the participation of EES personnel in outside research as a direct conflict of interest. Feelings then were so strong that this, coupled with budgetary issues, caused the resignation of the EES director in 1952.

During that same time, graduate education at Georgia Tech was expanding. As an essential corollary, research was receiving added emphasis from the administration. Because of the research impetus, a Georgia Tech chapter of Sigma Xi was granted in 1953, whereas it had been vetoed by the society in 1950 because of an inadequate "climate for research." At this time there were forty-six doctoral students at Georgia Tech, and the overall graduate enrollment had increased 865 percent since 1940. Many of these graduate students conducted thesis and dissertation research in conjunction with EES, where several faculty members had joint appointments. The Engineering College generally supported these arrangements, but many of the hard-science units were not in favor of it. The attack was led by the Department of Chemistry, centering around the question of whether or not basic research could be conducted within the context of contract work.

One member of the Board of Regents took the position that Georgia Tech "should employ the highest type of combination teachers and researchers that are obtainable within your budget so that our boys can receive both instruction and research training from the most outstanding men we can employ." The Georgia Tech president was somewhat ambivalent. He felt on the one hand that teaching loads should be realistic enough to support research programs directed by academicians, but at the same time he believed that the only way to foster research at Georgia Tech was to make use of contract dollars funneled to EES through GTRI.

There was considerable concern about the flow of funds and the financial management of EES, which culminated in a key agreement worked out among Georgia Tech, GTRI, and the Board of Regents in 1953. It spelled out the duties and responsibilities of all three bodies and specified a precise method of reporting of EES budgetary transactions. For its services, GTRI would receive $\frac{10}{46}$ of overhead collected on contracts. Any funds that were left over after operating costs had been paid would be left in trust in GTRI accounts to promote research at Georgia Tech and the station. This agreement has remained in force since.

Another sticky point of contention came to a head in 1953. This had to do with the faculty rank assigned to full-time EES staff not engaged in teaching. On the one hand, academic faculty resented that station personnel who were not teaching held professorial rank. At the same time, station employees were getting turned down for advancement by the Regents because they did not hold Ph.D. degrees or otherwise did not meet promotion or tenure qualifications. A policy was established in the spring of 1953 which defined a parallel range of titles for research faculty that did not have the same requirements for advancement in faculty rank or limitations on their salary. In exchange, research faculty were eliminated from the possibility of tenure. Research faculty remained members of the General Faculty but were excluded from membership in the Academic Senate, the body dealing with all academic matters. This arrangement left Georgia Tech's professional researchers with a substantial role in faculty governance. The problem of disenfranchisement relative to academics that haunts researchers on so many campuses was avoided at Tech.

There were other problems between the academic and research faculty. In 1954, a faculty committee expressed concern that the station budget (then \$2 million) represented 83 percent of research support from government agencies, about two-thirds of which was classified. The committee also indicated a "lack of liaison between EES and the academic departments."

The desire for separate arrangements to permit individual academic faculty to conduct research without doing it through EES continued to grow over the next ten years. The Defense Department represented large funding, but the relatively new National Science Foundation offered basic research grants that were far more attractive to academic faculty.

Meanwhile, the cold war of the 1950s and the advent of Sputnik in 1957 contributed to efforts to expand research and graduate programs in engineering and the physical sciences, both at the national level and at Georgia Tech. In 1961, the president of Georgia Tech, in a major policy statement, focused heavily on research as being "the most discussed and least understood" concern of the institute. He advocated a unification of effort in the areas of teaching, research, and graduate study. Paradoxically, the best way to accomplish this seemed to be to separate research done in the academic units from that done in the station. This was accomplished in 1964. The decision was greeted with enthusiasm by many faculty members, while being disapproved by many in the station.

The decision did not resolve continuing debates over the nature and control of research at Tech, but institute research continued to grow, especially in EES. In November of 1969, a report noted that during the previous fiscal year, various divisions of the station held twelve hundred contracts with industry, especially in Georgia, about half of which were extended contracts with the companies concerned. The report also noted that twenty-nine companies, with annual sales of $25 million, could be considered as spinoffs of Georgia Tech and that eighteen of those, including Scientific Atlanta, were started by EES personnel.

An event of continuing importance to Georgia Tech research was the organization of the first interdisciplinary research center in 1963: the Water Resources Center, whose name was changed in 1970 to the Environmental Resources Center. A second interdisciplinary research center, the Bioengineering Center, was established in 1969. In 1973, the Office of Interdisciplinary Programs was established to coordinate the management of existing centers and to encourage the development of new ones. The centers' program was meant to be flexible so that, as well as establishing new centers, existing centers without a viable program could be abolished. This would ensure timely and flexible response to intellectual and sponsorship opportunities. Typically, a center's program involves researchers from three or more major Georgia Tech units and requires identifiable solid sources of external funding, as internal funding is spartan.

An important ingredient of the centers' philosophy at Georgia Tech is that they report directly at the same level of administration as EES and the academic units. Essentially, all of their professional members retain their administrative homes within existing established units. Participation in the centers is voluntary on the part of faculty, who are not prohibited from writing their own proposals and doing their own research outside the center umbrella. On the other hand, additional visibility, equipment, and discretionary funding are often at the disposal of center directors, which adds a powerful incentive for both research and academic faculty to participate. Indeed, many of the most able researchers at Georgia Tech have elected to involve themselves with center activities.

In 1970, the underlying conflict between academic and station personnel again surfaced. There were not only old antagonisms over organizational and budgetary prerogatives, but new pressures brought matters to a point of confrontation. Some external sources were encouraging the station to become more self-supporting from research and development contracts, while other sources counseled further induction of the station into academic programs, particularly at the graduate level, without discontinuing provision of technical assistance to Georgia industries. Both the station and the instructional side were suffering from overall cutbacks in funds for military research and the space program. In the fall of 1970, the Georgia Tech president set out to dismantle EES and integrate it into Tech's academic units.

Response from the station was immediate and adamant. There was talk of breaking away from the institute. From the academic side there was apathy—essentially no interest in absorbing elements of EES, since their work was seen as being too applied and the management requirements for their contracts too onerous. Two things prevented the dissolution of EES. First, the assistance of key legislators was sought to prevent the university from unilaterally eliminating an organization which the state government had created independently. The second event was the resignation of the president to take another position, coupled with the subsequent appointment of Dr. Joseph M. Pettit as the new president. Dr. Pettit had been the dean of engineering at Stanford University, where he had recently witnessed the separation of the Stanford Research Institute from Stanford University. He was determined that Georgia Tech's EES would remain directly on the campus and work in harmony with the institute. Shortly after taking office in 1971, he created the position of vice-president for research and selected Dr. Thomas E. Stelson, who had been dean of engineering at Georgia Tech, for this position. All research in EES and the academic units, as well as in the centers, came under Stelson's purview. In this position, he controls the financial side of research administration, including allocation of research funds and indirect revenues of all research contracts at Georgia Tech. His office also serves as the focal point for resolving differences among research units and encouraging interdisciplinary and cross-organizational interaction.

In 1986, fifteen years after the unsuccessful attempt to dismantle the EES, the organization, sporting its new name as the Georgia Tech Research Institute, is in its strongest position ever, and the ties with its academic colleagues have never been closer. There are eighty-five graduate research assistants from academic units working in GTRI. Additionally, one hundred and twenty-five full-time GTRI researchers are also part-time graduate students under our program of offering tuition waivers toward advanced degrees. Dissertation work is being supervised by GTRI researchers on behalf of a number of academic schools, most notably Electrical Engineering, Chemical Engineering, Physics, and Mechanical Engineering.

There is a relatively fundamental difference between the organization of academic units, which typically must be chartered along disciplinary lines, and the seven laboratories that comprise GTRI, where the organization is more along functional lines (e.g., the Radar and Instrumentation Laboratory and the Economic Development Laboratory). This enhances its ability to have researchers from many different disciplines organized into the same administrative units. Certainly, the research centers previously mentioned are also organized along functional rather than disciplinary lines; indeed, that is a prime reason for forming them.

As an example, a proposal has recently been submitted for a $10 million, three-year program to develop and administer autonomously piloted helicopters. The proposal was generated by a team of researchers from Aerospace and Mechanical Engineering on the academic side, the Radar and Electromagnetic Laboratories within GTRI, and a commercial organization. Interestingly enough, there was early agreement that the management of such a large and complex project should be placed within GTRI. In fact, the idea was originally voiced by one of the senior academic researchers.

Alternatively, the College of Engineering and GTRI are currently working on a proposal to establish the Laboratory for Information Technology, which will be headquartered within the College of Engineering. This organization will solicit participation by industrial firms and will involve elements of teaching, research, and technology transfer.

THE FUTURE

Long-range planning has been in vogue during the past several years at Georgia Tech. Individual units have prepared their own, and they have been interactively matched with those from the president down. In the area of research, GTRI expects to double its current volume within the next fifteen years. This is the same growth scale that the academic side of the house has established for its research. The centers, now nineteen in number, which represent about 8 percent of the total, also anticipate increasing in number and research volume. However, three centers have been abolished in the past three years, while an even larger number were established. Tomorrow's centers may not be today's centers. These plans have all been cross-briefed and are acceptable to all parties. Another specific goal of Georgia Tech will be to significantly increase the number and throughput of Ph.D's. This goal will require interaction and support from GTRI, which it is quite prepared to give. With regard to students, GTRI's plan calls for having two hundred and fifty graduate research assistants and an additional two hundred and fifty full-time employees attending graduate school part-time. That will be a total of five hundred, out of the anticipated three thousand graduate students, certainly a significant fraction.

As we look toward the next fifteen years, we will need to double the total volume of research space. Current thinking calls for the development of buildings that would use combinations of academic and GTRI personnel with similar research interests (e.g., an Environmental Science Building and a Manufacturing Technology Building). This will enhance the opportunity for interdisciplinary activity among the faculties of both organizations, as well as with outside industrial firms.

As Georgia Tech and EES have grown, the need for space has become a factor in the rate and direction of growth. The subject of space can generate heated discussion, especially among faculties. There was a time when research buildings would be provided by legislative appropriation, but the last such building for EES was built in 1969. The demand for academic buildings is now so great that the likelihood of EES expansion through the legislature became infinitesimal. In some desperation, EES leased 125,000 square feet from Lockheed Missiles and Space Company, which had been designed for research and development use, at a distance of sixteen miles from the campus eight years ago. Following the lead of Colorado State University, a more effective means for adding research buildings was evolved. An arm's-length, not-for-profit corporation—the Georgia Scientific and Technology Research Foundation (GSTRF)—was formed in Georgia to float tax-exempt bond issues for the purpose of building research and development facilities. One of these bond issues was used to build the 191,000-square-foot Centennial Research Building on campus. The premises are leased back to Georgia Tech at commercial rates, and the lease costs are added to the overhead burden. It is anticipated that this mechanism will be used for further expansion of research facilities.

Of course, one solution can often lead to another problem. The expenses incurred in leasing these two properties caused the Georgia Tech overhead to rise significantly, to the dismay of academic researchers. That most recent problem was resolved, in part, at the beginning of fiscal year 1986 by establishing separate overhead rates for GTRI and for the academic structure in order to achieve more equitable cost recovery for sponsored research activities. While this is a move of fiscal separation, it is almost certain to reduce friction and misunderstanding between academic and GTRI researchers in the long run, just as establishing a new title structure for researchers did in 1953. The bugs still need to be worked out of the new system. It seems painful to have to compute separate overhead and fringe-benefit rates for different parts of the same proposal. However, the benefits to both groups are clear. GTRI can now recover its costs so that it does not have to subsidize other parts of Georgia Tech. The academics can lower their rate relative to a single, combined rate.

In the long run, in addition to mutual research interests, two factors should serve to keep ties close between GTRI and the academic units. These are the centers, which cross-cut GTRI and the academic units, and the involvement of graduate (especially Ph.D.) students in the GTRI research program, with the corresponding supervision of them by GTRI personnel. The cross-fertilization in such areas as the Microelectronics, Materials Handling, and Bioengineering centers, and in the Physics and Electrical Engineering Ph.D. programs, helps maintain a more cohesive and flexible environment across disciplinary and organization boundaries.

We look forward to an exciting, interactive future for all of the elements of Georgia Tech. There will be new problems to be met by innovative solutions. But the total enterprise will always be greater than the sum of the parts. We intend to remain interactive and interdisciplinary, and to be a model for the twenty-first century of university-government-industry cooperation.

11

The Development of an Interdisciplinary University-Based Microelectronics Research Center

JOHN W. HOOPER
FREDERICK A. ROSSINI

This paper describes a cooperative university-based program of research in the cross-disciplinary field of microelectronics. Specific organizational and management features patterned to address the cultural characteristics of the university are described. Particular emphasis is placed on the relative impact of each factor on the overall performance of the center.

Microelectronics is a research area of such scope that it requires the participation of scientists and engineers from a number of disciplines. To establish an effective program of microelectronics research in a university environment requires a substantial measure of cross-disciplinary, cross-organizational cooperation which is often not easy to attain in an academic environment. Yet the importance of microelectronics research as the foundation of developments in information technology is so great that a number of major research universities have established substantial research efforts in that area. This paper discusses, as a case study, the development and structure of the Microelectronics Research Center at Georgia Tech. While no single organizational form is ideal in every context, the institutional learning resulting from this activity has been beneficial for Georgia Tech, and parts of it may be transferrable to other universities as well. This paper first considers the organization, funding, and oversight of the center. Then it discusses the development and administration of research projects. Technology transfer is treated next. A concluding section discusses the status and prospects of the center.

ORGANIZATION, FUNDING, AND OVERSIGHT

Microelectronics research at Georgia Tech is conducted on a cooperative basis by an interdisciplinary group of researchers from various academic units and research laboratories. Focus for this overall effort is provided by the Microelectronics Research Center (MRC). The center also engages in the acquisition, housing, and maintenance of certain specialized facilities required by campuswide research teams. Approximately thirty-five to forty professional-level personnel conduct a broad spectrum of theoretical and experimental research programs in areas including, but not limited to, materials, modeling, discrete device fabrication, testing, chip design, computer architecture, algorithm development, and computer graphics. Research programs thus encompass specific aspects of microscience, microstructures, complex systems design, and applications. This research is supported by external sources, with approximately 45 percent of such sponsorship provided by industrial firms. The MRC is established as a center administratively located in Georgia Tech's Office of Interdisciplinary Programs which reports directly to the vice-president for research. This arrangement provides for maximum coordination of the related campuswide activities. Georgia Tech is committed through its management approach to the provision of quality facilities, contemporary research equipment, and effective guidance to the development of the MRC.

A new Microelectronics Research Center Building with approximately fifty thousand square feet of faculty offices, graduate student offices, laboratories, clean rooms, and support space was available in 1988. Funds for construction of this facility have been made available by the state of Georgia as part of a development plan directed toward bringing Georgia Tech into the first rank in microelectronics research and education. The state appropriation of $15 million will be invested in a building and equipment. In addition, Georgia Tech will develop matching nonstate resources of $15 million over the next five years to further support the program.

To emphasize the importance of microelectronics research to Georgia Tech, the director of the MRC reports directly to the vice-president for research, who in turn reports to the president. This provides direct access to the research management structure of Georgia Tech, since the vice-president for research is administratively responsible for all research conducted within Georgia Tech, both within the academic units and within laboratories of the Georgia Tech Research Institute (GTRI). Since all faculty performing research in MRC hold their appointments in an academic school or a laboratory of GTRI, it is important to communicate and coordinate with the unit heads, the dean of the College of Engineering, the dean of the College of Sciences and Liberal Studies, and the director of GTRI. This is facilitated since the center retains no overhead from the research income. Research funds are budgeted through the academic schools and GTRI laboratories. To enhance this coordination and communication, the director of MRC has a Management Advisory Committee. This committee is composed of the line administrators most closely related to individuals and groups within the schools and laboratories participating in the work of the MRC. The Management Advisory Committee assists the director in the establishment of all basic MRC policy and provides guidance regarding specific ways in which the effectiveness of the MRC may be increased within the context of overall Georgia Tech objectives. The MRC director also has a Technical Advisory Committee composed of representatives from each research area encompassed by MRC programs. The Technical Advisory Committee evaluates opportunities for new research initiatives and determines facilities requirements for existing and expanded program activities. The Technical Advisory Committee also serves as the interdisciplinary academic program coordinating committee as provided for by establishment Georgia Tech academic procedures. In addition, a new oversight group is contemplated. This External Review Panel, composed of three industrial, three university, and three government representatives, will be formed to provide an independent review of MRC program. External Review Panel members will be selected based on their technical knowledge of specific MRC activity areas. They will assist in the establishment of MRC development directions and will retroactively evaluate the selection of specific research tasks. The External Review Panel's actions will be advisory in nature. However, it will brief a key Georgia Tech administrative group composed of the vice-president for academic affairs, the vice-president of research, the Management Advisory Committee, and the MRC director on its findings and recommendations. Each faculty and staff participant involved in MRC programs has an appointment within a school or laboratory. This arrangement provides a mechanism for performance evaluation of each individual within the unit corresponding to his or her professional discipline, thus providing an advocacy position for each participant's contributions whether they take place through an academic school, GTRI laboratory, or the MRC. Georgia Tech also has a policy that requires each major activity manager to provide each line management evaluator with a critical assessment of each faculty member's contributions to the work of that activity center. Georgia Tech experience has proved that this approach is helpful to the individual in obtaining full consideration for promotion, salary increases, and tenure.

Not only is participation in MRC considered in advancing the faculty member's career, but its presence also makes Georgia Tech a more attractive environment for researchers. The symbiotic relationships among researchers involved in MRC's programs have facilitated the hiring by Georgia Tech units of a number of outstanding researchers from industry and academia.

Approximately 45 percent of current sponsored programs related to the research agenda of the MRC are supported by industry, and substantial contributions of equipment have been received from industrial firms. Research and development activities under industrial sponsorship are conducted on the traditional one-on-one basis. This method has proved superior to "pooled research" in the highly proprietary area of microelectronics. Industrial participants are more willing to provide access to proprietary scientific, engineering, and marketing information essential to the effective definition and conduct of the research. Experience indicates that this access does not preclude the definition of generic research and development of the type most compatible with the university environment. Rather, the direct involvement of research and engineering personnel from the sponsoring industrial concerns serves to protect the unique university needs, while at the same time providing an effective mechanism for the translation of publishable basic findings into specific products of interest to the sponsor.

While progress to date has been impressive, it is recognized that full utilization of these capabilities for research and academic purposes requires the addition of several key personnel in selected research areas. An expanded sponsored-program base will also be required. For these reasons, Georgia Tech has initiated an Industrial Partners/Microelectronics Research Center program as an essential component of the continued development program. Through the industrial partners program, now in the formative stage, the MRC will negotiate cooperative research and development relationships with six to eight companies that are representative of the industry and which in broad terms are complementary rather than competitive in their business activities. These cooperative arrangements are in addition to established sponsored relationships with industry and government and do not preclude extensive interactions with sponsors other than the industrial partners. The industrial partners arrangements are distinguished by their relatively large financial commitments and by the longevity of the relationship. Each industrial partner has the privilege of locating up to five professional personnel in facilities provided by Georgia Tech. All costs for these personnel, including office space rental, are paid by the industrial partner. Research and development performed by this corporate group is directly managed by the industrial partner and may be proprietary in nature. The MRC will provide access to required support facilities including specialized laboratories of the type described above. The industrial partner provides sponsored support for five years under a nonbinding agreement in support of MRC-conducted research and development. Ninety percent of these funds are applied to research mutually defined by the industrial partner and Georgia Tech. Ten percent of these funds will be used at the discretion of the MRC for exploratory research in areas complementary to the mutually defined program. The MRC will provide research staff as required for the cooperative program and basic facilities. While not a requirement for the relationship, each industrial partner is asked to consider provision of either one endowed chair in an area appropriate to its interests or equivalent endowment support for long-term facilities operations and maintenance. A model of this type should result in mutual advantage to both the industrial partner and Georgia Tech. Rapid translation of both generic and specific research results should be possible through the on-campus presence of industrial partner personnel. Sustained program effort will be possible on the part of Georgia Tech, permitting staff development and undergraduate and graduate student involvement at levels not normally possible. A unique feature will be the provision of full facilities by Georgia Tech, permitting directed application of industrial partner resources to the conduct of research programs of interest to individual sponsors. The industrial partner will in effect be making an investment at Georgia Tech, in contrast to making a donation to Georgia Tech.

DEVELOPING AND ADMINISTRATING RESEARCH

Georgia Tech has identified the area of compound semiconductors and the application of these materials to the development of electronic and integrated optics devices and systems for principal research emphasis. This research niche was selected because of its great intrinsic importance to the nation's technological future and the extensive demonstrated performance of the Georgia Tech research activities in the area. A commitment to building on this demonstrated strength has resulted in the development of extensive related research facilities. These long-term objectives will be implemented through the advice and counsel of the Technical Advisory Committee, the Management Advisory Committee, and the External Review Panel. These groups will identify and review the dimensions of the total MRC research and academic program and will then act to encourage activities that will fill the interstices left by the externally sponsored program pattern. Internal funds for exploratory research and academic activities will also be provided to stimulate the development of new research initiatives and to establish a base of performance from which additional external industrial and government agency funding may be sought.

The strength of this approach to program identification is derived from its bottom-up character. Those persons involved in the definition of missing elements in the overall program or involved in the identification of new research directions are the same individuals who are involved in either the program prosecution or the internal evaluation of those ideas. The External Review Panel provides a more global perspective evaluation of program definition and performance.

The majority of the research projects are engineering applications driven in keeping with the systems concept stressed in each MRC activity. This is a natural method for program selection. For instance, the need for a new optoelectronic device or system begins with a need for materials characterization of the type provided by the physics participants in the MRC. Materials modeling is necessarily followed by device modeling, provided by electrical engineering associates. An appropriate device model leads to the need for specific device design, conducted under the auspices of the electrical engineering and computer science associates. Implementation of device and system design through fabrication results in involvement by materials scientists, process engineers, and materials engineers. Systems implementation and tests may involve a variety of disciplines, including, for instance, personnel from modern optics, electrical engineering, and computer engineering. Systems-driven programs of the type described above are implemented through a research and/or design team approach. The total program needs are defined by a design team made up of personnel from all required disciplines. The overall program is divided into projects, each pursued within the context of the overall program needs. A program director is responsible for intragroup communications and the establishment of program reviews. The Technical Advisory Committee and External Review Panel provide periodic assessments of the productivity of the team and the continue appropriateness of the program. In some cases an industrial sponsor may wish to support related but independent projects in different areas. For example, a single contract covering compound semiconductor materials growth and characterization in GTRI, theoretical and experimental research on thermal cooling of semiconductor devices in mechanical engineering, and development of network protocols in information and computer sciences was placed through MRC.

All MRC funds and equipment allocations are made by the director, subject to advice and consent of the Management Advisory Committee. Project budgets are formulated in keeping with the standard procedures employed for all of Georgia Tech's sponsored activities. The majority of research activities are expected to be conducted in the MRC building within which the MRC participants will have complete access to all specialized facilities. In those instances where only a limited number of persons are involved in a specific project, equipment provided through the MRC may be placed in the academic school or GTRI laboratory requiring that capability. However, most activities involve the use of specialized, expensive facilities acquired and maintained within the MRC. This shared facility is expected to enhance the interaction among participants from the various disciplines and industrial organizations and thereby achieve one of the principal objectives of the MRC. It is frequently easier in the university environment to acquire and establish specialized facilities and equipment than it is to maintain those resources. Georgia Tech has addressed this issue by providing through centers such as the MRC for the maintenance of multiuser specialized equipment and access to that equipment by users from various units on the campus. Such facilities, established in support of specific activity areas such as microelectronics, frequently have even broader application by faculty, research staff, and students. Mechanisms have therefore been developed to provide needed access while at the same time ensuring effective operation and maintenance of the equipment. This approach provides for the housing of specialized resources broadly needed by campus researchers within a specific location, such as the MRC. Maintenance contracts and/or in-house maintenance are provided by the center.

A systems manager is identified for each specialized system (e.g., an Auger microprobe, a computer-aided design system, a molecular beam epitaxial growth system). Trained support staff operate the equipment under policies developed in cooperation with the systems manager on behalf of campuswide users, or, in those cases where hands-on utilization by an individual researcher is appropriate, provide certification training sufficient to permit productive work by the individual. A priority system is employed to ensure that access is available to meet commitments to sponsored research and to address the general academic research and program needs. A common user fee is shared for access to these specialized facilities. The fee is set at a level sufficient to cover the basic operating costs of the facility, including operator services where required. Fees are established at sufficiently low levels to encourage use, while at the same time providing for responsible continuing management of the facility. Special grants from the Georgia Tech Foundation and other sources are sought in behalf of those users (e.g., an unsupported faculty member's graduate students) who would otherwise be unable to utilize the resource. The maintenance of the common use fee has proved very effective in ensuring both effective control and continued serviceability of equipment.

TECHNOLOGY TRANSFER

Information developed through the MRC is disseminated in four principal ways: (1) through the industrial sponsor's on-campus participants; (2) through conventional journal publications and meeting presentation and book-publishing avenues; (3) through periodic research reviews to which broad industrial, university, and government representation are invited; and (4) as projected for the future, through a report's distribution program involving both hard copy and computer disk media.

As noted elsewhere in this paper, current experience shows that approximately 45 percent of the sponsored programs conducted through the MRC are supported by industry. Continued extensive industry equipment contributions, cooperative interchanges of data and software, and use of industry facilities by Georgia Tech research personnel are anticipated. On-campus presence of personnel from each of the industrial partners will provide additional linkages between Georgia Tech and industrial colleagues. This industrial interaction results in effective technology transfer between Georgia Tech and potential technology users.

Generic university research can be quickly exploited by industry through the development of proprietary products. Georgia Tech personnel are made aware of substantive industrial problems and proposed solutions before such awareness would be possible through normal information channels. Students benefit from exposure to contemporary problems and to both industrial and university approaches to solution development.

While these mechanisms do not lead to a formal codification of knowledge, they are especially valuable in real-time technology development and application of the type that is experienced today. Archived materials such as publications, meeting transactions, and books are particularly valuable means of codifying new knowledge. Current abstracting and computer search services make this resource increasingly valuable.

The MRC continues to work with others in the field to ensure that keyword and other citation mechanisms continue to be refined and expanded in a manner that will enhance the capabilities of computer searches. Periodic research reviews serve not only to present current findings for critical evaluation but also to provide a forum through which the university's capabilities to perform specific research may be shared with potential sponsors. Broad presentations of this type, as well as highly focused technology-transfer symposia, constitute a key component of the MRC's information-dissemination program. Reports and preprints provide a timely exposure of new research findings in a manner that cannot be accomplished through formal publication. Details of experimental procedure or theoretical analysis can best be conveyed through the report format. The MRC uses this medium to share research findings with other university and industrial research centers and with appropriate individuals. Production and distribution costs for reports make the dissemination of information on computer disks increasingly attractive. Disk storage and management is also frequently more convenient and cost-effective for the user. The computer disk medium will therefore be used in the future to the greatest extent possible by the MRC as a substitute for printed hard-copy reports.

STATUS AND PROSPECTS

Georgia Tech intends that the MRC develop a comprehensive quality program of research and education of leading national stature. This objective is being accomplished through a cooperative venture involving many elements of Georgia Tech through established administrative units. Experience acquired to date has established the attainability of this objective. Long-term MRC objectives can be realized only through the development of a strong base of basic research and exploratory development. While these activities do not always lend themselves to a broad team approach of the type described here, they can be integrated within the MRC framework. The ultimate objective is that MRC be one of the six to eight top comprehensive programs of microelectronics research in U.S. universities. Two crucial means to achieving this goal are the maintenance and enhancement of the cross-disciplinary, cross-organizational interactions crucial to its success.

III
INTERDISCIPLINARY RESEARCH IN BRAZIL

The Southern Hemisphere is often terra incognita to researchers from the United States and Western Europe. Yet these nations face the same sorts of problems in developing the research and development culture that have confronted other countries. The papers by Eduardo Vasconcellos study in detail interdisciplinary research projects in Brazilian government R&D organizations. He emphasizes conflicts between research and development project organizations and the functional organizations within which they reside. Because the role of the project manager in Brazilian government R&D organizations is not well defined compared to that of the functional manager, conflicts between these managers in such areas as resources are likely. An additional source of conflict is between line management and administrative staff. The different roles and worldviews of these two groups create the demand for good communication between them if they are to function effectively together. Vasconcellos's studies lead to an understanding of factors that promote the success of interdisciplinary research projects. While his work is in the Brazilian context, many of the identified factors and findings are good candidates for a broad range of other environments.

12

Organization Design for Interdisciplinary Research: Conflicts and Performance

EDUARDO VASCONCELLOS

This paper presents the results of a study on the performance of interdisciplinary research projects in Brazilian government research institutes. Thirty R&D projects had their performance evaluated. Projects of high and low performance are compared in terms of conflict level, formalization, communication pattern, size, and level of interdisciplinarity.

The management of interdisciplinary research has been studied with a higher level of interest because of four basic reasons. First, problems are being recognized increasingly as interdisciplinary. Second, the undisciplinary problems are easier to solve; therefore, the remaining ones are frequently interdisciplinary. The third reason is the trend toward higher levels of specialization. Fourth and finally, there is a growing need for management tools to integrate the work of different areas of knowledge, to solve complex problems (Birnbaum 1982).

This paper deals with the management of interdisciplinary projects in Brazilian industrial-government research institutes matrix structures. There are many studies about the use of the matrix design to develop interdisciplinary projects. Roman (1980) presents the advantages of this type of structure to accomplish at the same time specialization and effective cooperation among the several technical units. Davis and Lawrence (1977) analyze the conditions for the matrix utilization. Other authors such as Galbraith (1973) and Vasconcellos (1979) present models differentiating the several types of matrices. The roles of the project manager and the functional manager are discussed by Cleland and King (1972) and Sbragia (1984). The approaches of Gunz and Pearson (1977) and Vasconcellos and Hemsley (1981) are more in the direction of the designing process of the matrix structure. Pitts and Daniels (1984) analyze a sample of industrial

The author acknowledges the valuable cooperation of research assistant Ines Massumi Iwashita.

firms and arrive at the conclusion that the matrix design is not being used as predicted ten years ago. For the purpose of this study, *matrix* is defined as an organizational form that uses two or more types of departmentalization on the same resources, creating a double or multiple subordination.

Several authors have studied the measurement of the performance of R&D projects. Benton (1976) studied the measure of the performance of interdisciplinary research and identified the following indicators: teamwork, competence of professionals, morale, feedback, and organization structure flexibility. De Cotiis and Dyer (1979) utilized five factors to measure the performance of R&D projects: manufacturability and business performance, technical performance, efficiency, personal growth, experience, and technological innovativeness. Sbragia (1984) studied the performance of R&D projects in matrix structures. The following indicators were utilized: technical performance, cost, schedule attainment, and client satisfaction.

The research method and the results obtained are described below. Several aspects such as conflicts, formalization, communication, and level of interdisciplinarity will be analyzed in projects of higher and lower levels of performance.

METHOD

This is the second phase of research that began in 1976. In the first phase, seventeen R&D government research organizations operating in a matrix mode were identified. Data were collected from 211 respondents of fifty interdisciplinary projects about conflicts, formalization, communication, and size.

This paper presents the results of the second phase of this study, in which thirty terminated projects are evaluated and classified in groups of high and low performance levels. Then a comparison is made between these groups in terms of the following variables: conflict, formalization, communication, size, and level of interdisciplinarity.

Data were collected by survey questionnaire on the existence of conflict between project and functional managers, between project manager and the research team, between functional manager and the research team, project managers among themselves, and, finally, among the functional managers. The respondents were asked to give the reasons for the conflicts between the functional and the project manager. The following alternatives were presented as conflict reasons: human resources, schedules, equipment, quality standards, technical content, and definition of authority and responsibility. Respondents were asked to rate the extent of conflict associated with each alternative on a scale from 1 (low level of conflict) to 10 (high level of conflict).

The formalization level was measured by a question that presented three alternatives related to the existence of manuals to define authority and responsibility of the project and functional managers.

The communication pattern was also one of the project characteristics measured and was assessed by a question with four alternatives attempting to measure the extent to which the communication between the project manager and the research team was direct.

Level of interdisciplinarity is the extent to which the research team has to interact to achieve the project goals. This variable was measured on a 1-to-10 scale where 1 represented a situation in which there was no need for interaction between researchers of different areas of knowledge, and 10 indicated the other extreme.

Project performance was measured by the following indicators: schedule, client satisfaction about the quality of the project, client satisfaction about schedule attainment, spinoff contracts, utilization of the results of the project, and attainment of technical specifications.

Respondents were asked to rate their projects using a 1-to-10 scale. For each project, data were collected from the project manager, from his or her boss, and from one of the researchers. The average of all these factors was considered as a general evaluation grade for each project.

RESULTS

The management of interdisciplinary projects in a matrix design is a conflict-generation process. Table 12.1 shows the conflict possibilities among the several roles of the matrix. The figures represent percentages of respondents that answered positively to each alternative. The bottom line of Table 12.1 shows the average of all frequencies for each column. This figure is considered as the average level of conflict presented by that group.

Table 12.1. Conflict level and project performance

		Performance (%)					
	TOTAL	Average		Quality		Schedule	
Conflicts	N=30	High N=7	Low N=7	High N=13	Low N=13	High N=12	Low N=12
Between project and functional managers	50	29	43	33	50	42	60
Between project manager and research team	50	57	29	38	50	50	40
Between functional manager and research team	33	0	43	15	50	16	40
Among project managers	16	29	14	15	20	16	30
Among functional managers	13	14	14	15	10	16	10
Average level of conflict	22	26	29	23	36	28	42

As the figures in Table 12.1 show, conflicts are more frequent between the project and the functional managers, and between the project manager and the research team. The project and functional managers share the same resources, with different goals. The functional manager is concerned with efficient distribution of staff among the several projects, development of technical capabilities, quality control, and other administrative duties related to the department. The project manager is mainly concerned with the project and its goals. Therefore, a high level of conflict between them is to be expected.

The conflicts between the project manager and the research team are also high because in Brazilian R&D government organizations, the role of the project manager is not as formalized as it should be. The project manager tends to have responsibility for the project but not enough authority over the resources. The research team considers their "second boss" to have low priority. The data collected on communication pattern and formalization support these statements. These aspects are discussed below.

The projects with lower performance level present a higher average of conflicts: 29 percent against 26 percent. The difference in the level of conflict is even higher between the project and functional managers: the projects with lower performance present 43 percent of the conflict between these two roles, while projects in the higher group present 29 percent.

Data in Table 12.1 also indicate that the projects with lower performance in terms of quality present a higher level of conflict: 36 percent against 23 percent. The same thing happens when the projects with a higher rate of schedule attainment are compared with the projects that didn't perform as well according to this factor. The first group presented 28 percent of conflict level, while the second one showed 42 percent.

Several factors can be considered to explain the inverse relationship between performance and conflicts found in this study. Researchers in Brazil usually do not have sufficient management training for interdisciplinary projects. Besides, the matrix design has a high potential of conflict, and it is usually implemented in a very informal way. These factors result in a tense situation where the project manager has the responsibility over the project but insufficiently defined authority over the resources. This ambiguity raises the level of conflict, decreasing the project performance.

As Table 12.2 indicates, project size is another factor that helps to explain the inverse relationship between performance and conflict level. The projects with lower performance and higher frequency of conflicts involved more man-months: 15 against 9. A larger group has a higher potential of conflict, and it is more difficult to manage.

Conflicts between the project manager and the researchers showed an inverse result. The high-performance projects also presented a high level of conflict. A possible explanation for this finding is the level of interdisciplinarity. The projects with higher performance had a higher level of interdisciplinarity: 8.1 against 6.5. Therefore, the projects with high performance demanded more interaction between the project manager and

Table 12.2. Project characteristics and performance

Characteristics	Performance (%) High	Low
Size (average number of man-months)	9	15
Number of technical units involved in the project (average)	4.4	3.7
Level of interdisciplinarity (average)	8.1	6.5

the research team. This explains the higher level of conflict. It should be noted that the higher-performance projects involved more technical units: 4.4 against 3.7.

The analysis of the data on the question related to the reasons for the conflicts shows that the project technical content was considered the main reason for conflicts between the project and the functional managers: 50 percent. The next most important conflict reason was quality standards (40 percent), followed by schedules (38 percent). Definition of authority and responsibility was considered a reason for conflict by 36 percent of the respondents. This factor was higher in low-performance projects: 57 percent against 14 percent.

Table 12.3 shows the results related to the level of formalization of authority and responsibility of the project and functional managers. The level

Table 12.3. Formalization and project performance

	TOTAL	Performance (%) Average		Quality		Schedule	
Formalization	N=30	High N=7	Low N=7	High N=13	Low N=10	High N=12	Low N=10
There are no manuals, but there is an informal definition of authority and responsibilities of project and functional managers.	87	100	57	84	90	91	90
There are no manuals and no informal definition of authority and responsibilities of project and functional managers.	10	0	29	8	10	9	10
There are manuals defining authority and responsibilities of project and functional managers.	3	0	14	8	0	0	0

of formalization is relatively low. The most frequent alternative (87 percent) indicates that there are no manuals of procedures. The definition of authority and responsibility is done informally. One can notice that the lowest level of formalization is associated with low performance. This level of formalization is represented by the alternative "There are no manuals and no informal definition of authority and responsibilities . . ."

The respondents of the lower-performing projects selected this alternative with higher frequency: 29 percent against 0 percent. These findings are consistent with the analysis on conflicts that were made on the previous topic, expect for alternative 1, "There are manuals defining authority and responsibilities of the project and functional managers." Table 12.3 shows that the existence of these manuals (14 percent against 0 percent) is associated with low performance. This might be the case since techniques for managing interdisciplinary projects aren't well known in Brazilian R&D government institutes.

Table 12.4 shows the data on the communication pattern. The most frequent procedure is the direct communication between the project manager

Table 12.4. Communication and project performance

		Performance (%)					
	TOTAL	Average		Quality		Schedule	
Communication Patterns		High	Low	High	Low	High	Low
	N=30	N=7	N=7	N=13	N=10	N=12	N=10
The project manager communicates directly with the project team, keeping the functional manager informed.	64	71	57	61	70	58	80
The project manager communicates with the project team through the functional manager. Direct communication with the project team is done only informally.	23	14	14	23	10	33	0
The project manager communicates directly with the project team, independently of the functional manager.	33	0	43	15	50	16	40
The project manager communicates with the project team through the functional manager. There is no direct communication with the project team.	0	0	0	0	0	0	0

ager and the research team: 64 percent. The project manager keeps the functional manager informed. This communication pattern is more frequent in high-performance projects: 71 percent against 57 percent. The high-performance projects present a higher level of interdisciplinary, which demands more frequent interaction between the project manager and the research team; therefore, the direct communication pattern tends to be more effective. However, if the direct communication occurs without any involvement of the functional manager, then performance will be lower. Data in Table 12.4 confirm this statement. The lower-performance projects present this pattern with more frequency than the high-performance ones: 29 percent against 14 percent.

This can be explained by several factors. First, the matrices in R&D institutes in Brazil present a low level of formalization; therefore, direct communication between the project manager and the research team without informing the functional manager tends to increase the level of conflict, reducing the performance level. Since the projects are interdisciplinary, the project manager is not able to control the quality without the cooperation of the functional managers. Another aspect is the low level of commitment to the project by the functional manager who hasn't been kept informed. All these elements contribute to a low level of performance.

CONCLUSIONS

The R&D government institutes have a strategic role in the industrial development of Brazil because most companies don't have the necessary resources to invest in technological innovation. In the last decade, efforts have been made by these institutes to help industry in solving their technological problems. One important barrier to this goal is the interdisciplinary nature of these problems and the lack of effective management tools to integrate the efforts of several technical areas. This paper is an attempt to deal with this question. The main conclusions are summarized as follows:

- The most frequent conflicts in matrix structures occur between the project and the functional managers and between the project manager and the research team.
- Projects with lower performance present higher levels of conflict.
- The technical content of the project was found to be the main reason for conflict between the project and the functional managers.
- Projects with higher performance present higher levels of interdisciplinarity.
- Projects with higher performance involve fewer researchers but more technical units.
- The level of formalization of the project and functional managers roles is low.
- The most frequent communication pattern is the direct communication between the project manager and the research team. The functional manager is kept informed by the project manager. Projects with higher performance presented this pattern of communication.

These results are not intended to be conclusive because of limitations of these types of studies; however, I expect that these findings will contribute positively to the complex science of managing interdisciplinary research projects.

REFERENCES

Benton, D. 1976. Management and effectiveness measures for interdisciplinary research. *Journal of the Society of Research Administrators* 7(4):36–45.

Birnbaum, P. H. 1982. The organization and management of interdisciplinary research, a progress report. *Journal of the Society of Research Administrators* 13(4):11–23.

Cleland, D., and W. King. 1972. *Management: A systems approach*. New York: McGraw-Hill.

Davis, S. M., and P. R. Lawrence. 1977. *Matrix*. Reading, Mass.: Addison-Wesley.

De Cotiis, T. A., and L. Dyer. 1979. Defining and measuring project performance. *Research Management* 22(1):17–22.

Galbraith, J. 1973. *Designing complex organizations*. Reading, Mass., Addison-Wesley.

Gunz, H. P., and A. Pearson. 1977. *Matrix organization in R&D*. Research report to the Manchester Business School, Manchester.

Pitts, R. A., and J. D. Daniels. 1984. Aftermath of the matrix mania. *Columbia Journal of World Business* (Summer):48–54.

Roman, D. D. 1980. *Science, technology and innovation: A systems approach*. Columbus, Ohio: Grid.

Sbragia, R. 1984. Clarity of manager roles and performance of R&D multidisciplinary projects in matrix structure. *R&D Management* 26:56–64.

Vasconcellos, E. 1979. A model for a better understanding of the matrix structure. *IEEE Transactions on Engineering Management* 26:56–64.

Vasconcellos, E., and J. Hemsley. 1981. The design of the matrix structure for R&D organizations. Paper presented at Joint Symposium Project Management Institute/Internet, Boston, September 28–30.

13

Managing Conflicts Between Line and Staff in Interdisciplinary R&D Projects

EDUARDO VASCONCELLOS

This paper presents the results of a study on the conflicts between line and administrative staff in the development of interdisciplinary projects in industrial government research institutes in Brazil. Data on the reasons for conflict and the instruments to manage them were collected from 150 respondents.

R&D organizations are formed by two main subsystems. The first (line) is responsible for the development of the main activity of the organization, which is research. The other (staff) supplies a set of support functions making it possible for the line units to accomplish their tasks. Purchasing, cost control, training, and personnel evaluation are examples of staff activities. The effective attainment of the organization goals depends on a high level of cooperation between line and staff. Unfortunately, this doesn't happen very frequently. These two groups are exposed to many conflicting situations in the process of developing their daily activities.

This paper deals with the management of conflicts between line and administrative staff in R&D industrial government organizations. The focus on interdisciplinary research projects was selected because of its importance to the success of an R&D organization. The high level of technological specialization creates the need for managerial tools to integrate effectively several areas of knowledge to solve complex problems (Birnbaum 1982).

Conflicts are not necessarily bad for the organization; in some situations, they might stimulate a higher level of performance (Butler 1973). This view is also shared by Coser (1986), Paltridge (1971), and Pondy (1967). However, above a certain level conflicts can be very destructive, creating a negative organizational climate. According to Newman and Warren (1961), there are five reasons for the organizational conflicts: competition over resources, organization design, task characteristics, differ-

The author acknowledges the valuable cooperation of research assistant Ines Massumi Iwashita.

ences in values and goals, and ambiguity. The reasons for interdepartmental conflicts can be classified in two groups: rational and emotional (Longenecker 1981).

METHODS

The purpose of this study is to answer the following research questions:

1. What are the reasons for conflict between line and staff in the development of interdisciplinary projects?
2. What can be done to reduce the conflict level?
3. At what extent do line and staff have the same views about these questions?

A set of conflict determinants and a list of techniques to manage them were identified from the literature. The following conflict factors were considered: line doesn't cooperate with staff, line doesn't understand the importance of the management practices, line considers staff as a "cost" to the organization, line doesn't trust staff efficiency, staff implements unfeasible procedures, staff doesn't understand its role as a support function, line treats staff as inferiors, line and staff have different perceptions about the organization objectives and priorities, budgets are cut by the government and line puts the blame on staff, and line doesn't know that a great deal of staff red tape is required by government regulations and are out of staff's control.

The following measures were considered as means to reduce the conflict level: meetings between line and staff, participation of line people when the administrative staff is designing new procedures, more involvement of the administrative staff in line activities so that they will understand better the nature of the research activities, training program on interpersonal relations for line and staff, definition of organization objectives and priorities, utilization of quality of the interaction between line and staff as one of the criteria for performance evaluation and promotion, improvement of staff quality, training program for line people about the importance of staff to the organization effectiveness.

A questionnaire based on the above statements was prepared. A sample of 150 respondents (77 line and 73 administrative staff) of an industrial government research institute answered the questionnaire. A 1-to-5 scale was used. The higher the score, the higher the level of agreement with each statement. For the purpose of analyzing the data, scores of 4 and 5 were considered as agreement with the statement. Respondents were asked to answer the questionnaire for the interdisciplinary projects, according to the following definition: interdisciplinary projects are those projects that demand frequent interaction among researchers of different technical sections. This methodology was utilized by Vasconcellos and Kalinowsky (1985) in a study on line and staff conflicts in an agriculture research organization.

RESULTS

Table 13.1 shows the results on the questions related to the reasons for conflict between line and staff. The figures indicate the percentage of respondents who agree with each statement. The main conflict reason (77 percent) was the difference in perception between line and staff about the organization objectives and priorities. The administrative staff provides a great variety of support services to the line. Since the resources are usually insufficient, a lack of agreement around priorities tends to be a strong reason for conflict.

The last two columns of Table 13.1 compare data obtained from the line group of respondents with those of the staff group. The figures show a difference in perception about the causes of conflict. This is an important conflict reason by itself. The main conflict reason according to the staff group is that "line doesn't know that a great deal of staff red tape is required by government regulations . . ." (90 percent); however, less than half of the line group (47 percent) agrees with this statement.

The second most important conflict reason (77 percent) from the staff point of view was that "line doesn't understand the importance of the management practices." Only 27 percent of the line respondents agreed with that. On the other hand, more than half of the line respondents (66 percent) agreed that "staff implements unfeasible procedures"; however,

Table 13.1. Reasons for conflict between line and staff

	Total (%) N=150	Line (%) N=77	Staff (%) N=73
Line and staff have different perceptions about the organization objectives and priorities.	77	84	70
Line doesn't understand that a great deal of staff red tape is required by government regulations.	68	47	90
Line doesn't have confidence in administrative staff efficiency.	57	64	51
Staff doesn't understand their role as a support function.	51	71	29
Line doesn't cooperate with administrative staff, resisting new administrative procedures.	49	29	71
Staff implements unfeasible procedures because they don't understand the nature of line activities.	46	66	25
Line considers administrative staff as a "cost" to the organization.	45	30	60
Line treats staff as inferiors.	37	16	60
Budgets are cut by the government, and line puts the blame on staff.	35	17	53

only 25 percent of the staff had the same opinion. The line respondents (71 percent) complained that the administrative staff doesn't recognize its role as a support function. Only 29 percent of the staff respondents had the same opinion.

The statement that "line treats staff as inferiors" had the lowest level of agreement (16 percent) among the line group; however, 60 percent of the administrative staff respondents agreed with it. In R&D organizations, this factor tends to be stronger because of the high technical level of the line personnel. Table 13.1 also shows different perceptions between line and staff about the statement that "line considers staff as a 'cost' to the organization." Sixty percent of the staff respondents agreed with it; however, only 30 percent of the line respondents had the same opinion.

The different views between line and staff over the conflict reasons are a strong barrier to the effective management of those conflicts. Study by Vasconcellos and Kalinowsky (1985) on an R&D agriculture research institute confirmed this finding.

Table. 13.2 shows the results from the items that identify methods for reducing the conflict level between line and staff. The results indicate that "definition of organization objectives and priorities" was considered by the respondents as the most important instrument (91 percent) to reduce the line-staff conflict. The second most valuable conflict-management tool (77 percent) was the realization of meetings between line and staff. When the same methodology was applied to an R&D agriculture institute (Vasconcellos and Kalinowsky 1985), this method was considered as the most important.

The respondents considered the participation of the line in the designing

Table 13.2. Instruments to reduce conflict between line and staff

	Total (%) N=150	Line (%) N=77	Staff (%) N=73
Definition of organizational objectives and priorities.	91	91	90
Meetings between line and staff.	77	91	85
Participation of line personnel when administrative staff is designing new procedures.	75	78	71
More involvement of administrative staff in line activities.	64	58	70
Using the quality of the interaction between line and staff as one of the criteria for evaluation and promotion.	62	52	73
Improvement of staff quality.	61	62	59
Training program for line people about the importance of the administrative staff to organizational effectiveness.	56	34	79
Training program on interpersonal relations for line and staff.	54	47	62

of new procedures by the administrative staff as the third most useful method (75 percent) for conflict management. Many times the staff creates new planning and control systems, for example, without sufficient knowledge of the tasks performed by the line. This tends to result in inadequate techniques that very often become conflicting issues. The participation of the line in the design of these procedures has two main advantages: the procedure is usually better, and it is easier to implement. Training programs on interpersonal relations for line and staff had the lowest frequency of positive answers: 54 percent.

The last two columns of Table 13.2 show the answers by group of respondents. Line and staff shared the same view on the main solution to their conflicts: definition of organization objectives and priorities. The second most important conflict management tool according to the line respondents (78 percent) was the participation of line personnel in the designing of new procedures by the administrative staff. This factor occupied the fourth position in the view of the administrative staff.

Seventy percent of the administrative staff agreed that the involvement of the staff in the line activities is a useful tool to reduce conflict level. Only 58 percent of the line respondents shared the same perception. A great majority of the staff respondents agreed with the need for training programs for the line personnel about the importance of the administrative procedures to organization effectiveness. Only 34 percent of the line people had the same opinion.

CONCLUSIONS

The development of interdisciplinary R&D projects depends on several factors. One important determinant of success is effective support from the research institute staff. Therefore, there is a high need to anticipate and manage possible disruptive conflicts between these two groups.

This paper presents the results of a study on the reasons for conflict between line and administrative staff in the development of interdisciplinary projects. The main conclusions are summarized as follows:

- Different views of line and staff about organization objectives and priorities were considered as the main reason for conflict between the two groups.
- The line group considered the principal reason for conflict the fact that "line doesn't know that a great deal of staff red tape is required by government regulations."
- The great majority of the administrative staff considered an important reason for conflict the fact that line "treats staff as inferiors."
- The different perceptions between line and staff about the conflict determinants are an important reason for conflict.
- Definition of organization objectives and priorities was considered as the most powerful instrument to reduce the conflict level between line and staff.

- Meetings between line and staff were considered the second most valuable conflict management technique.
- Participation of the line personnel in the designing of new procedures by the administrative staff was considered another useful tool for conflict management.

These findings shouldn't be considered as conclusive because of the several limitations of these types of studies. I expect that these results will generate useful discussions, contributing to the difficult task of managing R&D interdisciplinary projects.

REFERENCES

Birnbaum, P. H. 1982. The organization and management of interdisciplinary research, a progress report. *Journal of the Society of Research Administrators* 13(4):11–23.

Butler, A. G. 1973. Project management: A study in organizational conflict. *Academy of Management Journal* 16(1):84–99.

Coser, L. A. 1986. *The functions of social conflict.* New York: Free Press.

Longenecker, J. 1981. *Introducão a Administracão: Uma abordagem comportamental.* São Paulo: Atlas.

Newman, W. H., and K. E. Warren. 1961. *The process of management: Concepts, behavior, and practice.* Englewood Cliffs, N.J.: Prentice-Hall.

Paltridge, J. G. 1971. Organizational conflict in academia. *California Management Review* 13:85–94.

Pondy, L. R. 1967. Organizational conflict: Concepts and models. *Administrative Science Quarterly* 12:296–320.

Vasconcellos, E., and L. F. Kalinowsky. 1985. Conflitos entre linha e apoio em organizacoes de pesquisa: Causas e sugestoes de solucão. *Revista de Administracão* 20(3):53–63.

IV
INTERDISCIPLINARY RESEARCH IN EASTERN EUROPE

Research in Eastern Europe is conducted largely through academies of science and institutes. In socialist countries, studies are centrally focused on conducting effective research. Furthermore, planning for the future is an important feature of these societies. Heinrich Parthey addresses the issue of correlations between the interdisciplinary structure of problems and research groups and the characteristics of cooperative behavior and output. Ana Marie Sandi draws some critical links between interdisciplinary and futures research. Important in socialist countries, futures work is becoming especially significant outside the United States, which presently lags in this area. Sandi's points are a reminder of the intrinsically interdisciplinary character of planning, forecasting (except for single variable, short-term projections), and impact assessment.

14

Relationship of Interdisciplinarity to Cooperative Behavior

HEINRICH PARTHEY

For the empirical study of research environments a questionnaire was sent to three academic institutes to assess the degree of their cooperative work. Cooperative interdisciplinary work was measured by the proportion of scientists in the group who derived their method from a field of science other than that in which the problem was formulated. The data were treated by rank-order correlation, showing some relationship between interdisciplinarity in research and coauthorship as well as cooperative behavior.

Empirical studies of interdisciplinarity often use the distribution of scientists in research groups by disciplines and fields of science as an indicator. For international comparisons, it has turned out to be useful to apply the International Standard Nomenclature for Fields of Science and Technology (UNESCO 1973). The distinction between disciplines follows the two-digit major category codes, that of fields of science the four-digit major category codes. I present here the results of a study made between late 1979 and early 1981 which involved scientists from seven disciplines (mathematics, physics, chemistry, life sciences, agricultural sciences, medical sciences, technological sciences) an thirty-six fields of science working in forty-one groups at three life science institutes of the Academy of Sciences of the German Democratic Republic.

The quotient between n_j as number of scientists in the group and m_{ik} as number of scientists in the discipline (or field of science) permits the introduction of the Shannon index, when N is the maximum number of possible disciplines (N=4) and fields of science (N=5) in the individual groups: $V_j = -(1n\ \mathrm{N})$.

From this point of view, analyses of research programs and problem fields have been carried out (Amir 1985). Problem fields of this type are certainly necessary for the development of interdisciplinary relations between scientists, though they cannot satisfy completely. Thus, groups engaged in problem fields are justly referred to as working more disciplinarily if the scientists solve the individual problems with the means of their own discipline. Interdisciplinary research, as compared to disciplinary research, occurs when methods are needed to work at a problem that are not rooted in the same field of science as the problem itself.

In this sense, a comprehensive empirical UNESCO study on the efficiency of basic research units asked: (a) In carrying out your research projects, do you borrow some methods, theories, or other specific elements developed in other fields, not normally used in your research? If No, write "0," and move to Part E of the questionnaire. If Yes, write "1" and continue. (b) Using the International Standard Nomenclature for Fields of Science and Technology, write the names of these other fields and their two-digit major category codes (Andrews 1979, p. 445).

Earlier interpretations attempted to obtain comparability between the twelve hundred groups surveyed by classifying them according to the distribution of the disciplines and institutional forms of organization they represent. The valuation of the statements made on part (b) of the above question for interdisciplinary orientation yielded little significant correlation with other group features, including coauthorship (Darvas and Haraszthy 1979).

METHODS

This study used another indicator referring, in the sense of part (a) of the above question, to the interdisciplinarity of problem and method. The question was: Are the methods used by your research team to tackle a problem (1) rooted in the same field of knowledge in which your problem is formulated; or (2) rooted in a field of knowledge that differs from the field in which your problem is formulated? (Parthey 1973, p. 44). The percentage of scientists who answered (2) related to group size was identified in our studies as level of interdisciplinarity in groups.

RESULTS

When correlating coauthorship with this indicator and the abovementioned indicators obtained with the help of the Shannon index, the coefficients of the Spearman correlation, as Table 14.1 shows, indicate a significant relation only between coauthorship and the new indicator introduced by us, though the various indicators for interdisciplinarity correlate significantly with each other.

Obviously, not the structure and distribution of competence according to various disciplines but the lacking prerequisites in the knowledge of the individual scientist to work at the problem and the ensuing search for methods to be transferred from other fields of science as well as a corresponding coauthorship are the main characteristics of the interdisciplinary research situation.

We also developed and tested indicators of problem development for the

Table 14.1. Correlation matrix: Interdisciplinarity and coauthorship

	1	2	3	4	5	6
1	1.00	.78++	.41++	.34+	.01	.16
2	—	1.00	.29+	.33+	.17	.08
3	—	—	1.00	.29+	.19	.26
4	—	—	—	1.00	.02	.39+
5	—	—	—	—	1.00	.00

Key to variables
1 Multidisciplinary structure of groups
2 Distribution of competence in disciplines
3 Distribution of competence in fields of science
4 Interdisciplinarity of problem and method
5 Output per scientist
6 Coauthorship

empirical analysis of the research situation: first, the dynamism of the problem field and, second, the time needed to react to new problems. The development of methods in research situations was registered mainly by the increase or decrease in the share of method and instrument innovations. A new indicator of the research situation was developed for the availability of knowledge and instruments, and a second one for relevance for knowledge and society. As Table 14.2 shows, the rank correlations among all indicators of the interdisciplinary research situation and of scientific output used by us confirm the dominance of a correlation between coauthorship and interdisciplinarity of problems and method.

Of these two indicators, however, only the interdisciplinarity of problem

Table 14.2. Correlation matrix: Interdisciplinarity research situation

	1	2	3	4	5	6	7	8	9
1	1.00	−.11	.0	.03	.14	.15	.03	−.15	.20
2	—	1.00	−.31+	−.14	.07	−.17	.06	.24	.03
3	—	—	1.00	.11	.17	.25	.14	−.06	.18
4	—	—	—	1.00	.22	.34+	−.01	.02	.39+
5	—	—	—	—	1.00	.35+	.26	.22	−.12
6	—	—	—	—	—	1.00	−.03	.01	.16
7	—	—	—	—	—	—	1.00	.38+	.03
8	—	—	—	—	—	—	—	1.00	−.03

Key to variables
1 Dynamic problem area
2 Time reaction of modern problems
3 Rate of methodical and instrumental innovation
4 Interdisciplinarity of problems and method
5 Availability of knowledge and instruments
6 Multidisciplinary structure in groups
7 Relevance for knowledge and society
8 Output per scientist
9 Coauthorship

Table 14.3. Correlation matrix: Interdisciplinarity and cooperative behavior

	1	2	3	4	5	6	7	8	9
1	1.00	.40+	.39+	.33+	.41+	.27+	.46+	.25	.21
2	—	1.00	.18	−.19	−.27+	−.26	−.10	−.21	−.27+
3	—	—	1.00	.22	−.13	.01	.08	.13	−.02
4	—	—	—	1.00	.21	−.03	.19	−.01	.20
5	—	—	—	—	1.00	−.21	−.09	−.29+	.02
6	—	—	—	—	—	1.00	.50++	.51++	.29+
7	—	—	—	—	—	—	1.00	.33+	.20
8	—	—	—	—	—	—	—	1.00	.20

Key to variables

1 Interdisciplinarity of problem and method
2 Distribution of competence among all functions in the division of labor
3 Coauthorship
4 Share of cooperative work in the total work
5 Ratio between cooperation within the group/with outside
6 Participation of group members in decision making with regard to their own research work
7 Participation with regard to the research work of other group members
8 Autonomy of group members
9 Acceptance by the head

Source: Geissler 1985.

and method has in almost all cases significant rank correlations with features of cooperative behavior, as can be seen from Table 14.3, which is based on an analysis of the work of heads of units carried out by Geissler in the same ensemble of groups (1985, pp. 83–85).

CONCLUSIONS

The interdisciplinarity of problem and method is a basic feature of interdisciplinary research situations with a determining influence on cooperative behavior. This is important because usual procedures for organizing research groups are based on the notion that efficiency is influenced by agreement between the problem's structure and the structure of the research groups (Hiebsch 1977, pp. 115–16). Our investigations, in contrast, underline the importance of the individual investigators' competence and the knowledge to work together with others as being of prime importance.

REFERENCES

Amir, S. 1985. On the degree of interdisciplinarity of research programs: A quantitative assessment. *Scientometrics* 8:117–36.

Andrews, F. M., ed. 1979. *Scientific productivity.* Cambridge: Cambridge University Press; Paris: UNESCO.

Darvas, G., and A. Haraszthy. 1979. Interdisciplinary orientation of research teams in six European countries. In R. T. Barth and R. Steck, eds., *Interdisciplinary research groups: Their management and organization*. Vancouver: IRGIP.

Geissler, U. 1985. Wissenschaftliche Tatigkeitsformen in ihrer Anforderungsspezifik fur die Leitung [Scientific forms of activity and the demands they make on management]. *Kolloquien* 50:78–93. Academy of Sciences of the GDR, Institute of Theory, History, and Organization of Science (Berlin).

Hiebsch, H. 1977. *Wissenschaftspsychologie* [Science psychology]. Berlin: VEB Deutscher Verlag der Wissenschaften.

Parthey, H. 1973. Forschungssituation interdisziplinarer Arbeit in Forschergruppen [Research situation of interdisciplinary work in research groups]. In H. Parthey and K. Schreiber, eds., *Interdisziplinaritat in der Forschung*. Berlin: Akademie Verlag, pp. 13–46.

UNESCO 1973. Proposed International Standard Nomenclature for Fields of Science and Technology. Paris: UNESCO.

15
Interdisciplinarity and Futures Research

ANA MARIE SANDI

The purpose of this paper is to look into the relationships existing between interdisciplinarity and futures research as emphasized by both the pragmatic view on futures studies and the philosophical view. The conclusion that futures research needs interdisciplinarity while interdisciplinarity is benefiting from exercises in futures research is based on this analysis as well as on the experience summarized from futures research projects developed at ICMFDS.

THE NEED FOR INTERDISCIPLINARITY IN FUTURES RESEARCH

We all forecast in our everyday lives, even without being aware of it, as Mr. Jourdain of Molière's *Le bourgeois gentilhomme* ignored as he was speaking in prose: "We could even believe that man is forecasting since always, if such an idea would not be questioned by the fact that not all languages had always future tenses, some of them, as the Hopi language, still ignoring it."

Future visions have been offered, in time, in various forms, by arts, religion, folklore, witchcraft, and prophecy. However, in our century, in an attempt to get ahead of the mere emotional reference to the future, a new type of research—"futures research"—was created.

The question "What is futures research?" leads to a whole range of different answers. Mostly, European researchers have been engaged in real philosophical debates concerning the possibility of scientifically studying the future. More pragmatic, the American attitude may be described by paraphrasing Descartes: it is practiced, thus it exists. Here the place of interdisciplinarity in futures research will be examined, as revealed by the two mentioned hypotheses.

THE PRAGMATIC FUTURES RESEARCH

The idea that futures research is what those who are practicing it are doing helps, for example, Marien (1985) to escape from difficult epistemological interrogations and leads him directly to a categorization of futurists into twelve types, according to "roles in the world of world-shaping ideas and how they are defined." The classes are established within three main categories: (1) mainstream futurists (synoptic generalist, general forecaster, normative generalist, pop futurist); (2) marginal futurists (futurized specialist, closet futurist, future futurist, forgotten futurist); and (3) nonfuturist futurists (pseudo-futurist, strawman futurist).

Although these types describe roles that may be assumed by individuals as well as by research teams, Marien restricts his considerations to futurist individuals. In addition, he thinks that "futures research . . . does not qualify as a field because, by almost any definition, its practitioners do not share a common academic background."

The consideration of the role and place of interdisciplinary approach and team in futures research leads to the following observations.

If the interdisciplinary character of futures studies is understood, it obviously follows that their practitioners do not share a common academic background. Even individual futurists are most of the time adopting an interdisciplinary approach in their analysis, and this is truer for interdisciplinary teams. The argument used to assert the impossibility of qualifying futures research as a field is, thus, no longer valid.

One of the most prolific producers of futures studies proved to be the interdisciplinary team. Many examples can be given. The MIT Project Team for "Limits to Growth" comprised specialists in pollution (three), agriculture (three), resources (two), population (three), sociopolitical trends (one), administration (two), capital (one), and documentation (one). The GAMMA research team, working on the report "The Conserver Society: A Workable Alternative for the Future," was formed from specialists in economics (six), anthropology, management, engineering, political science, sociology, psychology, demography, philosophy, and soil science. The Rumanian, American, and Moroccan national teams that worked on the project summarized in the report to the Club of Rome "No Limits to Learning: Bridging the Human Gap" had components of various qualifications; the Rumanian team, for example, was formed of a mathematician, an economist, a sociologist, an anthropologist, an engineer, and a psychologist. More numerous teams were engaged in the development of global forecasting studies, such as "Global 2000" and "Interfutures."

It is obvious that interdisciplinarity does not mean only providing the participation of specialists from various disciplines, which may be qualified as multi- or pluridisciplinarity. But, as demonstrated below, futures studies need interdisciplinarity, such that the teams already mentioned and equally others had an interdisciplinary character. In fact, such teams are an operational answer to Marien's search for a basis for "mutual respect and enrichment between the generalist and the specialist." And they also explain certain difficulties faced by futures research, difficulties that belong to interdisciplinary research.

FUTURES RESEARCH PHILOSOPHY

Futures research was associated in Europe with deep gnosiological and epistemological debates, which have known a historical evolution. The discussions initially regarded only the possibility and the specificity of future knowledge.

The views ranged between two extreme attitudes: (1) the future may not be known—it preexists; and (2) the future may not be known—it does not preexist but is born from choices.

H. G. Wells believed in the possibility of "knowing" the future, neglecting the importance of individual choices in history. In his already classical discourse of 1902, *The Discovery of the Future,* he confirmed his belief in the possibility of futures research: "I believe quite firmly that an inductive knowledge of a great number of things in the future is becoming a human possibility. I believe that the time is drawing near when it will be possible to suggest a systematic exploration of the future." But he also added that "in absolute fact the future is just as fixed and determinate, just as settled and inevitable, just as possible a matter of knowledge as the past."

In 1943, Flechtheim stated in his book *History and Futurology* his optimism related to the scientific study of the future, pleading for the creation of futurology, a science of future, analogous to history, the science of past.

Another classic, Bertrand de Jouvenel, maintained in his *The Art of Conjecture* that it is not possible to know the future which is completely open and must be created through choices. *Futures research* contains a contradiction in terms, as only facts can be known. Those concerned with the future could make (using their creative imagination) only conjectures of the type "If you do that, it will be so; if not, it will not be so." The controversies regarding future knowledge and scientific knowledge have moved in time to a different field. Is futures research a field? If so, is it a science? If a scientific field, is it autonomous?

Assessing futures research with strict positivist criteria, R. Jungk and J. Galtung did not deny, at a certain moment, the existence of a discipline of futures studies but doubted the possibility of considering it as a science capable of offering positive knowledge.

Even the acceptance of a possible scientific character of future studies is giving place to a controversy: in what frame to realize them. On one hand, some people are arguing that the already existing disciplines all have a prediction function; thus, an autonomous discipline does not have justification. On the other hand, reality confirms that such an autonomous discipline does exist and that it is developing all the time.

What follows is an attempt not so much at making a stand in the already mentioned controversies but at emphasizing certain new trends relevant to the subject of interdisciplinarity and futures research.

For the moment, it can be said that the epistemic difficulties facing futures studies are not in principle different from the ones with which social and particularly historical studies are confronted (what "reality" is studied, how "the truth" of statements is established). And if the acceptability of the "scientific" label is questioned, it can be remarked that meterology, which is in the same epistemic situation, is holding this label without great opposition.

If it is obvious that the future cannot be "known" in the same way as the past and the present, it is not that obvious that knowledge should be a copy, recollection, or simulation of a real object. Virtual, potential, and possible objects that may appear as the result of processes or practical actions can also be subject to knowing processes. The idea of an open future is directing futures research toward possibilities of evolution, possibilities emerging, however, from the existing reality. The last part of this sentence is essential, since in a voluntarist interpretation, free of any external determination, the future will be filled at will with extravagant images, wishes based only on subjective reasons, utopic projects. Such products of the mind, fascinating and tempting as they can be, are not acceptable if we try to advance futures research to the level of scientific knowledge. The past, the present, and the objective laws are highly reducing the area of the possible and do not allow for the statement of every objective, for qualitative leaps over evolutionary stages.

In addition, together with other factors, objective laws of science enable people to assign probabilities to the process of changing possibilities into reality (probable futures). On the other hand, futures research is not a gratuitous game with virtual events, but it offers studies responding to the needs of socioeconomic development. Thus, it is true that the future is built but subject to the existing economic, sociopolitical, and technological states and to the will of social forces to carry out what they consider necessary. Human wishes, aspirations, and values are finally defining the frame for preferable futures.

Classical, fragmentary approaches are of no use in identifying possible, probable, and preferable futures, generated by complex interactions between objective and subjective conditions. Holistic views on process developments in which one factor depends on others, reciprocal influences generate higher-order effects, and counterintuitive behaviors are often exhibited require systematic approaches and implicit interdisciplinarity. In other words, comprehensive and dialectic visions of the futures cannot be obtained by the simple justification of disciplinary projections. Moreover, they require the creation, in an interdisciplinary manner, of new concepts, methods, and instruments shared by several disciplines.

The above-mentioned aspects are revealed by various types of futures studies. In an attempt at classifying future studies (Sandy 1984), three dimensions with three levels were used. (See Table 15.1.) From the thirty-

Table 15.1. Dimensions and levels of futures studies

Dimensions	Level
1. Perspective	Local, regional, global
2. Scale of elaboration	National, international, worldwide
3. Range	Sectorial, problem-oriented, comprehensive

three types theoretically generated by level combinations, the necessity of interdisciplinarity is obvious for studies with a comprehensive or problem-oriented range. It must be demonstrated for sectorial future studies, as the idea that the internal logic of a sector is adequate for developing sectorial forecasts still prevails. Relationships among sectors and multiple interdependencies render unfeasible the attempt at projecting the future from a single perspective. This remark is valid when the sector is a scientific discipline, and more so when the sector is defined by complex social phenomena (human settlements, employment, etc.).

Economic forecasting, for example, cannot ignore the relationships between economy and technology and the social, political, and natural environment. Such forecasts will resort also to concepts and methods alien to economic science or shared with other disciplines.

The theoretical prediction specific to a scientific discipline has only certain elements in common with the scientific futures research related to that discipline. Predictions are in fact not related to time, as they are mainly concerned with the anticipation of a new fact, not necessarily a future one (the discovery of a planet, of an element, etc.).

Future studies are broader in scope, trying to identify future evolutions which are generated by multiple factors. In this attempt, they are using both conceptual elements belonging to theoretical predictions and concepts, theories, and methods belonging to an already existing field which may be called the general future research. The arguments used for denying the existence of such a field are of the same nature as those that might be called upon for denying the existence of an autonomous science of history. The general future research, a field in continuing development, has a marked interdisciplinary character, despite the fact that those contributing to its creation have sometimes acted from the standpoint of a specialized discipline (mathematics, sociology, politology). However, the synthesis that determined the present existence of concepts, theories, and methodologies for futures research was always made with an interdisciplinary view (sometimes by individuals, such as E. Jantsch, and sometimes by research teams).

THE IMPACT OF FUTURES RESEARCH ON INTERDISCIPLINARITY

If, until now, the necessity and utility of interdisciplinarity in futures research was advocated, the active role futures research plays in the development of interdisciplinarity will be emphasized here. The practice of interdisciplinarity while working out futures studies is pointing out new theoretical and methodological issues which have to be clarified.

Participation and Futures Research

Futures research has a broader significance than the one assigned by knowledge processes. The complexity of socioeconomic processes, the multiple perspectives from which they may be dealt with, were and are leading to the generation of contradictory future visions. In this situation, viable long-term projections cannot be obtained without a broad social dialogue, able to engage both specialists and decision makers and lay people. This is certainly a modality of grasping areas of agreement or disagreement, of persistent major uncertainties. A large participation contributes on one hand to remove disagreements or uncertainties and on the other hand to an increased social approval for forecasts, programs, and plans essential for their implementation. There is no doubt that the meaning of interdisciplinarity is extended in this case beyond the sense accepted in academic circles; it is enriched with elements reflecting new needs of reality.

The above-mentioned aspects are well emphasized by the way in which futures research is organized in Rumania. Since a comprehensive account of this problem could well be the subject of an independent paper, it will only be stressed that the forecasting and planning activity in Rumania is organized in a way that is, in fact, a comprehensive action to promote a democratic management of socioeconomic development. In this context, futures studies are no longer the product of experts isolated from reality but the result of a broad consultation with citizens at various levels of society.

The guidelines of the whole socioeconomic development of Rumania are stated in the "Program of the Romanian Communist Party," which has a long-term perspective and a normative character. Moreover, on the basis of various futures studies, specific programs have been developed: the Program of Scientific Research, Technological Development, and Application of Technical Progress for 1981–1990 and the Major Guidelines until 2000; the Energy Research and Development Program for 1981–1990 and the Principal Directions through the Year 2000; and others. For the field of water and forestry, the national programs have an extremely long time horizon, until the year 2025.

Besides the programs, long-term forecasts have an important role in establishing development directions and as a basis for the formulation of five-year plans. The institutional framework responsible for their development consists of a wide network of forecasting commissions, directly coordinated by the Supreme Council of Economic and Social Development. In order to understand the scope of this activity, it is sufficient to mention the futures studies on science and technology coordinated by the National Council for Science and Technology and developed in close cooperation by central research institutes, academies of sciences, ministries, and other central institutions.

Initially, forecasts for 1981–2000 were worked out for nearly seventy branches and fields and more than thirty integrative forecasts for groups of fields and branches and the whole R&D system. Afterward, some three hundred forecasts over 1986–2010 were finalized, focused on raw materials and energy sources, groups of products and products, activities, services, and technologies, as well as on subfields of exact sciences, natural and medical sciences, economics, social and political sciences, education, and interdisciplinary sciences.

Actually, forecasting is possible in Rumania because of a diversified, intense activity in the field of futures research. The International Center of Methodology for Future and Development Studies is one among the many organizational forms for this activity. The research team of the center was engaged in interdisciplinary future studies on subjects such as (1) societal and individual learning processes and mechanisms—their role in development processes; (2) the analysis of complex relationships between values, objectives, and processes of development (in the context of the interdependence between economic growth and human and social development); (3) impact studies (concerning the societal impact of scientific and technological developments), assessments of the impact of the new information technologies and of technologies for renewable energy sources; (4) the analysis of appropriate technologies in the frame of a self-reliant Rumanian development—future technologies for rural areas. Several themes were dealt with in the frame of international projects, which have emphasized the importance of multiple perspectives in research, contrasting various viewpoints in a cooperative manner. Moreover, the work in the frame of an interdisciplinary team pointed out certain obstacles and opportunities regarding both the scientific production and the organization of research.

The Interdisciplinary Team

Although interdisciplinary futures research is also possible at an individual level, the research team is more characteristic for this field. Work in a team has its own features, summarized by Malita (1972):

1. Two identical persons cannot form a team, hence the need for diversity.
2. The team is subordinated to the project.
3. Every team has a center; its denial leads to the destruction of the team.
4. The reasoning of a team is qualitatively different from individual reasoning.
5. The team spirit is qualitatively different from the individual one; in individual competition, what one is losing the other is gaining; in a team, the gain (loss) of someone may be a gain (loss) to the others too. The changed logic leads to cooperative strategies that replace the competitive ones.

The analysis of interdisciplinary teams engaged in futures research shows that they can belong to different types of organization:

1. The stable team has a stable structure (beyond certain insignificant variations) regardless of the project dealt with; researchers tend to acquire needed research skills rather than recruit collaborators who possess them.
2. The ad hoc team has a flexible organization, corresponding completely to the research needs of the ongoing project; it can be dissolved after completion of the project.

Each type of team has its own advantages and disadvantages, some of them summarized in Table 15.2.

Interdisciplinary Scientific Production

Besides the organizational problems of interdisciplinary teams, futures research also reveals problems related to the interdisciplinary scientific results and the status of those who are producing them. Certain problems were mentioned in other papers, such as difficulties in obtaining necessary funds to finance interdisciplinary projects. As Porter and Rossini (1985) pointed out, such difficulties are partly the result of paper review processes carried on in the frame of organizations designed to promote disciplinary research. Other problems can be also mentioned:

1. Reception difficulties. Most researchers, specialized in particular disciplines and engaged in thorough, narrow studies, do not trust researches in which their field is only superficially represented through its links with other fields. The lack of a general interdisciplinary education makes them less receptive to interdisciplinary subjects.

Table 15.2. Interdisciplinary research teams

Type	Advantages	Disadvantages
Stable team	Common view and language. Acquaintance with the same bibliography. Accommodation of the work with different personalities.	Possible superficiality in dealing with problems that need specialized knowledge. Danger of routine work, cliché research.
Stable-core team	Increased matching of research skills and specific needs of the project. Avoidance of superficiality. Contribution of fresh visions.	Possible diverging understanding and communication between the core and co-opted specialists. Possible conflict arising from varying degree of interpersonal relations.
Ad hoc team	Total matching between research skills and project needs. Fresh approach, increased chances for insights, creative work.	Longer time needed for personal accommodation. Communication barriers. Loss, once the project is finalized, of certain acquired qualities (common views, language, attitudes).

2. Communication difficulties. Interdisciplinary research tends to establish its own conceptual and even linguistic languages, unaccessible to outsiders.
3. Diffusion difficulties. These are caused by the prevalence of disciplinary conferences, symposia, and journals.
4. Indefinite status of those engaged in interdisciplinary research. This is caused mainly by the prevalence of disciplinary institutional forms. Following from this are comparatively reduced possibilities of promotion, obtaining doctoral or academic degrees, and so on.
5. Insufficient and inadequate education. The prevalence of the disciplinary education system results in a random manner of learning interdisciplinary subjects (eventually through apprenticeship stages in interdisciplinary teams). Besides the loss of time, the lack of an organized education system also becomes an obstacle to the rapid development of interdisciplinary fields of high social utility.

The new and important field of futures research reflects the benefits and the still existing shortcomings of interdisciplinarity. It also offers a vision of the possible future evolution of interdisciplinarity into a broader, "interperspectives" approach. Such an approach would allow for the confrontation and merging of various perspectives such as the scientific, organizational, and personal ones, as well as of different international viewpoints.

REFERENCES

Malita, M. 1972. Aurul cenusiu. *Editura Dacia* 2:126–32.

Marien, M. 1985. Toward a new futures research: Insight from twelve types of futurists. *Futures Research Quarterly* 1(1):13–35.

Porter, A. L., and F. A. Rossini. 1985. Forty interdisciplinary research projects: Multiple skills and peer review. In B. W. Mar et al., eds., *Managing high technology*. Amsterdam: North-Holland.

Sandy, A. M. 1984. Local, regional, and global future studies. *Journal of the National Committee of Rumania for UNESCO* 26(2):104–11.

V

INTERDISCIPLINARY RESEARCH IN JAPAN

Japan's rapid rise as a major technological power has been achieved through a variety of factors. This development is perhaps a forerunner of what is to come in a number of Pacific Rim countries. Masahiro Ikejima, relying on data obtained by Japan's Ministry of International Trade and Industry (MITI), reviews in detail research and development management practice in Japan. Through job rotation and interdisciplinary communication among research and development, production, and marketing, Japanese product development time and quality have been generally outstanding. Ikejima notes that decision-making style is a critical factor in Japanese firms. This is contrary to the commonly held belief that there is a single, consensus style in Japan. Finally, he points out the importance of using evaluation techniques and promotion criteria for researchers in Japan that are widely used in countries such as the United States.

16

R&D Management in Japanese Companies

MASAHIRO IKEJIMA

It is necessary to integrate innovative technological development into corporate strategy for corporate growth under changing technological environment. R&D management must be divided into a research stage and a development one. In the research stage, researchers should be encouraged by the evaluation system. Interdisciplinary research is also useful because new heterogeneous information is needed outside the company. In the developmental stage, positive participation in setting development objectives by top executives is most important. Then interdisciplinary collaboration among different departments inside the company is necessary to share the sense that development is important for business success. We investigated R&D management in Japanese companies from the viewpoint of corporate growth using a new statistical method and LISREL VI.

THE PROCESS OF CORPORATE GROWTH UNDER CHANGING TECHNOLOGICAL ENVIRONMENT

Product development is the most important factor for corporate growth. In the past, many Japanese companies have grown through product development by improved technology. Many Japanese companies have thoroughly improved technology that was first introduced by excellent American or European companies to make consumer-oriented products. Recently, many people refer to this phenomenon as Japanese-style management or quality control activity.

We can remember, however, that the development of high-quality and low-priced products was mainly accomplished by drastic process innovation. Typically, as in the work of Abernathy and Utterback (1975), the model of innovation is that products will be developed over time, in a predictable manner, with an initial emphasis on product performance, then an emphasis on product variety, and, later, emphasis on product standardization and costs. In the maturity stage, the bulk of significant innovation tends toward manufacturing process enhancements that minimize cost. One major reason for success in Japanese business is that many companies have thoroughly emphasized process innovation with product technology in its maturity stage in American or European industry. Furthermore, severe competition among companies promoted the development of good products based on this innovation and market information.

Recently, however, it has been difficult for Japanese companies to import innovative product technology onesidedly, because foreign companies required cross-license as well as the decrease in product innovation rate. In the future, therefore, development of innovative technology, especially the product itself, is absolutely necessary in order for Japanese companies to grow over a long period of time. Without this innovation, substantial product differentiation is almost impossible.

To make a success of this development, R&D strategy, with a great emphasis on innovative technological development, obviously should be established. Generally, companies tend to concentrate on the improvement of existing technology to gain profit for a short term. As more of a company's R&D effort goes into really innovative development, the probability of technological completion goes down, but financial performance, or corporate image, usually goes up. This also results in higher entry barriers if commercialization is successful.

R&D strategy is implemented through R&D management. It is necessary to divide this management into two stages. One is the research stage, which includes basic research and applied research. Basic research in a company, of course, is more practical than in a university. Many companies, therefore, concentrate on applied research in the research stage. The other stage is the development stage. The management practices in this stage are different from those in the research stage, because developmental research must be quickly accomplished and requires a great deal of capital investment. I suggest three important systems as management practices: (1) an objective-setting system that determines the concrete objective of R&D and resolves the dilemma between the freedom for researchers and the corporate strategic direction; (2) an evaluation system that balances and differentiates between the research and development stages, and (3) an information system that seeks the relevant information inside or outside the company that researchers and evaluators need. Free and open channels of communication should be established so that they are stimulated by diverse and useful information.

In the past, Japanese companies have emphasized the short-term cyclical process rather than the long one depicted in Figure 16.1. Though the former process cannot be disregarded because the innovative technological development is risky, the latter process must be consciously emphasized in the future. Through this long-term cyclical process, the technological information for product differentiation can be accumulated and updated to enhance R&D capability. Successful development results in enhanced corporate image, which attracts qualified workers, as well as enhanced eco-

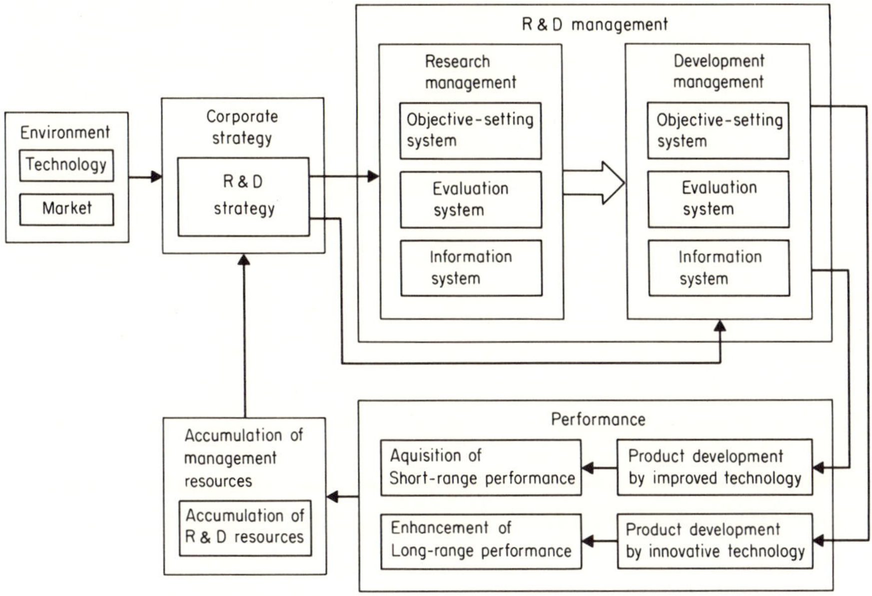

Figure 16.1. The process of corporate growth by R&D

nomic financial performance (Business Policy Forum 1985). I discuss R&D strategy and management so that a long-term cyclical process is revolving in a positive manner by empirical research.

EMPHASIS ON INNOVATIVE TECHNOLOGICAL DEVELOPMENT

It is necessary to integrate innovative technology into corporate strategy for overall corporate growth. However, as this strategy is risky, it is very difficult for companies with small R&D resources to exercise it. In fact, only about 30 percent of Japanese companies had emphasized innovative technological development in R&D strategy in 1984. Of course, large companies tend to emphasize it more than the medium ones. Moreover, in the situation where companies intensely compete with each other in technological development, great emphasis is placed on innovative R&D strategy. For example, 48.7 percent of companies in the chemical industry and 46.9 percent of companies in the electronics industry have emphasized this strategy. More importantly, those companies that place emphasis on innovative R&D strategy tend to have high financial performance, as shown in Table 16.1. This means that risk-taking behavior is of importance at a strategic level.

It is necessary to identify and develop a key technology that contributes

Table 16.1. R&D strategy and financial performance, morale (1984)

	Financial performance			Morale		
	All companies	Large companies	Medium companies	All companies	Large companies	Medium companies
Improved technology	4.883	4.905	4.846	3.227	3.344	3.030
Innovative technology	5.341*	5.457*	4.949*	3.541*	3.605*	3.324*

*$p < .05$, two-sided test.

to a future business domain and greatly affects the other product or technology. To develop this technology, a consistent R&D effort with an increased budget must be undertaken for a long period. R&D expenditure, as a percentage of sales, has been increasing a little every year. The average in 1984 was about 2.5 percent, and that of large companies (2.7 percent) is higher than that of medium ones (2.1 percent). Moreover, there is a positive relation between R&D expenditure/sales and financial performance, as shown in Table 16.2.

Basic research may be inevitable in developing innovative technology. Genuine basic research, when it is the original investigation for the advancement of scientific knowledge and does not have immediate commercial objectives, is next to impossible in a company's laboratory, except those having vast R&D resources. However, basic research in targeted areas seems to be necessary in joint research with other companies, universities, and so on. The number of basic researchers as a percentage is 6.47 percent. Although this figure is low, there is a positive relation between this ratio and the level of R&D activities against a competitor. Mansfield (1981) suggested that innovative output seemed to be directly related to the percentage of R&D expenditures going for basic research.

Table 16.2. R&D expenditure/sales and financial performance

	1982			1983			1984		
	All companies	Large companies	Medium companies	All companies	Large companies	Medium companies	All companies	Large companies	Medium companies
Less than 1%	4.839	4.976	4.647	4.663	4.748	4.553	4.656	4.670	4.635
1%–2%	4.934	4.957	4.900	4.943	4.910	4.989	4.716	4.855	4.991
2%–4%	5.247	5.169	5.511*	5.053	4.998	5.202	5.104	5.114	5.076
4% or more	5.308*	5.298*	5.337	5.424*	5.425*	5.420*	5.888*	5.845*	6.019*

*$p < .05$, two-sided test.

METHODS

About five hundred Japanese companies were surveyed annually from 1974 to 1986 by the Corporate Management Ability Committee in the Ministry of International Trade and Industry (MITI 1986), on which I participated as a member. Data was gathered using questionnaires. The 1984 sample consisted of 505 companies listed on the Stock Exchange. A large company is defined as one that is listed in the first section of the Stock Exchange, while a medium company is defined as one that is listed in the second section of the Stock Exchange. The 1984 sample size of large companies was 338, and that of medium ones was 167. Following the questionnaire survey, the chief executive officers and R&D managers of selected companies were interviewed.

The purpose of this research was to investigate the relationship between strategy, organization, and performance. This paper analyzes the R&D management of these firms by examining the responses to questions dealing with R&D.

Performance consisted of financial performance and employee morale. Financial performance here means the compound value of sales growth rate and ROI, with a minimum of 0 and a maximum of 10. Morale is measured by using the semantic differential method on a five-point scale compared with other companies in the same business. The minimum is 1 and the maximum is 5.

We use a D value analysis, which is a new statistical method created by the committee for the quantitative analysis of the contribution of qualitative items, such as those from R&D strategy and management, and quantitative performance. It is shown as the difference between the minimum and maximum of average performances in several categories within a certain qualitative item. Of course, an F test is used for each set of two categories in the item.

Besides the MITI data, data gathered in 1986 by the Business Policy Forum were also analyzed. The Business Policy Forum sample consisted of 111 companies which were listed on the Stock Exchange. LISREL VI (Jöreskog and Sörbom 1981) was used to investigate the causal relation between R&D management and performance.

A LISREL model is a mixture of simultaneous equation models in econometrics and a confirmatory factor analysis in psychometrics. The relations between endogenous latent and observable variables and between exogenous latent and observable variables are specified by each measurement model. A hypothesized causal relation between exogenous latent variables and endogenous latent variables is referred by the structural equation model. All of the parameters are simultaneously estimated. In this study, a maximum likelihood estimation was used. This program also gives *t* values to determine the statistical significance of individual estimates. The program then computes *chi*-square goodness-of-fit statistics, which may be regarded as a test of the specified model against the most general alternative.

The following exogenous observable variables *(x)* and endogenous observable variables *(y)* were analyzed:

x_1 = Growth rate of the industry (five years ago)
x_2 = Average age of executive officers
x_3 = Decision-making style of CEO (the degree of consensus of opinion in the executive team)
y_1 = Product innovation (the degree of positiveness of product innovation during the recent five years)
y_2 = Process innovation (the degree of positiveness of process innovation during the recent five years)
y_3 = Promotion through long service
y_4 = People-oriented coordination as a character required to be promoted to manager
y_5 = Level of product development against competitors
y_6 = Morale of employees

RESULTS

There are three important systems in the process of putting R&D strategy into action. I discuss these systems in different stages, namely the research stage and the development stage.

Objective-Setting System

We investigated the persons having great weight in setting researchers' objectives—namely "mainly self," "self and chief," and "mainly chief"—because researchers' ability or morale is influenced by this system.

First, in the research stage, researchers say that self-direction is essential to high performance, because they want freedom. Certainly, this philosophy seems to be suitable for the basic researcher. But a company needs ideas that contribute to future business or products. Thus, coordination of researchers, especially applied researchers, toward corporate strategic direction must be inevitable. They should talk about research objectives with their chief. In fact, most companies selected the "self and chief" category, as shown in Table 16.3. Moreover, financial performance was best when the researcher's objectives were decided jointly with the chief. This result is analogous to the empirical study of Ph.D.'s in developmental laboratories by Pelz and Andrews (1966). On the other hand, financial performance was lowest when self alone decided. This means that the researcher may spend his or her autonomy studying irrelevant research.

Thus, the chief should encourage the researcher to set innovative and relevant objectives as middle manager. Kanter (1982) suggested that the innovativeness depended, to a great degree, on how innovative middle

Table 16.3. Objective-setting system in research stage and financial performance (all companies)

	1982		1983		1984	
	%	Financial performance	%	Financial performance	%	Financial performance
Mainly self	11.3	4.752	13.0	4.747	11.5	4.758
Self and chief	79.2	5.114*	75.2	5.011	80.8	5.065
Mainly chief	9.5	4.825	11.8	4.835	7.7	4.962

*$p<.05$, two-sided test.

managers were. They may become key persons, or bridging persons, between researchers and top management, or the other manager, to implement the innovation. On the contrary, middle managers who are conservative discourage researchers from making innovative or creative studies.

Second, in the development stage, autonomy is lower. The chief or higher echelons have great influence on researchers concerning objectives, because development research requires a great deal of capital investment and integration between R&D, marketing, and production departments. Thus, the researcher who has a high spirit of cooperation is suitable for development research.

Furthermore, the success of this research depends, to a great degree, on how top executives positively participate in setting objectives. Though top executives generally make only some degree of change in the overall research budget in the research stage, they should concentrate the budget on some researches that come to good and let those gain momentum in the development stage. It seems that they should have extra money and invest it in a timely manner in good researches at any time. In addition, they should aggressively appeal to key persons, so as to push the researcher's idea and get it done well. Though the presence of a product champion is an important factor for the success of product development (Chakrabarti 1974), it is necessary for top executives to perform the role of product champion themselves.

In fact, financial performance and employee morale were always best when the top executives positively participated in setting objectives, as shown in Table 16.4 (Shimizu 1980). Relevant objectives can be settled because decision making by top executives is made observing future market trends as well as technological development, and researchers and related persons can be directed toward the success of development by great leadership. Researchers are motivated and make greater efforts because they are recognized as important persons in the company.

Evaluation System

This system is related to two problems. One is to evaluate the contents of research to judge whether one research should be implemented or not and

Table 16.4. Objective-setting system in development stage and financial performance, morale (all companies)

	1982			1983			1984		
	%	Financial performance	Morale	%	Financial performance	Morale	%	Financial performance	Morale
Positive participation in setting objectives by top executives	30.2	5.139*	3.483	27.7	5.164*	3.417	31.2	5.353*	3.598
Ordinary participation in setting objectives by top executives	59.2	5.055	3.420	65.4	4.904	3.330	58.5	4.893	3.253
Delegation of authority to researchers	10.6	4.554	3.250	7.9	4.669	3.337	10.3	4.704	3.106

* $p < .05$, two-sided test.

then continued or not. The other is to evaluate the researcher's effort. It seems that the researcher's effort evaluation is emphasized more in the research stage, because there is little relation between the researcher's effort and result. An innovative research effort must be appropriately evaluated so that researchers can devote themselves to their work with enthusiasm. On the other hand, in the development stage the evaluation of the content of the research is emphasized more because the success of development depends on the content of research, with a transition from the research stage to the development one.

First, in terms of research management, it is desirable that the research be original and applicable to the applied research at the basic research level. But it is very difficult to evaluate the content of basic research, because the time horizon involved in the activity is so long, or there may be cases where a flash of insight into the possibilities of wholly unanticipated experimental results may lead to great discoveries (Ansoff and Stewart 1967). Thus, a superior should judge whether a researcher can be entrusted with this task or not and then not penalize risky behavior for about three years, even if the researcher cannot obtain excellent results. Tolerance for risky behavior is probably one of the prerequisites for creativity (Steiner 1965).

It is also difficult to evaluate applied research, because the solutions are not always obvious. Thus, several research projects should not be rigidly evaluated but proceed in parallel. Quinn (1985) states, "Recognizing the inadequacies of theory, innovative enterprises seem to move faster from paper studies to physical testings than do noninnovative enterprises." Honda encourages heterogeneous approaches to creative innovative climates through competing principles.

Of course, concrete research management is influenced by the environment and research resources. If a company belongs to a growing industry such as electronics, many research themes tend to be listed as objectives. As all objectives cannot be implemented, some hopeless ones must be deleted by quantitative methods for research evaluation. Such a company needs systematic management so that hopeful research themes can be promptly selected as objectives because of competitive product development. At Hitachi, the chief evaluates the researchers' themes in terms of research level and contribution to the organization. After that, the higher echelon roughly and promptly ranks the themes by evaluating the originality and potential capacity of the laboratory.

Such systematic management is proceeding on the assumption that there are some good evaluators who can judge the originality of themes. Fortunately, Hitachi has many excellent middle managers as good evaluators, because the researchers have been nurtured with care since the company was established, under the philosophy that the prosperity of future business depends on R&D. Some themes are settled as objectives through the procedure. Then the objectives are executed in parallel and qualitatively judged on the way, observing accumulated data and external environmental change.

Because uncertainty is high in the research stage, it is very important that small failures be tolerated in the process of materializing innovative ideas. Honda places high value on challenging spirit. It even commends a valuable failure, considering that a person who does not try anything does not even fail. Such a system can help to enhance a researcher's morale, because a sense of competence (Lorsch and Morse 1974) can be generated.

According to the questionnaire responses, many companies employ award systems by chief executive officers (69.2 percent), research reporting systems (65.9 percent), and reward systems (64.7 percent) as means to raise the morale of researchers. About half of the companies employ the system to encourage the researcher to insert his paper in the company newspaper (55.6 percent), the system to develop research ability (46.9 percent), and the system to encourage the researcher to publish his paper in an academic journal (45.7 percent).

A few companies employ special post systems to set great value on qualified research (11.1 percent). Generally, large companies (e.g., electronics and chemical companies) positively employ these systems, as such companies probably have many researchers as compared to the other ones. The number of researchers averages 235 to a company. Of course, the researcher staff of a large company (341 on the average) is larger than that of a medium one (25 on the average). And those of an electronics company (836) and a chemical company (202) are also larger.

In addition, there is a positive relation between the number of systems employed and research levels; that is to say, the level is high when these systems are positively employed. Sometimes companies have informal schemes as well as the above-mentioned formal ones. For example, the chief executive officer hears directly what the younger researchers say, even in large companies. Consequently, some researchers are stimulated and encouraged.

Second, the research themes in the development stage should be evaluated in terms of marketability as well as the originality of technology. The selected researches are then executed on schedule to ensure that they are effectively achieved within the planned time. Failures tolerated in the early research stage should not be tolerated in the late development stage.

Thus, the work to be done in the development stage should be strictly evaluated at every step. Furthermore, some people in marketing and production departments, besides the R&D department, should give objective evaluations from each expert point of view. It is then important to investigate whether the plant is satisfactorily in production or not and if sales and profit are satisfactory. Of course, if the results are not satisfactory, the cause of failure should be thoroughly investigated. Generally, it is difficult to relate the result of each research to individual researcher effort, because researchers team up together, and the result of the research is different according to each research area.

Information System

An information system must be established so that researchers and evaluators can get relevant information inside and outside the company, because they are confronted with uncertainty. It seems that outside information is more important for research management than information from the inside. On the contrary, the inside information is more important for development management than outside information.

First comes discussion of research management. Since researchers are confronted with high uncertainty in the research stage, they need new heterogeneous information from outside the company to explore the problem from every kind of viewpoint. They must elaborate creative work by combining such information with the existing knowledge. In addition, a suspension of judgment, with which several researchers proceed in parallel in the early stage, keeps researchers open to new important information (Shapero 1985).

According to the questionnaire responses, most often technological cooperation with another research institute (78.0 percent) and units for gathering patent information, etc. (77.6 percent) are employed. More than half of the companies employed the system to help researchers attend the meetings of academic societies (55.3 percent). Furthermore, a company tends to mix one kind of technology with different ones through loose interorganizational networks (53.5 percent). It seems that such networks lead to interdisciplinary research. Generally, large companies (e.g., chemical and electronic companies which place emphasis on research) employ these systems.

At Kureha, the patent researching unit staff constantly summarizes patent information and presents summary reports to top executives as well as the researchers. The top executives develop the institution of evaluation investigating such reports. At Toore, a research planning unit manager also holds the post of management of the unit for gathering technological information. The goal is for relevant technological information to be promptly reflected in the research. This is interesting, as this manager is systematically playing the role of gatekeeper.

Second comes development management. As top executives must set development objectives with related persons in the early stage of development, they need market and production information as well as technological information. The executive committee (71.2 percent) is often employed to gather information from every department. Most often, electronics companies employ this committee because of timely development.

In implementing a stage of development, project team, or task force, formal and informal channels of communication among related unit members are usually built because the interdisciplinary collaboration among R&D, marketing, and production departments is of critical importance. A sense of which development is very important for business success can be shared among members.

Verbal communication is a particularly effective medium for the exchange of information and ideas, since it permits rapid feedback of information (Tushman and Nadler 1980). Good communication channels must be built so that there is no NIH ("not invented here") problem. In Japanese companies, job rotation is most often executed, or some researchers who develop a technology often change to a production department with technology transfer.

METHODOLOGY

A LISREL model was used to investigate the causal relation between the external environment, R&D strategy, the evaluation system that is the most important for R&D management, and performance. I made a special model of LISREL in which each exogenous observable variable was treated as a valid measure of a latent variable, as shown in Figure 16.2.

Since the units of measurement in the observed variables were diverse, a correlation matrix was used, as shown in Table 16.5. As *t* values for parameters are almost larger than 2 in magnitude, parameters are normally judged to be different from zero. Then *chi*-square goodness-of-fit and GFI show that this model is as good as whole.

It was found that the growth rate of the industry affected technological development. Those companies whose product life cycle is in the growth stage must emphasize innovative technological development against their competitors. The parameter estimate relating the process innovation to technological development is then larger than that relating to product innovation. This means that Japanese companies mainly place emphasis on process innovation.

Then, the company's uniqueness is inevitable to make a success of technological development. Decision-making styles of CEOs sometimes play a role in allowing a company to be unique. Those companies in which the CEO makes a strategic decision he or she feels confident about, even when many other executive team members do not support it, tend to emphasize innovative technological development. Though many persons believe that the Japanese style of management must be consensus management, the decision-making style of the CEO is necessary to make a company unique at the strategic level. At Asahikasei, the CEO makes a decision to go ahead when 30 percent of the team supports it. But he does not make a decision to go ahead when less than 50 percent of the team supports it.

In order to implement innovative technological development, researchers should be fairly evaluated and encouraged by the evaluation system. Promotion through ability and performance, rather than promotion through long service which is the famous Japanese style of management, is necessary to researchers. Moreover, companies should emphasize task-oriented aggressiveness rather than people-oriented coordination as the characteristic required for a candidate to be promoted to manager. Kureha employs

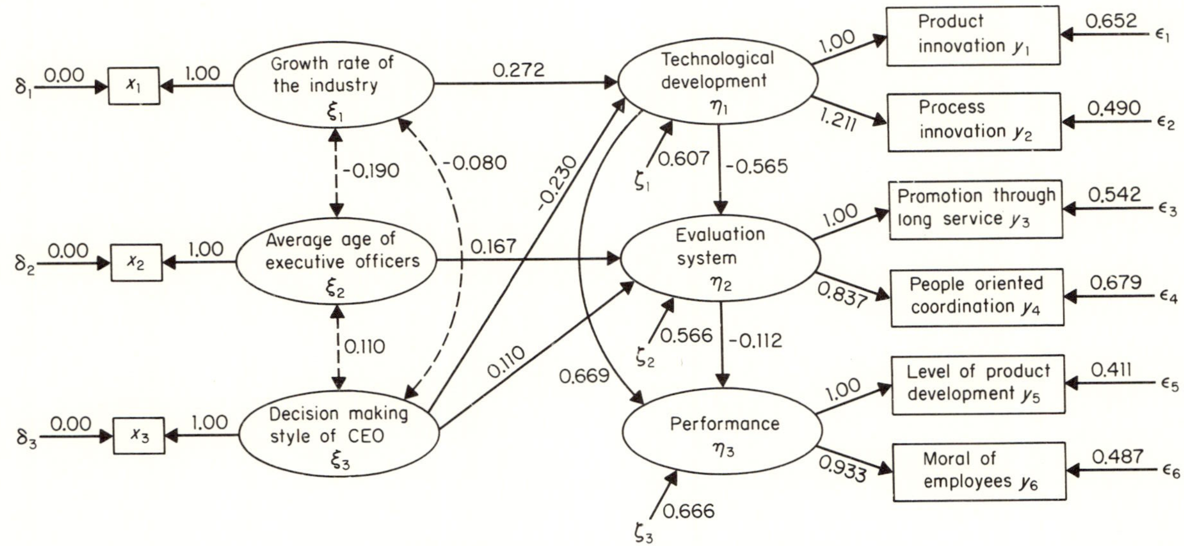

Measures of goodness-of-fit for the whole model:
χ^2 20.94 (prob. level = 0.401)
d.f. 20
GFI 0.960

Figure 16.2. LISREL model of R&D management

Table 16.5. Correlation matrix

	x_1	x_2	x_3	y_1	y_2	y_3	y_4	y_5	y_6
x_1	1.00								
x_2	0.42	1.00							
x_3	−0.27	−0.33	1.00						
y_1	−0.12	−0.17	0.38	1.00					
y_2	0.35	0.23	−0.17	−0.23	1.00				
y_3	0.25	0.30	−0.26	−0.13	0.55	1.00			
y_4	0.25	0.39	−0.17	−0.17	0.23	0.16	1.00		
y_5	−0.05	−0.04	0.23	0.15	0.00	0.03	−0.19	1.00	
y_6	−0.25	−0.30	0.20	0.33	0.24	−0.16	−0.08	0.11	1.00

Where:

x_1 = Growth rate of the industry (five years ago)
x_2 = Average age of executive officers
x_3 = Decision-making style of CEO (the degree of consensus of opinion in the executive team)
y_1 = Product innovation (the degree of positiveness of product innovation during the recent five years)
y_2 = Process innovation (the degree of positiveness of process innovation during the recent five years)
y_3 = Promotion through long service
y_4 = People-oriented coordination as a character required to be promoted to manager
y_5 = Level of product development against competitors
y_6 = Morale of employees

a special post system to set great value on excellent researchers. Those companies in which the executive officers are young and the CEO allows uniqueness in decision making tend to employ such an evaluation system, causing the level of product development and morale to rise.

CONCLUSIONS

In the past, many Japanese companies have grown through product development by improved technology. Recently, however, development of innovative technology was inevitable to corporate growth. To make a success of this development, R&D strategy, with a great emphasis on innovative technological development, should obviously be established.

Companies should emphasis R&D management, which is divided into a research stage and a development stage. There are three important systems—an objective-setting system, an evaluation system, and an information system—in each stage. It is very important to integrate the two different stages. Creative research should be smoothly transferred from the research stage to the development stage. In the research stage, researchers should be encouraged toward strategic direction by an evaluation system. In the development stage, top executives should aggressively support creative research.

REFERENCES

Abernathy, W. J., and J. M. Utterback. 1975. A dynamic model of process and product innovation. *Omega* 3:639–56.

Ansoff, H. I., and J. M. Stewart. 1967. Strategies for a technology-based business. *Harvard Business Review* 45:71–83.

Business Policy Forum 1985. Research and analysis of enterprise vitality. Interim report, March.

Chakrabarti, A. K. 1974. The role of champion in product innovation. *California Management Review* 17:58–62.

Jöreskog, K. G., and D. Sörbom. 1981. *LISREL VI: Analysis of linear structural relationships by the method of maximum likelihood.* Chicago: International Educational Services.

Kanter, R. M. 1982. The middle manager as innovator. *Harvard Business Review* 60:95–105.

Lorsch, J. W., and J. J. Morse. 1974. *Organizations and their members: A contingency approach.* New York: Harper and Row.

Mansfield, E. 1981. Composition of R and D expenditures: Relationship to size of firm, concentration, and innovative output. *Review of Economics and Statistics* 63:610–15.

MITI. 1986. *News from MITI* (Overseas Public Affairs Office), February.

Pelz, D. C., and F. M. Andrews. 1966. *Scientists in organizations: Productive climates for research and development.* New York: Wiley.

Quinn, J. B. 1985. Managing innovation: Controlled chaos. *Harvard Business Review* 63:73–84.

Shapero, A. 1985. Managing creative professionals. *Research Management* 28:23–28.

Shimizu, R. 1980. *The growth of firms in Japan.* Tokyo: Keio Tsushin.

Steiner, G. A. 1965. *The creative organization.* Chicago: University of Chicago Press.

Tushman, M. D., and D. A. Nadler. 1980. Communication and technical roles in R&D laboratories: An information processing approach. In B. V. Dean and J. L. Goldhar, eds., *Management of research and innovation.* New York: North-Holland.

Summary

Our knowledge of interdisciplinary research can be effectively divided into five areas: the environment external to the research team (consisting of institutional and societal considerations), the characteristics of the research team, the nature of the subject or problem to be studied, the characteristics of the individual participants in the research, and the impacts IDR has on the systems used and the new knowledge created.

The larger-scale societal considerations reflect the organization and funding patterns for research in a country. Each country has its predominant research performers. In Japan, industry is the principal performer. In France and the Soviet Union, research institutes play a central role. Research in the United States is divided among universities, industry, and government laboratories. There are various approaches to funding research, of which the three most common are institutional, program, and project.

From the IDR perspective, each type of institution and each funding arrangement has advantages and disadvantages. University reward structures have heavily favored individual, disciplinary contributions. Organized research units have been an alternative to traditional disciplinary departments. Problems with these units as viable homes for IDR include their permanence and the status of research faculty in a university. Their strength is that they conduct research in areas that cut across disciplines, though their internal organization may or may not favor actual IDR. Industry and government research organizations present a different range of opportunities and problems. The primary opportunity is that division by discipline is typically weaker than in academia, so that IDR can be encouraged in principle. However, turf problems exist in these organizations because of the advantage of managers of employing persons in their own organizations rather than importing talent from other groups. Small organizations without divisional barriers do not suffer from this latter problem.

Project-by-project funding arrangements tend to work against IDR when the projects are peer-reviewed. Reviewers tend to downgrade proposals with which they are not totally familiar, thus creating a bias against IDR. Program and institutional funding require less bureaucracy to manage but open the process to intrainstitutional turf wars and a higher level of managerial direction of research. If programs and institutions were organized for IDR, either of these mechanisms would be more supportive than funding by project with peer review.

Reward structures within organizations that are positive or neutral to IDR are necessary to allow individual researchers to participate. A very critical factor, especially in academia, is the openness of the host organization to new ideas and people from atypical backgrounds. This openness maintains an intellectual and personal dynamism that allows the organization to innovate by invasion as well as from within. This effectively allows a path of renewal for the substantive knowledge and skills contained within the organization.

Characteristics of the research team drive group success or failure on a particular project. The most critical team characteristic is leadership. Because no individual can be an expert in every part of a team IDR project, the leader cannot dominate as a dictator. Likewise, because of the degree of coordination and integration required for a successful IDR project, the laissez-faire approach to leadership is also undesirable. A democratic leader who communicates effectively and facilitates the conduct of the project by the team members is the most appropriate type of IDR team leader. It is important that the leader be ready and able to make timely bottom-line decisions after appropriate input from the team members. Also critical is the ability to communicate intellectually with the team members. Thus, the leader should be intellectually broad enough to relate to the range of skills involved in the project. At the same time, it is clear that a single individual cannot intellectually span a complex project.

Interteam communication is a critical factor in the process of IDR. Physical proximity of team members leads to increased interaction. Intellectual diversity of team members relative to the project is desirable. The combination of closeness and diversity anticipates a mutual learning experience at the beginning of the project to the extent that the participants are not familiar with one another and with the work to be done. Where physical closeness is not possible, systematic interactions among team members should be organized during the early period of the project so that communication links may be established. Projects in which the only communication links have been between the project director and the researcher without any researcher-to-researcher links have proved to be poorly integrated.

The characteristics of the subject to be studied or the problem to be solved constitute an important precondition of IDR. Each problem or project requires a set of skills. Skills can be divided into substantive knowledge and techniques. These skills serve as basic units of intellectual input into a project. For a complex project, a wide range of skills is required. Skills, rather than disciplines, are the intellectual building blocks of a project. In fact, skills are not in a one-to-one correspondence with disciplines. Using skills instead of disciplines to match researchers to the needs of a particular project allows an escape from ideological traps and turf issues relating to disciplines. The degrees of uncertainty and urgency involved in a project must be dealt with in the organization of the project. Projects whose outcome is predictable to a great degree allow for definitive schedule and budget as well as staffing. Researchers vary substantially among themselves in the level of uncertainty they find most desirable in a project. This ability and interest in dealing with uncertainty is critical in selecting researchers for particular project. Likewise, the ability and interest of researchers in working under the gun should be matched to the particular project. Academics have received very bad press, often deserved, regarding timely delivery of output. However, there are some university-based groups that can work under deadlines as well as industrial or contract research groups.

Individual participants in IDR need to possess a number of qualities if their efforts are to be unimpeded by negative intellectual baggage. They should be well grounded in their discipline or set of skills. Thus, they should possess intellectual confidence to the degree that they are not threatened by new and different ideas or approaches to familiar problems. They should be open not only to new ideas but also to new ways of organizing projects and team interaction. They should not be wedded to their own ideas or words, realizing that iteration can take the work of the individual and, while integrating it into the group effort, strengthen the output and enrich the individual participant at the same time. The participants should be ready and able to understand the general features of intellectual frameworks that are very different from theirs. They should be ready to engage in intensive intellectual give and take without ever letting it sink from the professional to the personal level. Finally, they should want to grow intellectually and personally and should see IDR as a vehicle for such growth. Obviously, being comfortable with both urgency and uncertainty helps. While this description is of a "water walker," it sets an ideal that researchers can approach.

The importance of understanding the preconditions and process of effective IDR rests in the human proclivity to reinvent the wheel. Researchers who would never dare to make a statement about a field with which they are not familiar often leap into IDR without ever thinking that a substantial body of knowledge may have been developed that will help the researcher and the project to succeed. Crashing ahead blindly without doing their homework on interdisciplinary research is the curse of beginning interdisciplinary researchers. Many of the obvious mistakes are well known and, in principle, preventable.

IDR has had enormous impact on the processes and structures used to conduct research generally as well as on the solution of basic and applied problems. IDR has spawned whole new programs and new approaches to supporting science within government agencies in nations such as the United States. These new programs have in turn affected the sites where research is conducted, such as research universities in the United States and institutes and academies of science in Eastern Europe. New organizational entities, incentive/reward systems, and educational programs to facilitate the IDR model and create a more goal-oriented mind-set among some researchers. These changes in the research establishment have also embraced the industrial sector since much of the federal funding available for IDR requires that funded university projects involve active interaction with and partial funding from the industrial sector. The presumption is that the academic-industrial collaboration ensures expedient transfer of the research results into applications generally beneficial to mankind and helpful to each nation's competitive position in the world marketplace.

Among the more significant impacts of IDR on the academic community is the advent of a variety of centers and institutes, referred to generically as organized research units (ORUs), through which to frame and carry out IDR programs. How to establish, operate, and evaluate such entities without unduly disrupting traditional academic values continues to be a significant challenge. In her paper, Martha Russell discussed several of the impacts of IDR as they directly affect the department/disciplinary environment. These range from redirecting faculty research interests and new approaches to the recruitment of graduate students to quite different interactions between universities and industrial firms that collaborate in IDR projects and provide partial funding for new facilities or instrumentation.

The papers by Donald Grace and Frederick Rossini also focused on the academic community through a case study describing the history and current status of a particular ORU within the Georgia Institute of Technology. The paper provided vivid insights into certain of the issues that frequently cause friction between regular faculty members and professional researchers that are generally key components of successful ORUs. Since the faculty member's base is in an academic department and the professional researcher's base is entirely within the ORU, the two hold quite different views about such fundamental matters as faculty status, space, and allocation of university resources.

The paper by Masahiro Ikejima provided helpful insights from the Japanese industry perspective by relating IDR to corporate R&D strategies and innovative technological development. A major theme of the paper stressed the importance of a smooth transition from research into the development stage. Ikejima asserts that this smooth transition is directly linked to a strategic plan made clear early in the process to all IDR team participants to ensure a common vision of the ultimate goal of their collective efforts.

In his paper, Heinrich Parthey made a key point by stressing the importance of a careful, well-founded decision to use the IDR model. He noted a crucial relationship between the problem and the structure of the group to work on it. The nature of the problem dictates not only the choice of disciplines required among the IDR team members but also the nature of what Parthey referred to as cooperative behavior required among team members.

The very thoughtful paper by Israel Dror presented some provocative observations about the interplay between science and technology on the one hand with social and economic forces on the other. He acknowledged the impact of this interplay to be long-term (fifty to sixty years) and asserted that over that long term research modes, especially IDR, coincide with the evolutionary phases of different disciplines. His paper presented certain cyclic patterns that he related particularly to the interplay between long-term technology and economic forces. Like others, Dror noted that problem-focused research generally requires the IDR model to ensure that the research team brings a sufficient range of knowledge and technical skills to solve the problem. Overall, the Dror paper forced us to consider some very long-term impacts of IDR by describing several environmental parameters and the possibility of a recurrent and cyclic pattern of those parameters.

Finally, the paper by Ana Marie Sandi attempted to help us extend what we know about IDR to the future through what she referred to as futures research. In so doing, she led us through some interesting discussions of European and American research views about the possibility of scientifically studying the future. She characterized the European view as philosophical and the American view as pragmatic and examined the place of IDR in the two approaches to futures research. Through the paper, Sandi used the discussion of futures research to show the benefits and shortcomings of IDR. In the end, she asserted that the new field of futures research offers a vision of the possible evolution of IDR into a broader interperspectives approach that will allow for the merging of scientific, organizational, and personal perspectives as well as different international viewpoints.

Bibliography

This is a bibliography for individuals who are interested in problem-focused interdisciplinary research (IDR). It is divided into three sections:

Interdisciplinarity (bibliographies, books, special issues, and important additional references)

Problem-focused research

Interdisciplinary medical care, education, social science, and science

All documents, papers, and publications accompanied by an ERIC identification number are generally available in academic libraries in the United States. They may also be ordered in either microfiche or paper copy from the Educational Resources Information Center in Washington, D.C.

INTERDISCIPLINARITY

Bibliographies

Chubin, D., A. Porter, and F. Rossini. 1986. Annotated bibliography. In D. Chubin, A. Porter, F. Rossini, and T. Connolly, eds., *Interdisciplinary analysis and research: Theory and practice of problem-focused research and development.* Mt. Airy, Md.: Lomond, pp. 441–70.

Cunningham, F., and S. Wolfe. 1982. Selected bibliography. In Stephen Dill, ed., *Integrated studies: Challenges to the college curriculum.* Washington, D.C.: University Press of America, pp. 133–42.

Grandberg, A. 1975. *The problem of interdisciplinarity: A bibliography.* Lund, Sweden: Research Policy Program, Lunds Universitet, April.

Humphreys, L. 1975. Interdisciplinarity: A selected bibliography for users. ERIC document ED 115-536.

Klein, J. T. 1984. Interdisciplinary literature. *Perspectives: Journal of the Association for General and Liberal Studies* 14(3):36–47. Reprinted 1984, *Institute for Renaissance Interdisciplinary Studies Newsletter* 5:1–11. Expanded version 1985: The interdisciplinary concept: Past, present and future. In L. Levin and I. Lind, eds., *Inter-disciplinarity revisited: Re-assessing the concept in the light of institutional experience.* Stockholm: OECD/CERI (Linköping) pp. 123–66. Reprinted 1985, *Interstudy Bulletin* 6(14):5–33.

———. 1989. Selected bibliography. In *Interdisciplinarity: History, theory, and practice.* Detroit: Wayne State University Press, pp. 229–325.

Mahan, J. L. 1970. Selected bibliography. In Toward transdisciplinary inquiry in the humane sciences. Unpublished dissertation, United States International University, San Diego, pp. 198–211.

Mayville, W. V. 1978. Bibliography. In *Interdisciplinarity: The mutable paradigm.* Washington, D.C.: American Association for Higher Education. Report no. 9, pp. 63–72.

Palmer, J. C. 1983. Interdisciplinary studies: An ERIC review. *Community College Review* 11(1):59–64.

Relations interdisciplinaires. *Social Science Information.* 1968, 7(2); 1969, 8(2); 1972, 10(2); 1975, 14(2).

Russell, M. G., and J. Cornwell. 1982. Selected annotated bibliography. In M. G. Russell, ed., *Enabling interdisciplinary research: Perspectives from agriculture, forestry, and home economics.* St. Paul: Agricultural Experiment Station, University of Minnesota, pp. 175–82.

Selected bibliography. 1979. In J. Kockelmans, ed., *Interdisciplinarity and higher education.* University Park: Pennsylvania State University Press, pp. 361–64.

Selected bibliography, references in interdisciplinary social science (mimeograph) 1981. Compiled by faculty and students of social science (Interdisciplinary Studies), with R. C. Miller, ed. San Francisco State University.

Books

Barth, R. T., and R. Steck, eds. 1979. *Interdisciplinary research groups: Their management and organization.* Vancouver: International Research Group on Interdisciplinary Programs. Papers from the First International Conference on Interdisciplinary Research.

Bayerl, E. 1977. *Interdisciplinary studies in the humanities: A directory.* Metuchen, N.J.: Scarecrow Press.

Bechtel, W., ed. 1986. *Integrating scientific disciplines.* Dordrecht: Martinus Nijhoof.

Boyer, E., ed. 1981. *Common learning: A Carnegie colloquium on general education.* Washington, D.C.: Carnegie Foundation for the Advancement of Teaching.

Case studies in interdisciplinarity. 1975. London: Group for Research and Innovation in Higher Education, Nuffield Foundation. Printed by the University of York. Vol. 1: *Environmental sciences and engineering.* 1975 (September). Vol. 2: *Science, technology and society.* 1975 (October). Vol. 3: *Integrated social sciences.* 1975 (September). Vol. 4: *National and international studies.* 1975 (September). Vol. 5: *Humanities and cognitive studies.* 1975 (September).

Chubin, D. E., A. L. Porter, F. A. Rossini, and T. Connolly, eds. 1986. *Interdisciplinary analysis and research: Theory and practice of problem-focused research and development.* Mt. Airy, Md.: Lomond.

Dill, S. H., ed. 1982. *Integrated studies: Challenges to the college curriculum.* Washington, D.C.: University Press of America.

Epton, S. R., R. L. Payne, and A. W. Pearson, eds. 1983. *Managing interdisciplinary research.* Chichester: John Wiley.

Fonseca, J. W., ed. 1985. Non-traditional and interdisciplinary programs. Fairfax, Va.: Division of Continuing Education, George Mason University. Selected papers from the Third Annual National Conference on Non-Traditional and Interdisciplinary Programs, Arlington, July 1–3.

Hanisch, T. E., and W. Vollman, eds. 1983. *Interdisciplinarity in higher education.* Bucharest: European Center for Higher Education.

Holzhey, H., ed. 1974. *Interdisciplinär. Philosophie aktuell.* Basel: Schwabe.

Interdisciplinarity. 1977. Papers presented at the Society for Research into Higher

Education European Symposium on Interdisciplinary Courses in European Education, London, September 1975. Surrey: SRHE at the University of Surrey. ERIC document ED 165-512.

Interdisciplinarity: A report by the Group for Research and Innovation. 1975. Regents Park: Group for Research and Innovation, Nuffield Foundation, July.

Interdisciplinarity: Problems of teaching and research in universities. 1972. Paris: Organization for Economic Co-operation and Development.

Jurkovich, R., and J. Paelinck, eds. 1984. *Problems in interdisciplinary studies: Issues in interdisciplinary studies,* no. 2. Hampshire: Gower, Steering Committee in Interdisciplinary Studies, Erasmus University, Rotterdam.

Klein, J. T. 1989. *Interdisciplinarity: History, theory, and practice.* Detroit: Wayne State University Press.

Kockelmans, J., ed. 1979. *Interdisciplinarity and higher education.* University Park: Pennsylvania State University Press.

Levin, L., and I. Lind, eds. 1985. *Inter-disciplinarity revisited: Re-assessing the concept in the light of institutional experience.* Stockholm: OECD/CERI (Linköping).

Luszki, M. B. 1958. *Interdisciplinary team research: Methods and problems.* Washington, D.C.: National Training Laboratories. Printed by New York University Press. Research Training Series no. 3.

Mar, B. W., W. T. Newell, and B. O. Saxberg, eds. 1985. *Managing high technology: An interdisciplinary perspective.* Amsterdam: North-Holland.

Margenau, H., ed. 1972. *Integrative principles of modern thought.* New York: Gordon and Breach.

Mayville, W. 1978. *Interdisciplinarity: The mutable paradigm.* Washington, D.C.: American Association for Higher Education. Report no. 9.

Milicic, V. 1973. *Symposium on interdisciplinary aspects of academic disciplines.* Bellingham: Western Washington University.

Newell, W. H., ed. 1986. *Interdisciplinary undergraduate programs: A directory.* Oxford, Ohio: Association for Integrative Studies.

Nyiri, N., and R. Preece, eds. 1977. *Unity in diversity: Proceedings of the interdisciplinary research seminar at Wilfrid Laurier University.* Waterloo, Ont.: Wilfrid Laurier University Press.

Palmade, G. 1977. *Interdisciplinarité et idéologies.* Paris: Editions Anthropos.

Piaget, J. 1973. *Main trends in interdisciplinary research.* New York: Harper and Row.

Russell, M. G., J. M. Barnes, and J. R. Cornwell, eds. 1982. *Enabling interdisciplinary research: Perspectives from agriculture, forestry, and home economics.* St. Paul: Agricultural Experiment Station, University of Minnesota. Miscellaneous Publication no. 19.

———. 1986. *Bridging disciplinary strengths.* St. Paul: Agricultural Experiment Station, University of Minnesota. Miscellaneous Publication no. 39.

Sherif, M., and C. Sherif, eds. 1969. *Interdisciplinary relationships in the social sciences.* Chicago: Aldine.

White, A., ed. 1981. *Interdisciplinary teaching.* San Francisco: Jossey Bass. New Directions for Teaching and Learning Series no. 8.

Special Issues

American Behavioral Scientist. 1976 (September–October). Political decision making: Interdisciplinary development from a microanalytic perspective.

Change Magazine. 1978 (August). Report on Teaching 6: Interdisciplinary studies. ERIC document ED 157-461.

Current Issues in Higher Education. 1981 (2). Creating an integrated curriculum: The "higher" in higher education. ERIC document ED 213-324.

Eighteenth Century Life. 1979. 5(3) (Spring). Eighteenth-century studies.

Forum for Liberal Education. 1986. 8(4) (March). Interdisciplinary education.

German Quarterly. 1989. 62(2) (Spring). Germanistik as German studies, interdisciplinary theories and methods.

Improving College and University Teaching. 1982. 30(1) (Winter). Interdisciplinary studies.

International Social Science Journal. 1964. 16(4):477–602. Problems of surveying the social sciences and humanities.

———. 1968. 2(20):192–210. Multidisciplinary problem-focused research.

———. 1977. 29(4):571–670. Facets of interdisciplinarity.

Journal of Canadian Studies. 1980. 15 (Fall). Thoughts on interdisciplinarity.

Liberal Education. 1979. (Spring). Interdisciplinary education.

New Literary History. 1980. 12(1) (Autumn). Psychology and literature: Some contemporary directions.

Policy Studies Journal. 1973. 2(1). Interdisciplinary approaches to policy studies.

R&D Management. 1984. 14(2) (April).

Social Science Information. Periodic special sections on interdisciplinary research.

Social Science Journal. 1975–76. (12–13) (October–January). U.S.-Mexico borderlands studies.

Social Science Quarterly. 1969. 50(1) (January): 6–58. Some convergences in history and sociology.

Soundings. 1971. 54(1) (Spring):82–123. Experimental interdisciplinary programs.

———. 1975. 58(2). Structuralism: An interdisciplinary study.

SRA, Journal of the Society of Research Administrators. 1981. (Fall). Management of interdisciplinary research.

Teacher's College Record. 1971. 73(2) (December). Curriculum: Interdisciplinary insights.

Technological Forecasting and Change. 1979. 2.

Important Additional References

Allan, A. 1980–1981. A method for determining interdisciplinary activities within a university. *Library Research* 2(1):83–94.

Arnoff, S. 1969. Interdisciplinary scholarship. Address to the Ninth Annual Meeting of the Council of Graduate Schools in the United States, December 5. ERIC document ED 035-365.

Bahm, A. J. 1977. *The specialist: His philosophy, his disease, his cure.* Delhi: Macmillan Company of India.

———. 1980. Interdisciplinology: The science of interdisciplinary research. *Nature and System* 2(1):29–35.

Bailey, M. J. 1978. Selecting materials for interdisciplinary programs. *Special Libraries* 69(12):468–74.

Bailis, Stanley. 1984–1985. Against and for holism: A review and rejoinder. *Issues in Integrative Studies* 3:17–41.

Baker, P. T. 1982. Human population biology: A viable transdisciplinary science. *Human Biology* 54(2):203–20.

Barmark, J., and G. Wallen. 1980. The development of an interdisciplinary project. In K. D. Knorr, R. Krohn, and R. Whitley, eds., *The social process of scientific investigation*. Vol. 4 of *Sociology of the Sciences*. Dordrecht and Boston: D. Reidel, pp. 221–35. See also 1979. Interaction of cognitive and social factors in steering a large interdisciplinary project. In R. T. Barth and R. Steck, eds., *Interdisciplinary research groups*. Vancouver: IRGIP, pp. 180–90.

Bateson, G. 1979. The pattern which connects. In *Mind and nature: A necessary unity*. New York: Dutton.

Beam, R. D. 1983. Fragmentation of knowledge: An obstacle to its full utilization. In K. Boulding and L. Senesh, eds., *The optimum utilization of knowledge*. Boulder: Westview, pp. 160–74.

Berk, R. A. 1981. On the compatibility of applied and basic sociological research: An effort in marriage counseling. *American Sociologist* 16(4):204–11.

Berthel, J. H. 1969. Twentieth century scholarship and the research library: A marriage of convenience. *University of Tennessee Library Lectures* 20:25–27.

Binder, A. 1987. Criminology and interdisciplinarity. *Issues in Integrative Studies* 5:41–67.

Birnbaum, N. 1969. The arbitrary disciplines. *Change* (July–August):10–21.

Blaschke, D. 1976. *Probleme interdisziplinärer forschung*. Wiesaden: Franz Steiner Verlag.

Borsodi, R. 1967. *The definition of definition: A new linguistic approach to the integration of knowledge*. Boston: Porter Sargent. See especially A. Brody, Toward integration of the social sciences, pp. 112–17.

Boulding, K. 1977. Peace research. *International Social Science Journal* 29(4):601–14.

Caldwell, L. K. 1983. Environmental studies: Discipline or metadiscipline? *Environmental Professional* 5:247–59.

Campbell, D. 1969. Ethnocentrism of disciplines and the fish-scale model of omniscience. In *Interdisciplinary relationships in the social sciences*. Chicago: Aldine, pp. 328–48.

Casey, B. 1986. The quiet revolution: The transformation and reintegration of the humanities. *Issues in Integrative Studies* 4:71–92.

Cassell, E. J. 1977. How does interdisciplinary work get done? In H. T. Engelhardt and D. Callahan, eds., *Knowledge, value, and belief*. New York: Hastings Center, pp. 355–61.

Chapman, I., and F. Chummer. 1980. The funding of interdisciplinary research in Canada. *Journal of Canadian Studies* 15(3):30–33.

Chen, R. S. 1981. Interdisciplinary research and integration: The case of CO_2 and climate. *Climate Change* 3(4):429–48.

Chubin, D., A. Porter and F. Rossini. 1984. "Citation classics" analysis: An approach to characterizing interdisciplinary research. *Journal of the American Society for Information Science* 35(6):360–68.

Cluck, N. A. 1980. Reflections on the interdisciplinary approaches to the humanities. *Liberal Education* 66(1):67–77.

Communities have problems, universities have departments. 1982. In *The univer-*

sity and the community: The problems of changing relationships. Paris: Organization for Economic Co-operation and Development, pp. 127–31.

Darden, L., and N. Maull. 1977. Interfield theories. *Philosophy of Science* 44 (March):43–64.

Darvas, G. 1981. Paradox of interdisciplinarity. Paper presented at the Sixteenth Meeting of the International Congress of the History of Science in Bucarest.

DeBie, P. 1968. Introduction to the special section on multidisciplinary problem-focused research. *International Social Science Journal* 20(2):192–210.

Delkeskamp, C. 1977. Interdisciplinarity: A critical appraisal. In H. T. Engelhardt, Jr., and D. Callahan, eds., *Knowledge, value, and belief.* New York: Hastings Center, 324–54.

Derrida, J. 1983. The principle of reason: The university in the eyes of its pupils. *Diacritics* (Fall), response section:3–20.

DeWachter, M. 1982. Interdisciplinary bioethics: But where do we start? A reflection on epochè as method. *Journal of Medicine and Philosophy* 7(3):275–87.

Dinges, N. 1977. Interdisciplinary collaboration in cross-cultural social science research. *Topics in Culture Learning* 5 (August):136–43.

Dluhy, M., and K. Chen, eds. 1978. *Interdisciplinary planning: A perspective for the future.* New Brunswick, N.J.: Transactions Books (Rutgers).

Firestone, F. N. 1971. Academic structures and the integration of the social sciences. In M. Rubin, ed., *Man in systems.* New York: Gordon and Breach Science Publications.

Fryxell, R. 1977. The interdisciplinary dilemma: A case for flexibility in academic thought. Rock Island, Ill.: Augustana College Library. Occasional Paper no. 13. ERIC document ED 146-102.

Gaff, J. G., and R. C. Wilson. 1971. Faculty cultures and interdisciplinary studies. *Journal of Higher Education* 42(3):186–201.

Garfield, E. 1981. Discipline-oriented citation indexes and data bases: Bridging the interdisciplinary gap via multidisciplinary input. *Current Contents* (3):5–8.

Geertz, C. 1980. Blurred genres: The refiguration of social thought. *American Scholar* 49(2):165–79.

Gelwick, Richard. 1983. Truly interdisciplinary study and commitment in relativism. *Soundings* 66(4):422–36.

Gordon, M. D. 1981. Language barriers, literature usage and the role of reviews: An international and interdisciplinary study. *Journal of Information Science* 3(4):185–89.

Govan, J. F. 1976. Community analysis in an academic environment. *Library Trends* 24 (January):541–56.

Gozzer, G. 1982. Interdisciplinarity: A concept still unclear. *Prospects: Quarterly Review of Education* 12(3):281–92.

Grele, R. 1975. A surmisable variety: Interdisciplinarity and oral testimony. *American Quarterly* 27 (August):275–95.

Gusdorf, G. 1963. Project for interdisciplinary research. *Diogenes* 42 (Summer):119–42.

———. 1977. Past, present and future in interdisciplinary research. *International Social Science Journal* 29(4):580–99.

Hadač, E., et al. 1977. Complex interdisciplinary investigation of landscape. *Landscape Planning* 4(4):333–48.

Hagstrom, W. O. 1965. The differentiation of disciplines. In *The scientific community.* New York: Basic Books, pp. 222–26.

Hall, S. 1984. Cultural studies and the Centre: Some problematics and problems. In S. Hall et al., eds., *Culture, media, language*. London: Hutchinson, pp. 16–47.

Hareven, T. 1971. The history of the family as an interdisciplinary field. *Journal of Interdisciplinary History* 2(2):339–414.

Harvey, J. H., ed. 1981. *Cognition, social behavior and the environment*. Hillsdale, N.J.: Lawrence Erlbaum Associates. See especially B. Fischoff, No man is a discipline, pp. 579–83.

Hermeren, G. 1985. Interdisciplinarity revisited: Promises and problems. In L. Levin and I. Lind, eds., *Inter-disciplinarity revisited: Re-assessing the concept in the light of institutional experience*. Stockholm: OECD/CERI (Linköping), pp. 15–25.

Hershberg, T., ed. 1981. *Philadelphia—Work, space, family and group experience in the nineteenth century: Essays toward an interdisciplinary history of the city*. New York: Oxford University Press.

Huerkamp, C., et al. 1981. Criteria of interdisciplinarity. In *Center for Interdisciplinary Research, University of Bielefeld: Annual Report 1978 and Supplement 1979–1981*. Bielefeld: Zentrum fur Interdisziplinäre Forschung (supplement to the 1978 edition), pp. 23–24.

Ichimura, S. 1975. Interdisciplinary research and area studies. *Journal of Southeast Asian Studies* (Singapore) 6(2):112–20.

Internationales Jahrbuch fur Interdisziplinäre Forschung. 1974. Vol. I: *Wissenschaft als Interdisziplinaries Problem*. Berlin: De Gruyter.

Jantsch, E. 1972. Interdisciplinary and transdisciplinary university: A systems approach to education and innovation. *Higher Education* (1 (February):7–37. Also in *Ekistics*. 1971. 32:430–37; and in *Policy Sciences*. 1970. 1:403–28.

———. 1980. Interdisciplinarity: Dreams and reality. *Prospects: Quarterly Review of Education* 10(3):304–12.

Jeffery, C. R. 1978. Criminology as an interdisciplinary behavioral science. *Criminology: An Interdisciplinary Journal* 16(2):149–69.

Kallen, H. M. 1951. The meanings of unity among the sciences. In P. Henle, H. Kellen, and S. Langer, eds., *Structure, method and meaning: Essays in honor of Henry M. Sheffer*. New York: Liberal Arts Press.

Kann, M. E. 1979. The political culture of interdisciplinary explanation. *Humanities in Society* 2(3):185–200.

Karpinski, A., and M. Samson. 1972. *Interdisciplinarité*. Montreal: University of Quebec, International School Book Service.

Kermoade, A. L. 1979. The interdisciplinary approach and its comparative effectiveness. Seattle: University of Washington College of Education. ERIC document ED 064-238.

Kim, C., and N. Yerkey. 1980. Impact of other disciplines on information retrieval and librarianship. Paper presented at the midyear meeting of the American Society for Information Science. Pittsburgh, May 14–17. ERIC document ED 191-467.

Klein, J. T. 1983. The dialectic and rhetoric of disciplinarity and interdisciplinarity. *Issues in Integrative Studies* 2:35–74.

———. 1985a. The evolution of a body of knowledge: Interdisciplinary problem-focused research. *Knowledge: Creation, Diffusion, Utilization* 7(2):117–42.

———. 1985b. The interdisciplinary concept: Past, present and future. In L. Levin and I. Lind, eds., *Inter-Disciplinarity revisited: Re-assessing the concept in the light of institutional experience*. Stockholm: OECD/CERI (Linköping), pp. 104–36.

———. 1986. The broad scope of interdisciplinarity. In D. E. Chubin, A. L. Porter, and F. Rossini, eds., *Interdisciplinary analysis and research: A book of readings*. Mt. Airy, Md.: Lomond, pp. 409–24.

Kochtanek, T. B. 1982. Bibliographic compilation using reference and citation links. *Information Process and Management* (U.K.) 18(1):33–39.

Kroker, A. 1980. Migration across the disciplines. *Journal of Canadian Studies* 15 (Fall):3–10.

Kuhn, A. 1979. A manifesto for system-based unified knowledge. *Association for Integrative Studies Newsletter* 1.

Landau, H. R. 1983. Evolution of a secondary service to an information supermarket. *Online Review* (U.K.) 7(5):407–12.

Landau, M., H. Proshansky, and W. Ittelson. 1962. The interdisciplinary approach and the concept of behavioral sciences. In N. F. Washburne, ed., *Decisions, values and groups*. Proceedings of a conference held at the University of New Mexico. Oxford and New York: Pergamon Press, pp. 7–25.

Laszlo, E., and H. Margenau. 1972. The emergence of integrative concepts in contemporary science. *Philosophy of Science* 39(2):252–59.

Leary, L. G., ed. 1955. *The unity of knowledge*. New York: Doubleday.

LePair, C. 1980. Switching between academic disciplines in universities in the Netherlands. *Scientometrics* 2 (May):177–91.

Lipton, M. 1970. Interdisciplinary studies in less developed countries. *Journal of Development Studies* 7(1):5–18. See also reply by M. P. Moore. 1974. The logic of interdisciplinary studies. *Journal of Development Studies* 11(1):98–106.

Luyten, N. A. 1973–1974. Interdisciplinarité: Un imperatif de la recherche scientifique. *Civitas* 29:221–42.

Lynton, E. 1985. Interdisciplinarity: Rationales and criteria of assessment. In L. Levin and I. Lind, eds., *Inter-disciplinarity revisited: Re-assessing the concept in light of institutional experience*. Stockholm: OECD/CERI (Linköping), pp. 137–52.

McCorcle, M. D. 1982. Critical issues in the functioning of interdisciplinary groups. *Small Group Behavior* 12(3):291–310.

Mahan, J. L., Jr. 1970. Toward transdisciplinary inquiry in the humane sciences. Unpublished dissertation, United States International University, San Diego.

Maruyama, M. 1974. Paradigmatology and its application to cross-disciplinary, cross-professional and cross-cultural communication. *Dialectica* 28:135–56, 237–81.

Mead, M., discussant. 1977. Can research institutions accommodate interdisciplinary researchers? (taped transcript). Symposium at the 143rd Annual Meeting of the American Association for the Advancement of Science, Denver, February 20–25.

Meadows, A. J. 1976. Diffusion of information across the sciences. *Interdisciplinary Science Reviews* 1(3):259–67.

Miller, R. C. 1982. Varieties of interdisciplinary approaches in the social sciences. *Issues in Integrative Studies* 1:1–37.

Mitroff, I. I., and R. O. Mason. 1981. Dialectical pragmatism: A progress report on an interdisciplinary program of research on dialectical inquiring systems. *Synthese* 47:29–42.

Mucklow, N. H. 1980. Grounds for grouping the disciplines. *Journal of Philosophy of Education* 14(2):226–37.

Murray, T. 1986. Confessions of an unconscious interdisciplinarian. *Issues in Integrative Studies* 4:57–70.

Nelson, N. 1980. Issues in funding and evaluating interdisciplinary research. *Journal of Canadian Studies* 15(3):25–29.

Neurath, O. 1938. Unified science as encyclopedic integration. In *International encyclopedia of unified science. Vol. I: Foundations of the unity of science*, no. 1. Chicago: University of Chicago Press.

Palmer, M., L. Stern, and C. Gaile. 1974. *The interdisciplinary study of politics.* New York: Harper and Row.

Peston, M. 1978. Some thoughts on evaluating interdisciplinary research. *Higher Education Review* 10(2):55–60.

Peterson, F. E. 1980. Exploring the relationships between academic disciplines: A fresh perspective at the Smithsonian. *Teacher's College Record* 82(2):311–16.

Petrie, H. G. 1976. Do you see what I see: The epistemology of interdisciplinary inquiry. *Journal of Aesthetic Education* 10 (January):29–43.

Phillips, D. C. 1976. *Holistic thought in the social sciences.* Stanford: Stanford University Press.

Physics Survey Committee, National Research Council. 1975. *Physics in perspective. Vol. I.* Washington, D.C.: National Academy of Sciences.

Pilet, P. E. 1981. The multidisciplinary aspects of biology: Basic and applied research. *Scientia* 116:629–31.

Pomerance, L. 1981. The need for guidelines in interdisciplinary meetings. *American Journal of Archaeology* 75(4):428–31.

Porter, A. 1973. The expansion of transdisciplinary studies. *Transactions of the Royal Society of Canada* 11:11–20.

Potter, G. 1977. The promise of interdisciplinarity and its problems. *Ramapo Papers* 1:1–23.

Pye, L. W., ed. 1975. *Political science and area studies: Rivals or partners?* Bloomington: Indiana University Press.

Radnitzky, G. 1968. *Continental schools of metascience.* Vol. I: *Anglo-Saxon schools of metascience.* Vol. II: *Continental schools of metascience.* Goteborg: Akademiforlaget.

Reiser, O. L. 1958. *The integration of human knowledge.* Boston: Porter Sargent.

Rich, D., and R. Warren. 1980. The intellectual future of urban affairs: Theoretical, normative and organizational options. *Social Science Journal* 17(2):53–66.

Rickson, R. E., and S. T. Rickson. 1982. Problems and prospects of crossdisciplinary research. *Rural Sociologist* 2 (March):95–103.

Riesman, D. 1974. The scholar at the border: Staying put and moving around inside the American university. *Columbia Forum* (Spring):26–31.

Rigney, D., and D. Barnes. 1980. Patterns of interdisciplinary citation in the social sciences. *Social Science Quarterly* 61(1):114–27.

Ripley, S. D. 1978. Smithsonian: Interdisciplinary institution 150 years after its conception by Smithson, James. *Interdisciplinary Science Reviews* 3(2):89–98.

Rose, R. 1976. Disciplined research and undisciplined problems. *International Social Science Journal* 28(1):99–121.

Roy, R. 1977. Interdisciplinary science on campus: The elusive dream. *Chemical and Engineering News* (August 29):28–40. Also in J. J. Kockelmans, ed. 1979.

Interdisciplinarity and higher education. University Park: Pennsylvania State University Press, pp. 161–96.

Salmon-Cox, L., and B. Holzner. 1977. Managing multidisciplinarity: Building and bridging epistemologies in educational R&D. Paper presented at the American Educational Research Association Annual Meeting, New York, April 4–8. ERIC document ED 135–760.

Schneider, S. N. 1977. Climate change and the world predicament: A case study for interdisciplinary research. *Climatic Change* 1:21–43.

Scholarly disciplines: Breaking out. 1986. *New York Times* (April 25):A18–19.

Schwartz, B. I. 1980. Presidential address: Area studies as a critical discipline. *Journal of Asian Studies* 40(1):15–25.

The search for absolute values in a changing world. 1978. Vols. I and II. New York: International Cultural Foundation.

Sinaceur, M. A. 1977. What is interdisciplinarity? *International Social Science Journal* 29(4):571–79.

Skinner, Q., ed. 1985. *The return of grand theory in the human sciences.* Cambridge: Cambridge University Press.

Smith, L. C. 1974. Systematic searching of abstracts and indexes in interdisciplinary areas. *Journal of the American Society for Information Science* 25:343–53.

Snyder, S. H. 1984. Neurosciences: An integrative discipline. *Science* 225 (September 21):1255–57.

Stoddard, E. R. 1982. Multidisciplinary research funding: A "Catch-22" enigma. *American Sociologist* 17 (November):210–16.

Stoddard, E. R., ed. 1975–1976. The status of U.S.-Mexico borderlands studies: A multidisciplinary symposium. *Social Science Journal* 12–13:1–112.

Sweet, A. 1980. Intersubjective Reference. *Nature and System* 2 (March):21–28.

Tagliacozzo, G. 1961. The literature of integrated knowledge. *American Behavioral Scientist* 4(10):3–11.

Taylor, A. M. 1969. Integrative principles and the educational process. *Main Currents in Modern Thought* 25(5):126–33.

Tenopir, C. 1982. Distribution of citations in databases in a multidisciplinary field. *Online Review* (U.K.) 6(5) (October):399–419.

Thomas, D. S. 1952. Experiences in interdisciplinary research. *American Sociological Review* 17 (December):663–69.

Toulmin, S. 1982. *The return to cosmology: Postmodern science and the theology of nature.* Berkeley: University of California Press.

Trent, J. E. 1978. Internationalization? Interdisciplinarity? Development? The social sciences from 1952–1977. *Social Science Information* 17(2):337–42.

Twining, W. 1973. Law and anthropology: A case study in inter-disciplinary collaboration. *Law and Society Review* 7(4):561–84.

Van Verlaan, A., and A. A. Winters. 1984. Use of information in a changing world: Proceedings of the Forty-Second FID Congress, The Hague, September 24–27. Amsterdam: North-Holland.

Vlachy, J. 1971a. The measures of interdisciplinarity research. *Teorie a Metoda* (June):51–66.

———. 1971b. More data on interdisciplinarity. *Teorie a Metoda*, 3:63–80.

———. 1982. Interdisciplinary approaches in physics. The concepts. *Czechoslovakian Journal of Physics* B32(11):1311–18.

Vosskamp, W. 1986. From scientific specialization to the dialogue between the disciplines. *Issues in Integrative Studies* 4:17–36.

Walker, R. 1978. Holistic knowledge and the politics of fragmentation—An image of the whole: Knowledge and curriculum in an age of fragmentation. Proceedings of a series of symposia, Queen's University, Kingston (Ont.), February. ERIC document ED 153-817.

Wescott, R. W. 1982. The plight of the interdisciplinarian. *Academy Notes* (Academy of Independent Scholars) (April):4.

White, I. L. 1975. Interdisciplinarity. In S. R. Arnstein and A. N. Christakis, eds., *Perspectives on technology assessment.* Jerusalem: Science and Technology Publishers, pp. 87–96.

———. 1979. Interdisciplinary approach to applied policy analysis. *Technological Forecasting and Social Change* 2:95–106.

Winkler, K. 1987. Interdisciplinary research: How big a challenge to traditional fields? *Chronicle of Higher Education* 7(October):A1, 14–15.

Winthrop, H. 1964. Methodological and hermeneutic functions in interdisciplinary education. *Educational Theory* 14 (April):118–27.

Note the following unique series of papers by individuals who participated in Cornell University's Center for International Studies project for the Improvement of Undergraduate Education, with insight into their perceptions of working relationships. Presented at the Annual Meeting of the American Educational Research Association, Chicago, April 1975:

D. B. Macklin. Impacts on a social psychologist-consultant. ERIC document ED 107-677.

A. Brown. Impacts on an intellectual historian. ERIC document ED 107-678.

S. C. Brock. Impacts on an educationist/administrator. ERIC document ED 107-679.

S. P. Whiton. Impacts on an educational researcher. ERIC document ED 107-680.

PROBLEM-FOCUSED RESEARCH

Abestalo, M. 1979. Interdisciplinarity in the light of the development of science and the actual research work. In J. Farkas, ed., *Sociology of Science and Research.* Budapest: Akademiai Kiado.

Allen, T. H. 1978. Cross impact analysis: A technique for managing interdisciplinary research. *Journal of the Society of Research Administrators* 10 (Summer):11–18.

Allen, T. J., J. M. Piepmeier, and S. Cooney. 1971. The international technological gatekeeper. *Technology Review* (March):37–43.

Alpert, D. 1969. The role and structure of interdisciplinary and multidisciplinary research centers. Address to the Ninth Annual Meeting of the Council of Graduate Schools in the United States, Washington, D.C., December 4–6. ERIC document ED 035-363.

———. 1973. University research on problems posed by society. Paper presented at the Annual Conference on Special Emerging Programs in Higher Education, St. Louis, October 17. ERIC document ED 083-002.

Anbar, M. 1973. The "bridge scientist" and his role. *Research/Development* 24 (July):30–34.

Anderson, J. 1977. Organizing for interdisciplinary team research. *Hortscience* 21(1):33–35.

Andrews, F. M. 1979. Motivation, diversity, and the performance of research units. In F. M. Andrews, ed., *Scientific productivity: The effectiveness of research groups in six countries*. Cambridge: Cambridge University Press.

Armstrong, D. L., C. W. Laughlin, and G. S. Ayers. 1977. Administration of interdisciplinary activities. *Hortscience* 12(1):35–36.

Arnstein, S. R., and A. Christakis, eds. 1975. Perspectives on technology assessment. Washington, D.C.: Academy for State and Local Governments. See especially J. B. Taylor, Building an interdisciplinary team, pp. 45–60; and I. L. White, Interdisciplinarity, pp. 87–96.

Background material and summary report for a workshop on the management of interdisciplinary research, July 9–10, 1974, University of Southern California. Grant no. NM-39528, NSF Research Management Improvement Program. Principal investigator Z. A. Kaprielian, co–principal investigator J. M. Nilles.

Baer, W. S. 1976. Interdisciplinary policy research in independent research centers. *IEEE Transactions on Engineering Management* 23 (May):74–78.

Baldwin, D. R., and B. J. Faubian. 1975. Interdisciplinary research in the academic setting. *Journal of the Society of Research Administrators* 6 (Spring):3–8.

Barker, W. T., et al. 1980. Environmental implications of coal development: An interdisciplinary research team approach. *North Dakota Farm Research* 38(1):22–26.

Barmark, J., and G. Wallen. 1980. The development of an interdisciplinary project. In K. D. Knorr, R. Krohn, and R. Whitley, eds., *The social process of scientific investigation*. Dordrecht and Boston: D. Reidel, pp. 221–35. See also: 1979. Interaction of cognitive and social factors in steering a large interdisciplinary project. In R. T. Barth and R. Steck, eds., *Interdisciplinary research groups*. Vancouver: IRGIP, pp. 180–90.

Barnette, B. D., et al. 1978. Interdisciplinary directory of scientists engaged in the study of choice and perceived control (abstract). *Catalogue of Selected Documents in Psychology* 8 (August):58.

Barth, R. T., and R. Steck, eds. 1979. *Interdisciplinary research groups: Their management and organization*. Vancouver: IRGIP.

Bartlett, C. D. S. 1983. Interdisciplinary co-operation to identify innovations for small farmers: The role of the economist. *Agricultural Administration* 13(3):123–35.

Bass, L. W. 1975. *Management by task forces: A manual on the operation of interdisciplinary teams*. Mt. Airy, Md.: Lomond. See especially Categories of interdisciplinary activities; Environment and benefits of interdisciplinary teams; and Appendix: How to start task force systems.

Bawden, R. J. 1978. A perspective for parasite management. *Agriculture and Environment* 4(1):43–56.

Bella, D. A., and K. J. Williamson. 1976–1977. Conflicts in interdisciplinary research. *Journal of Environmental Systems* 6(2):105–24.

———. 1979–1980. Diagnosis of chronic impacts of estaurine dredging. *Journal of Environmental Systems* 9(4):289–311.

Bennis, W. G. 1956. Some barriers to teamwork in social research. *Social Problems* 3(4):223–35.

Benton, D. A. 1975. Management and effectiveness measures for interdisciplinary research. *Journal of the Society of Research Administrators* 6 (Spring):37–45.

Benton, D. A., et al. 1977. Organization and personnel management for effective interdisciplinary research projects. Ft. Collins, Colo.: Colorado State University NTIS item no. PB 271-796.

Berg, S. V., et al. 1983. An interdisciplinary approach to cost benefit analysis of innovative electric rates. *Resources and Energy* (Neth.) 5(4):313–30.

Bewersdorff, A., ed. 1985. *Materials science in space.* Proceedings of the topical meeting of the COSPAR Interdisciplinary Scientific Commission G meeting of the COSPAR 25th plenary meeting. Oxford: Pergamon Press.

Birnbaum, P. H. 1977. Assessment of alternative management forms in academic interdisciplinary research projects. *Management Science* 24(3):272–84.

———. 1978. Academic contexts of interdisciplinary research. *Educational Administration Quarterly* 14(2):80–97.

———. 1979a. A theory of academic interdisciplinary research performance: A contingency and path analysis approach. *Management Science* 25(3):231–41.

———. 1979b. Academic interdisciplinary research: Problems and practice. *R&D Management* 10(1):17–22.

———. 1981a. Academic interdisciplinary research: Characteristics of successful projects. *Journal of the Society of Research Administrators* 13(1):5–16.

———. 1981b. Integration and specialization in academic research. *Academy of Management Journal* 24(3):487–503.

———. 1981c. Contingencies for interdisciplinary research: Matching research questions with research organizations. *Management Science* 27(11):1279–93.

———. 1982a. The organization and management of interdisciplinary research: A progress report. *Journal of the Society of Research Administrators* 13(4):11–23.

Birnbaum, P. H., and D. Gillespie. 1979. Status and performance in small professional organizations: The case of scientific research projects. *Social Science Quarterly* 60(1):105–12.

Birnbaum, P. H., W. T. Newell, and B. O. Saxberg. 1979. Managing academic interdisciplinary research projects. *Decision Sciences* 10(4):645–65.

Black, R. G. 1969. The interdisciplinary communication problem: Its etiology and therapy. *Trend in Engineering* 21(1):10–18.

Blackwell, G. W. 1955. Multidisciplinary team research. *Social Forces* 33(4):367–74.

Blaschke, D. 1980. Management problems of interdisciplinary basic research in the social sciences. *Interstudy Bulletin* 1 (August).

Bonnicksen, T. M., and R. H. Becker. 1983. Environmental impact studies: An interdisciplinary approach for assigning priorities. *Environmental Management* 7(2):109–17.

Bradley, R. T. 1982. Ethical problems in team research: A structural analysis and an agenda for resolution. *American Sociologist* 12 (May):87–94.

Branin, F. H., Jr., and K. Huseyin. 1977. *Problem analysis in science and engineering.* New York and London: Academic Press.

Burdge, R. J., and P. Opryszek. 1981. Interdisciplinary problems in doing impact assessment. In *Coping with change: An interdisciplinary assessment of the Lake Shelbyville reservoir.* Urbana: University of Illinois at Urbana, Institute for Environmental Studies (June), pp. 349–59.

Burdick, N. S. 1981. The evolution of environmental consciousness in nineteenth century America: An interdisciplinary study. *DAI* 41(11):4752-A. Unpublished dissertation, Case Western Reserve University.

Bush, G. P., and L. H. Hattery, eds. 1953. *Teamwork in research*. Washington, D.C.: American University Press.

Cameron, A. 1979. Lubrication: Interdisciplinary subject. *Lubrication Engineering* 35(12):670–71.

Capener, H. R., and R. J. Young. 1975. Interdisciplinary research in the university. In K. S. Porter, ed., *Nitrogen and phosphorus: Food production, waste and the environment*. Ann Arbor, Mich.: Ann Arbor Science Publishers.

Cassell, E. J. 1977. How does interdisciplinary work get done? In H. T. Engelhardt and D. Callahan, eds., *Knowledge, value and belief*. New York: Hastings Center, pp. 355–61.

Caudill, W., and B. H. Roberts. 1951. Pitfalls in the organization of interdisciplinary research. *Human Organization* 10(4):12–15.

Chambers, A., P. Crabbe, and I. Spry, eds. 1973. *Natural resource development in Canada: Multidisciplinary seminar*. Ottawa: University of Ottawa Press.

Chen, R. S. 1981. Interdisciplinary research and integration: The case of CO_2 and climate. *Climatic Change* 3(4):429–48.

Chubin, D. E., A. L. Porter, F. A. Rossini, and T. Connolly, eds. 1986. *Interdisciplinary analysis and research: Theory and practice of problem-focused research and development*. Mt. Airy, Md.: Lomond.

Chubin, D. E., F. A. Rossini, A. L. Porter, and I. I. Mitroff. 1979. Experimental technology assessment: Explorations in processes of interdisciplinary team research. *Technological Forecasting and Social Change* 15:87–94.

Cohen, B. P., R. J. Kruse, and M. Anbar. 1982. The social structure of scientific research teams. *Pacific Sociological Review* 25:205–32.

Compton, W. D. 1971. Multidisciplinary research. *Physics Today* 24:11.

Computerising a multi-disciplinary team (building industry). 1984. *Building* (U.K.) 247(47):49.

Coyne, D. P. 1979. Horticulture and interdisciplinary research. *Hortscience* 14 (December):686.

Cravens, D. W., K. W. Heatherington, and R. A. Mundy. 1976. Organizing for interdisciplinary research in a university setting. *Journal of the Society of Research Administrators* 8(1):3–10.

Crusberg, T. C., A. H. Hoffman, and L. J. Morse. 1983. The water quality resource study group: An interdisciplinary community effort in Worcester, Massachusetts, USA. *Environmental Professional* 5(2):162–67.

Cunningham, D. E. 1969. *Federal support of interdisciplinary research in universities*. U.S. Department of Commerce National Bureau of Standards, no. N70–21072 (October).

Dailey, R. C. 1978. The role of team and task characteristics in R&D collaborative problem solving and productivity. *Management Science* 24(15):1579–88.

———. 1980. A path analysis of R&D team co-ordination and performance. *Decision Sciences* 1(2):357–69.

Darbellay, C. 1982. Ecological problems in the Swiss Alps: The Pays d'Enhaut project. *International Social Science Journal* 34(3):427–39.

Davis, W. E., III. 1970. Interdisciplinary research in theory and practice: A view from the university. M. A. thesis, Syracuse University (April). National Technical Information Service, no. N70-33934.

Day, D. H., Jr. 1977. The management of organized research units at the University of California, Berkeley: Size, politics and interdisciplinarity. Working paper no. CP-399, Center for Research in Management Science, University of California, Berkeley. Revised March.

DiCastri, F. 1976. International, interdisciplinary research in ecology: Some problems of organization and execution—The case of the Man and the Biosphere (MAB) Programme. *Human Ecology* 4(3):235–46.

Eaton, J. W. 1951. Social processes of professional teamwork. *American Sociological Review* 16 (October):707–13.

Ellis, R. H. 1974. The planning and management of problem-oriented, interdisciplinary research at academic institutions. Hartford, Conn.: Renssalaer Hartford Graduate Center.

Epton, S. R., A. W. Pearson, and R. L. Payne. 1984. The management of cross-disciplinary research. *R&D Management* 14(2):69–79.

Epton, S. R., A. W. Pearson, and R. L. Payne, eds. 1984. *Managing interdisciplinary research*. Chichester: John Wiley.

Everest, F. H. 1979. How to demonstrate the importance of fishing resources to interdisciplinary planning teams. *Fisheries* 4(1):15–20.

Fenner, E. H. 1980. A project accounting system that encourages multidisciplinary research. *Engineering Education* 71 (November):167–69.

Fennell, M. L., and G. D. Sandefur. 1983. Structural clarity of interdisciplinary teams: A research note. *Journal of Applied Behavioral Science* 19(2):193–202.

Floret, C., and M. S. Hadjej. 1977. An attempt to combat desertification in Tunisia. *Ambio* 6(6):366–68.

Fundamental research on estuaries: The importance of an interdisciplinary approach. 1983. Washington, D.C.: National Academy Press.

Giacomini, V. 1978. Man and the biosphere: An amplified ecological vision. *Landscape Planning* 5(2–3):193–211.

Gillespie, D. F., and P. H. Birnbaum. 1980. Status concordance, coordination, and success in interdisciplinary research teams. *Human Relations* 33(1) (January):41–56.

Gillespie, D. F., and B. Mar. 1977. Interdisciplinary team preproposal management. *Journal of the Society of Research Administrators* 9 (Fall):33–40.

Golubev, G., and O. Vasiliev. 1978. Interregional water transfers as an interdisciplinary problem. *Water Supply and Management* 2(2):67–77.

Gulf Universities Research Consortium. 1981. Methods to support multidisciplinary university interdisciplinary research program. *Interstudy Bulletin* 2(4).

Gummick, J. L., S. G. Appan, and C. S. Dunn. 1982. Computerized mind support to interdisciplinary consensus formation processes. *Journal of Energy and Environment* 1 (September):37–60.

Gunz, H. P., and A. W. Pearson. 1977. Introduction of a matrix structure into an R&D establishment. *R&D Management* 7(3):173–81.

Hagstrom, W. O. 1964. Traditional and modern forms of scientific teamwork. *Administrative Science Quarterly* 9(3):241–63.

Hargis, W. J., Jr. 1981. A benchmark multidisciplinary study of the interaction between the Chesapeake Bay and adjacent waters of the Virginian sea. NASA-CP2188:1–14. Chesapeake Bay Plume Study, N82-10622:1–14.

Harriott, B. L. 1983. Interdisciplinary research: The USDA-ARS plan. *Agricultural Engineering* 64(9):7.

Harrold, A. H. 1981. Multidisciplinary engineering in the process industries. *Radio and Electronic Engineering* 51(9):416.

Helmer, O. 1983. The need for interdisciplinarity. In *Looking forward: A guide to future research*. New York: Sage.

Henschel, R. L. 1975. Effects of disciplinary prestige on predictive accuracy: Distortions from feedback loops. *Futures* 7(2) (April):92–106.

Hoddeson, L. 1981. The discovery of the point-contact transistor. *Historical Studies in the Physical Sciences* 12(1):41–76.

Holton, G. 1986. Niels Bohr and the integrity of science. *American Scientist* 74(3):237–43.

Hopeman, R. J., and D. L. Wilemon. 1969. Reflection on interdisciplinary research (mimeograph). Occasional paper no. 2. Syracuse University, April. Also available as: Reflecting on interdisciplinary research, NASA document N70-18480 (1970).

Ikenberry, S. I., and R. C. Friedman. 1972. *Beyond academic departments: The story of institutes and centers*. San Francisco: Jossey Bass.

Interdisciplinary research tools. Santa Barbara, Calif.: ABC-CLIO, no. MNUG83-B48082.

Jackson, F. H. 1981. Interdisciplinary environmental analysis for timber sale planning. *Water Resources Bulletin* 17(2):301–6.

Jeffs, G. W. 1979. Space shuttle: Its interdisciplinary design and construction. *Interdisciplinary Science Reviews* 4(3):208–38.

Jurkovich, R., and J. H. P. Paelinck, eds. 1984. *Problems in interdisciplinary studies*. Issues in Interdisciplinary Studies, no. 2. Hampshire: Gower. (Steering Committee in Interdisciplinary Studies, Erasmus University, Rotterdam.)

Kade, G. 1970. Introduction: The economics of pollution and the interdisciplinary approach to environmental planning. *International Social Science Journal* 22(4):563–73.

Kamen, C. S. 1977–1978. The effect of a "social problem" orientation on the organization of scientific research. *Journal of Environmental Systems* 7:309–22.

Kappeler, T. 1979. The world ecotoxicology watch. *Environmental Science and Technology* 13(4):412–15.

Kash, D. E., and I. L. White. 1971. Technology assessment: Harnessing genius. *Chemical Engineering News* 49:36–41.

Kast, F. E., J. E. Rosenzweig, and J. W. Stockman. 1970. Interdisciplinary programs in a university setting. *Academy of Management Journal* 13(3) (September):311–24.

Kendall, S., and E. E. Mackintosh. 1978. *Management problems of polydisciplinary environmental research projects in the university setting*. Guelph, Ont.: University of Guelph. Centre for Resources Development Publication no. 86 (May). Also listed as Canada/Man and the Biosphere Committee Report no. 13 (November 31, 1979).

Khush, G. S., and W. R. Coffman. 1977. Genetic evaluation and utilization (GEU) program: The rice program of the International Rice Research Institute. *Theoretical and Applied Genetics* 51(3):97–110.

Klassen, W. 1978. Interdisciplinary programs in insect mass rearing and in insect population management. *Entomology Society of American Bulletin* 24(1):63–65.

Klein, J. T. 1985. The evolution of a body of knowledge: Interdisciplinary problem-focused research. *Knowledge: Creation, Utilization, and Diffusion* 7(2):117–42.

Kloza, M., C. Sztukowski, and R. Wasniowski, eds. 1980. Management of research, development and education. *Fourth International Conference proceedings*. Wroclaw, Poland: Futures Research Center of Wroclaw Technical University, no. 13.

Knott, K., and B. Feuerbacher. 1982. Spacelab-1: An early space station for science and technology. *Acta Astronautica* 9(6–7):347–52.

Kruse, R. J., et al. 1975. Interdisciplinary research teams as status systems. Technical report no. 56, Laboratory for Social Research, Stanford University. Paper presented at the Annual Meeting of the American Society for Engineering Education, Ft. Collins, Colo., June 16–19. ERIC document ED 118–450.

Kruse, R. J., M. Anbar, and B. Cohen. 1977. Threats to the promise of synergy in interdisciplinary research. Technical report no. 57, Laboratory for Social Research. Stanford University.

Larsson, P., et al. 1978. The lake ecosystem of Ovre, Heimdalsvatn, Norway. *Holarctic Ecology* 1(2–3):304–20.

Linstone, H. A., et al. 1981. The multiple perspective concept with applications to technology assessment and other decision areas. *Technological Forecasting and Social Change* 20:275–325.

Little, Arthur D., Inc. 1978. *Into the information age: A perspective for federal action on information*. Chicago: American Library Association.

Loeb, E. 1960. Some concepts for interdisciplinary practice. *Social Work* 5:83.

Lomas, T. 1981. Multidisciplinary engineering in the process industries. *Radio and Electronic Engineer* 51(9):417.

London, M., and W. Bruce Walsh. 1975. The development and application of a model of long-term group process for the study of interdisciplinary teams. *Catalog of Selected Documents in Psychology* 5 (Winter):1–35.

Long, F. A. 1971. Interdisciplinary problem oriented research in the university. *Science* 171 (March 12):961.

Loveday, D. 1984. Factors affecting the management of interdisciplinary research in the pharmaceutical industry. *R&D Management* 14(2):93–103.

Luszki, M. B. 1958. *Interdisciplinary team research methods and problems*. New York: New York University Press.

McCorcle, M. 1982. Critical issues in the functioning of interdisciplinary groups. *Small Group Behavior* 13 (August):291–310.

McDole, R. E., and S. A. Reinertsen. 1983. Steep: An interagency, multidisciplinary approach to soil conservation. *Journal of Soil and Water Conservation* 38(3):244–45.

MacDonald, W. R. 1982. The management of interdisciplinary research teams: A literature review. Report for Department of the Environment and Department of Agriculture, Government of Alberta, Edmonton (January).

McEvoy, J., III. 1972. Multi- and interdisciplinary research: Problems of initiation, control, integration and reward. *Policy Sciences* 3 (July):201–8.

McGrath, D. C., Jr. 1971. Multidisciplinary environmental analysis: Jamaica Bay and Kennedy Airport. *Journal of the American Institute of Planners* 37(4):343–52.

Mar, B. 1974. Problems encountered in multidisciplinary resources and environmental simulation model development. *Journal of Environmental Management* 2:82–100.

Mar, B., et al. 1983. Applied interdisciplinary, interdepartmental management. *Interstudy Bulletin* 4:3.

Mar, B. W., W. T. Newell, and B. O. Saxberg. 1976. Interdisciplinary research in the university setting. *Environmental Science and Technology* 10 (7) (July:650–53.

Mar, B. W., W. T. Newell, and B. O. Saxberg, eds. 1985. *Managing high technology: An interdisciplinary perspective.* Amsterdam: Elsevier Science Publishers.

Martin, J. N., et al. 1981. The structural engineer in a multidisciplinary practice. *Structural Engineer* 59(5):177–80.

Martino, J. P. 1978. Managing interdisciplinary research teams. *Proceeding of the IEEE 1978 National Aerospace and Electronics Conference* #1(May):280–85.

Materials Science and Engineering. 1979. 37 (January):56–70. Case studies.

Meadows, A. J. 1974. Scientific collaboration and status. *Communication Science:*172–206.

Meechan, C. 1978. Interdisciplinary problem solving: Some actual teaming experiences. *Journal of the Society of Research Administrators* 10(1):19–25.

Michaelis, A. R. 1978. Great problems and interdisciplinary solutions. *Interdisciplinary Science Reviews* 3(1):1–2.

———. 1984. Interdisciplinary disaster research. *Interdisciplinary Science Reviews* 9(3):193–94.

Missouri Agricultural Experiment Station. 1974. An administrative structure for interdisciplinary research involving animal nutrition, physiology, and metabolism (May) (mimeograph). An administrative structure for interdisciplinary research in forage breeding, management, and utilization (September) (mimeograph).

Mitchell, R. 1977. The maintenance of personal integrity in the interdisciplinary team research effort. *Hortscience* 12(1):36–37.

Mooney, G. H., and A. H. Williams. 1980. Economists in multidisciplinary teams: Some unresolved problems in the conduct of health services research. *Social Science and Medicine* 14:217–21.

Morphet, C. 1981. Positivist and political approaches to interdisciplinarity. *Science and Science Policy* (February):18–22.

Morris, J. W. 1980. The United States Army Corps of Engineers: Two centuries of interdisciplinary engineering. *Interdisciplinary Science Reviews* 5(4):269–80.

Murray, K. A., and B. J. Rothschild. 1972. *Policy issues in resource management. World Fisheries Policy: Multidisciplinary Views,* Vol. 4. Seattle: University of Washington Press.

Narayan, L. R. A., and B. Sahai. 1983. Integrated resources survey and applications: Proceedings of the Indian Academy of Sciences. *Engineering Sciences* 6(4):287–95.

Neumann, K.-K. and H.-J. Neumann. 1983. Interdisciplinary chemical engineering: Present and future. *Interdisciplinary Science Reviews* 8(3):231–34.

Newell, W. T., et al. 1975. Management of interdisciplinary research in universities faces problems. Paper presented at the annual meeting of the American Society for Engineering Education, Colorado State University, Ft. Collins. (June 16–19). ERIC document ED 118-395.

———. 1980. Guidelines for applied interdisciplinary research in the university: How to manage the university role in solving society's problems. Project report no. 11 (July). Seattle: Graduate School of Business Administration, College of Engineering, University of Washington, NSF grant no. NM 44380. See also in the *Interstudy Bulletin,* 1980.

Newell, W. T., B. O. Saxberg, and P. H. Birnbaum. 1975. Measures of effectiveness and efficiency for university interdisciplinary research organizations. Working paper no. 3, Research Management Improvement Program, University of Washington.

Nicholas, D. D. 1981. Multidisciplinary approach to the development of new wood preservatives. *Forest Products Journal* 31(9):28–33.

Nilles, J. M. 1975. Interdisciplinary research management in the university environment. *SRA, Journal of the Society of Research Administrators* 6(9):9–16.

———. 1976. Interdisciplinary research and the American university. *Interdisciplinary Science Reviews* 1(2):160–66.

———. 1978. Interdisciplinary policy research and the universities. *IEEE Transactions on Engineering Management* 23(2) (May).

Norman, C. 1985. NSF readies new engineering program: A major effort to establish multidisciplinary centers on university campuses is being viewed with some apprehension. *Science* 227 (4 January):38.

Odhner, F. 1970. Group dynamics of the interdisciplinary team. *American Journal of Occupational Therapy* 24 (October):484–87.

Oeschger, H. 1980. The carbon-dioxide problem: An interdisciplinary survey. *Experimentia* 36(7):808–12.

Pal, Y. 1978. The singular success of SITE: How satellites can teach Indian villages by television. *Interdisciplinary Science Reviews* 3(1):55–57.

Paquin, M. J. 1971. Multidisciplinary progress and the need for the behavioral sciences in environmental affairs. Report prepared for the Policy, Planning, and Research Service, Environment Canada, Ottawa (September).

Peston, M. 1978. Some thoughts on evaluating interdisciplinary research. *Higher Education Review* 10 (Spring):55–60.

Pignataro, L. J., and W. R. McShane. 1979. Interdisciplinary research: Transcending departmental conflicts. *Engineering Education* 69(4):349–51.

Polishuk, P. 1976. Problems in interdisciplinary policy research and management in government. *IEEE Transactions on Engineering Management* 23 (2) (May):92–100.

Porter, A. L. 1983. Interdisciplinary research: Current experience in policy and performance. *Interdisciplinary Science Reviews* 8(2):158–67.

Porter, A. L., et al. 1980. Between disciplines. *Science* 209 (August 29): 966.

Porter, A. L., and F. A. Rossini. 1984. Interdisciplinary research redefined: Multiskill problem-focused research in the STRAP framework. *R&D Management* 14(2) (April):105–11.

Potchen, E. J., et al. Management of large-scale interdisciplinary activities in medicine. Final report, NSF grant NM 44353-109, PB 262-205.

Povsner, A. D. 1976. Interdisciplinary research project as a system. *Systems Research* (Yearbook):91–103. Moscow: Nauka. (In Russian.)

Purschwitz, M. A. 1983. National diary housing conference attracts wide interdisciplinary support. *Agricultural Engineering* 64(5):15.

Quinn, T. F. J. 1983. NASA interdisciplinary collaboration in tribology: A review of oxidational wear. NASA Contract. Rep. no. 3686, E-1573, NAS1.26.3686.

R&D Management. 1984. Special Issue. 14(2) (April).

Rajagopal, R. 1979. Interdisciplinary research and education for ecosystems management. *Urban Systems* 4(1):43–52.

Redding, D. S. 1981. Setting up the maintenance organization in a multidisciplinary project. *Terotechnica* 2(2):105–19.

Regier, H. A. 1978. *A balanced science of renewable resources with particular reference to fisheries*. Seattle: University of Washington Press.

Reisenburg, S. 1979. Interdisciplinary research groups: International comparison of their organization and management. *R&D Management* 10(1):35–41.

Riesenhuber, H. 1982. Interdisciplinary co-operation between industry and government in the FRG. *Interdisciplinary Science Reviews* 8(2):102–4.

Riley, M. W. 1980. Phases encountered by a project team. *IEEE Transactions on Education* 23 (November):212–13.

Robertson, I. T. 1981. Some factors associated with successful interdisciplinary research. *Journal of the Society of Research Administrators* 13 (Fall):44–50.

Roether, W. 1980. The carbon-dioxide problem—An interdisciplinary survey: The effect of the ocean on the global carbon cycle. *Experientia* 36(9):1017–25.

Rose, R. 1976. Disciplined research and undisciplined problems. *International Social Science Journal* 28(1):99–121.

Rossi, P. H. 1964. Researchers, scholars and policy makers: The politics of large-scale research. *Daedalus* 93 (Fall):1142–61.

Rossini, F. A., et al. 1979. Technology assessment. In P. T. Durbin, ed., *Research in philosophy and technology,* Vol. II. Greenwich, Conn.: JAI Press, pp. 341–56.

———. 1981. Interdisciplinary integration within technology assessments. *Knowledge: Creation, Diffusion, Utilization* 2(4):503–28.

Rossini, F. A., & A. L. Porter. 1979. Frameworks for integrating interdisciplinary research. *Research Policy* 8(1):70–79.

Rossini, F. A., and A. Porter. 1981. Interdisciplinary research: Performance and policy issues. *SRA, Journal of the Society of Research Administrators* 13(2) (Fall):8–24. See also in *Interstudy Bulletin* 1981 (August):2–5.

Roy, R. 1977. Interdisciplinary science on campus: The elusive dream. *Chemical and Engineering News* (August 29):28–40. See also under the same title in J. J. Kockelmans, ed. 1979. *Interdisciplinarity and higher education*. University Park: Pennsylvania State University Press, pp. 161–96.

Roy, W. R., and R. A. Griffin. 1982. A proposed classification system for coal fly ash in multidisciplinary research. *Journal of Environmental Quality* 11(4):563–68.

Russell, M. G., J. M. Barnes, and J. R. Cornwell. 1986. Bridging disciplinary strengths. St. Paul: Agricultural Experiment Station, University of Minnesota. Miscellaneous publication no. 39.

Russell, M. G., J. M. Barnes, and J. R. Cornwell, eds. 1982. Enabling interdisciplinary research: Perspectives from agriculture, forestry, and home economics. St. Paul: Agricultural Experiment Station, University of Minnesota. Miscellaneous publication no. 19.

Saxberg, B., W. T. Newell, and B. W. Mar. 1981. Interdisciplinary research: A dilemma for university central administration. *Journal of the Society of Research Administrators* 13(2):25–43.

Sbragia, R. 1984. Clarity of manager roles and performance of R&D multidisciplinary projects in matrix structures. *R&D Management* 14(2):113–28.

Scarff, J. E. 1977. International management of whales, dolphins and porpoises: An interdisciplinary assessment. *Ecology Law Quarterly* 6(3):571–638.

Schneider, S. H. 1977a. Climate change and the world predicament: A case study for interdisciplinary research. *Climatic Change* 1:21–43.

———. 1977b. Quality review standards for interdisciplinary research (transcript).

Paper presented at "Can research institutions accommodate interdisciplinary researchers?" Symposium at 143rd Annual Meeting of the American Association for the Advancement of Science, Denver, February 20–25.

———. 1982. Climatology and glaciology: An interdisciplinary opportunity—an editorial. *Climatic Change* 4(4):327–28.

Schyttt, V. 1983. Ymer-80: A Swedish expedition to the Arctic Ocean. *Geographical Journal* (U.K.) 149(1):22–28.

Scribner, R. A., and R. A. Chalk, eds. 1977. *Adapting science to social needs: Conference proceedings*. Washington, D.C.: American Association for the Advancement of Science. Report no. 76-R-8. See especially C. W. Churchman, Toward a holistic approach, pp. 11–24; D. E. Kash, Observations on interdisciplinary studies and government roles, pp. 147–67; W. A. Hahn, Observations on interdisciplinarity: Its need, management and utilization, pp. 253–63.

Semple, J. 1983. Smoke control: An interdisciplinary concept. *American Society of Heating, Refrigerating and Air Conditioning Engineers Journal* 25(5):60.

Sharp, J. M., and J. L. Gumnick. 1981. A method for peer group appraisal and interpretation of data developed in interdisciplinary research programs. *SRA, Journal of the Society of Research Administrators* 13(2):51–66.

Simeonova, K. 1973. *The inter-disciplinary movement and the organization of scientific research problems of the science of science, 1972–1973*. Ossolineum: Polish Academy of Sciences Press.

Simonton, D. K. 1975. Interdisciplinary creativity over historical time: A correlational analysis of generational fluctuations. *Social Behavior and Personality* 3(2):181–88.

Smythe, G. E. 1981. Multidisciplinary engineering in the process industries. *Radio and Electronic Engineer* 51(9):416–17.

SRA, Journal of the Society of Research Administrators. 1981. (Fall). Special issue on management of interdisciplinary research.

Stankiewicz, R. 1979. The effects of leadership on the relationship between the size of research groups and their performance. *R&D Management* 9:207–12.

Steck, R. 1976. How can research on research contribute to a better management of university research? *R&D Management* 6 (February):81–86.

Steck, R., and J. Sundermann. 1978. The effects of group size and cooperation on the success of interdisciplinary groups in R&D. *R&D Management* 8(2):59–64.

Stoddard, E. R. 1982. Multidisciplinary research funding: A "Catch-22" enigma. *American Sociologist* 17 (November):210–16.

Stone, A. R. 1969. The interdisciplinary research team. *Journal of Applied Behavioral Science* 5(3):351–65.

Stucki, J. C. 1979. A goal oriented pharmaceutical research and development organization: An eleven-year experience. In R. T. Barth and R. Steck, eds., *Interdisciplinary research groups*. Vancouver: IRGIP, pp. 77–96.

Technological Forecasting and Social Change. 1979. 2. Issue on problem-focused research.

Thomas, D. S. 1952. Experiences in interdisciplinary research. *American Sociological Review* 17 (December):663–69.

Thurman, E. M. 1983. Multidisciplinary research: An experiment. *Environmental Science and Technology* 17(11):511.

Toft, G., and R. T. Sparrow. 1984. University interdisciplinary engineering centers:

New directions—persistent organizational problems. Paper presented at the Third International Conference on Interdisciplinary Research, Seattle, August 1.

Tomczak, M., Jr. 1983. Some conclusions from the Port Hacking Estuary project. In *Synthesis and modelling of intermittent estuaries: A case study from planning to evaluation*. Berlin: Springer-Verlag, pp. 293–302. See also W. R. Cuff, An evaluation of the dynamic information for South West Arm, Port Hacking, pp. 233–58.

Törnebohm, H., et al. 1980. Researcher roles and the organization of interdisciplinary groups. In *R&D for higher education*. Stockholm: Research and Development Unit, National Swedish Board of Universities and Colleges. ERIC document ED 201-35.

U.S. Library of Congress. *Legislative reference series: Interdisciplinary research . . . an exploration of public policy*. NYPG734445477-B.

Valaskakis, K. 1975. Rewards and tribulations of interdisciplinary futures studies. *Industrialization Forum* 6:41–46.

Volker, E. J., and C. Schultz. 1978. Microbial conversion of D-sorbitol to L-sorbose: Interdisciplinary experiment illustrating an industrial process. *Journal of Chemical Education* 55(10):673–74.

Walker, B. H., et al. 1978. A procedure for multidisciplinary ecosystem research: With reference to the South African savannah ecosystem project. *Journal of Applied Ecology* 15:481–502.

Walsh, J. 1985. New R&D centers will test university ties: Interdisciplinary research labs are campus fixtures, but industry, government involvement gives a new twist. *Science* 227 (January 11):150–52.

Walsh, W. B., G. L. Smith, and M. London. 1975. Developing an interface between engineering and the social sciences: An interdisciplinary approach to solving societal problems. *American Psychologist* 30(11):1067–71.

Walters, C. 1975. Interdisciplinary approach to development of watershed simulation models. *Journal of the Fisheries Research Board of Canada* 32:177–95.

Warrick, R. A., and W. E. Riebsami. 1981. Societal response to Co_2-induced climate change: Opportunities for research. *Climatic Change* 3(4):387–446.

Weingert, J. M. 1977. Transdisciplinary science: Some recent experiences with solar energy conversion research (transcript). Paper presented at 143rd Annual Meeting of the American Association for the Advancement of Science, Denver, February 20–25.

Wheeler, L., and E. Miller. 1970. Multi-disciplinary approach to planning. Paper presented at the Council of Education Facilities Planners 47th Annual Conference, Oklahoma City, October 6. ERIC document ED 044-814.

White, I. L. 1979. An interdisciplinary approach to applied policy analysis. *Technological Forecasting and Social Change* 2 (September):95–106.

Wilbanks, T. 1979. Communications between hard and soft sciences. *Oak Ridge National Laboratory Review* (Spring):24–29.

Williams, A. S., et al. 1978. Guidelines for conducting interdisciplinary applied research in a university setting. *Review of Public Data Use* 6(2):3–12.

Wilson, R. R. 1970. My fight against team research. *Daedalus* (Fall):1076–87.

Winnicki, T., and B. Glowiak. 1978. Management of large-scale interdisciplinary environmental programs. *R&D Management* 8:127–32.

Wohl, R. R. 1955. Some observations on the social organization of interdisciplinary social science research. *Social Forces* 33:374–83.

Wohlwill, J. F., and E. M. Zube. The role of the social sciences with U.S. M.A.B. In E. H. Zube, ed., *Social sciences, interdisciplinary research and the U.S. Man and the Biosphere program: Workshop proceedings.*

Wolfle, D. L. 1981. Interdisciplinary research as a form of research. *Journal of the Society of Research Administrators* 13 (Fall):5–7.

Wymore, A. W. 1976. *Systems engineering methodology for interdisciplinary teams.* New York: Wiley.

For reports on the findings of the National Science Foundation's Research Management Improvement Program, original copies are filed with the National Technical Information Service of the U.S. Department of Commerce. A file of these and other reports on IDR management is also available in the Center for Technology and Administration at American University in Washington, D.C.

INTERDISCIPLINARY MEDICAL CARE, EDUCATION, SOCIAL SCIENCE, AND SCIENCE

Ackerman, L., et al. 1983. Role clarification: A procedure for enhancing interdisciplinary collaboration on the rehabilitation team. *Archives of Physical and Medical Rehabilitation* 64(10):514.

Ackoff, R. L. 1960. Systems, organizations, and interdisciplinary research. *General Systems* (Yearbook) 5:1–8.

Allen, K. E., V. A. Holm, and R. Schiefelbusch, eds. 1978. *Early intervention: A team approach.* Baltimore: University Park Press. See especially V. A. Holm and R. McCartin, Interdisciplinary child development team: Team issues and training in interdisciplinariness, pp. 99–122.

Appleyard, J., and J. G. Maden. 1979. Multidisciplinary teams. *British Medical Journal* 2:1305–07.

Ashby, W. R. 1958. General systems theory as a new discipline. *General Systems* (Yearbook) 3:2–6.

Assimopoulos, N., and C. H. Berlanger. 1978. Interdisciplinary policies and practices. Paper presented at the Eighteenth Annual Association for Institutional Research Forum, Houston, May 21–25. ERIC document ER 161-366.

Bailey, D. B., et al. 1983. Measuring individual participation on the interdisciplinary team. *American Journal of Mental Deficiency* 88(3):247–54.

Baker, F. W. G. 1982. A century of international interdisciplinary cooperation. *Interdisciplinary Science Reviews* 7(4):270–82.

Battista, J. R. 1977. The holistic paradigm and general systems theory. *General Systems* (Yearbook) 22:65–71.

Baumann, B. 1975. *Imaginative participation: The career of an organizing concept in a multidisciplinary context.* The Hague: Martinus Nijhoff.

Beardsley, R., et al. 1981. The interdisciplinary approach. *American Pharmacy* #21(11):54–55.

Benson, O., and C. M. Bonjean. 1970. *Social Science Quarterly*, 1920–1970: A case history in organizational growth. *Social Science Quarterly* 50(4):806–825.

Benson, T. L. 1982. Five arguments against interdisciplinary studies. *Issues in Integrative Studies* 1:38–48.

Beroza, M. 1977. Some techniques and interdisciplinary aspects of pesticide chemistry. *Abstracts of Papers of the American Chemical Society* 174 (September):46.

Binder, A., D. Stokols, and R. Catelano. 1975. Social ecology: An emerging multidiscipline. *Journal of Environmental Education* 7:32–43.

Blackburn, R. S., and M. Mitchell. 1981. Citation analysis in the organizational sciences. *Journal of Applied Psychology* 66(3):337–42.

Bloom, B., and H. Parad. 1976. Interdisciplinary training and interdisciplinary functioning. *American Journal of Orthopsychiatry* 46:669–76.

Blunt, P. 1981. Methodological developments in the social sciences: Some implications for interdisciplinary study. *New Zealand Psychologist* 10(2):55–70.

Boger, R. P. 1973. Organizational policy issues affecting interdisciplinary educational research and research training. Boulder: Colorado University (February). ERIC document ED 077-422.

Boulding, K. E., and L. Senesh. 1983. *The optimum utilization of knowledge: Making knowledge serve human betterment.* Boulder, Colo.: Westview.

Brequet, C. A. J. 1980. The Breguet dynasty: Two centuries of interdisciplinary scientists and engineers. *Interdisciplinary Science Reviews* 5(2):149–64.

Bronowski, J. 1956. *Science and human values.* New York: Messner.

Bunge, M. 1973. The role of forecast in planning. *Theory and Decision* 3:207–21.

———. 1977. General Systems and holism. *General Systems* 22:87–90.

Cain, S. 1967. Can ecology provide the basis for synthesis among the sciences? In M. E. Gurnsey and J. R. Hibbs, eds., *Social sciences and the environment.* Boulder: University of Colorado Press.

Charlesworth, J. C., ed. 1972. *Integration of the social sciences through policy analysis.* Philadelphia: American Academy of Political and Social Science.

Cook, E. E. 1974. An engineering educator's experience in interdisciplinary teaching. *Engineering Education* 6 (December):230–32.

Cope, R. G. 1981. *Strategic planning, management and decision making.* AAHE-ERIC research report no. 9. Washington, D.C.: American Association for Higher Education. ERIC document ED 217-825.

Cowie, G. B. A. 1983. The multidisciplinary team. *New Zealand Medical Journal* 96(731):359–60.

Crawford, B. 1969. The support of interdisciplinary and transdisciplinary programs. Address to the Ninth Annual Meeting of the Council of Graduate Schools in the United States, Washington, D.C., December 5. ERIC document ED 035-364.

Crow, J. 1978. Interdisciplinary research and arid lands studies. *Social Science Journal* 15(3):49–54.

David, E. E., Jr. 1979. Science futures: The industrial connection. *Science* 203 (March 2):837–40.

Day, D. W. 1981. Perspectives on care: The interdisciplinary team approach. *Otolaryngologic Clinics of North America* 14(4):769–75.

Developments in interdisciplinarity. 1974. *Group for Research and Innovation in Higher Education Newsletter* 4 (April). (Nuffield Foundation, London.)

DeWachter, M. 1976. Interdisciplinary team work. *Journal of Medical Ethics* 2:52–57.

Dobson, J. R. E., et al. 1982. The multidisciplinary team. *New Zealand Medical Journal* 95(707):319.

Doyal, L. 1974. Interdisciplinary studies in higher education. *Universities Quarterly: Higher Education and Society* 28(4):470–87.

Dragoun, O. 1984. Interdisciplinary applications of gamma-ray internal conversion. *Europhysics News* (Switz.) 15(4):11–13.

Ducanis, A. J., and A. K. Golin. 1979. *The interdisciplinary health care team: A handbook*. Germantown, Md.: Aspen Systems.

Duncan, W., W. Edwards, and J. Flynt. 1971. An experiment in large group interdisciplinary investigations into contemporary social issues. *Social Science* 46(4):216–22.

Durbin, P. T., and C. Mitcham, eds. 1979. *Research in philosophy and technology*. Greenwich, Conn.: JAI Press. See especially H. Lenk & G. Ropohl, Toward an interdisciplinary pragmatic philosophy of technology, pp. 15–52.

Eckhardt, C. D. 1978. *Interdisciplinary programs and administrative structure: Problems and prospects for the 80's*. University Park: Pennsylvania State University Press.

Feiger, S. M., and M. H. Schmitt. 1979. Collegiality in interdisciplinary health teams: Its measurement and its effects. *Social Science and Medicine: Medical Psychology and Sociology* 13(2A):217–29.

Fethe, C. 1973. A philosophical model for interdisciplinary programs. *Liberal Education* 59(4):490–97.

Firestone, F. N. 1971. Academic structures and the integration of the social sciences. In M. Rubin, ed., *Man in systems*. New York: Gordon and Breach.

Fitzsimons, R. M. 1977. Fostering productive interdisciplinary staff conferences. *Academic Therapy* 12:281–87.

Forbes, I. J., et al. 1984. Multidisciplinary approach to phototherapy of human cancers. *Progress in Clinical and Biological Research* 170:693–708.

Fordyce, W. E. 1981. On interdisciplinary peers. *Archives of Physical Medicine and Rehabilitation* 62(2):51–53.

Fox, W. M., and J. A. Stewart. 1978. Practitioners' views on interdisciplinary studies at the college level. Kansas Center for Faculty Evaluation and Development in Higher Education, Kansas State University (June). ERIC document ED 172-598.

Fry, L., and J. P. Miller. 1974. The impact of interdisciplinary teams on organizational relationships. *Sociological Quarterly* 15(3):417–31.

Goodwin, W. M., and W. K. LeBold. 1975. Interdisciplinarity and team teaching. *Engineering Education* 66 (December):247–54.

Greden, J. F., et al. 1979. Interdisciplinary differences on a general hospital psychiatry unit. *General Hospital Psychiatry* #1(1):91–97.

Grinker, R., ed. 1956, 1967. *Toward a unified theory of human behavior: An introduction to general systems theory*. New York: Basic Books.

Hackerman, N. 1978. Interdisciplinary chemistry. *Interdisciplinary Science Reviews*, 3(4):332–34.

Halliburton, D. 1981. Interdisciplinary studies. In A. Chickering, ed., *The modern American college*. San Francisco: Jossey Bass, pp. 453–71.

Heims, S. 1975. Encounter of the behavioral sciences with new machine-organism analogies in the 1940's. *Journal of the History of the Behavioral Sciences* 11(4):368–73.

Holton, G. 1975. On the role of themata in scientific thought. *Science* 188 (April 25):328–34.

Horwitz, J.J. 1970. *Team practice and the specialist: An introduction to interdisciplinary teamwork*. Springfield, Ill.: Charles C. Thomas.

Hutchinson, D. A. 1974. *A model for transdisciplinary staff development: A nationally organized collaborative project to provide comprehensive services to atypical infants and their families*. New York: United Cerebral Palsy Associates, technical report no. 8.

Jacobs, S. S. 1981. Interdisciplinary investigations in antarctic oceanography. *Antarctic Journal of the United States* 15(5):87–89.

Jantsch, E. 1968. Integrating forecasting and planning through a function-oriented approach. In J. Bright, ed., *Technological forecasting for industry and government*. Englewood Cliffs, N.J.: Prentice-Hall. See also: 1969. New organizational forms for forecasting. *Technological Forecasting* 1 (Fall).

———. 1969a. Integrative planning for the "joint systems" of society and technology: The emerging role of the university. Alfred P. Sloan School of Management, Massachusetts Institute of Technology, Cambridge (May). Substantial Extracts published under the same title in: 1969. *Ekistics* 28.

———. 1969b. *Integrative planning of technology: Perspectives of planning*. Paris: Organization for Economic Cooperation and Development.

Jantsch, E., ed. 1981. *The evolutionary vision: Toward a unifying paradigm of physical, biological and sociocultural evolution*. Boulder, Colo.: Westview Press.

Kapitza, S. P. 1982. Science and politics: Interdisciplinary co-operation essential. *Interdisciplinary Science Reviews* 7(4):257–60.

Kargon, R. H. 1977. Temple to science: Cooperative research and the birth of the California Institute of Technology. *Historical Studies in the Physical Sciences* 8:3–31.

Khush, G. S., and W. R. Coffman. 1977. Genetic evaluation and utilization program: The river improvement program of the International Rice Research Institute. *Theoretical and Applied Genetics* 51(3):97–110.

Kuhn, A. 1975. *Unified social science: A system-based introduction*. Homewood, Ill.: Dorsey Press.

Lacefield, G., et al. 1982. Interdisciplinary beef forage management demonstrations. *Journal of Animal Science* 55 (suppl. 1):206–7.

Laszlo, E. 1978. Systems philosophy. *Ultimate Reality and Meaning* 11(3):223–30.

Laszlo, E., and H. Margenau. 1972. Discussion: The emergence of integrative concepts in contemporary science. *Philosophy of Science* 39 (June):252–59.

Laudan, L. 1977. *Progress and its problems: Towards a theory of scientific growth*. Berkeley: University of California Press.

Lenk, H., and G. Ropohl. 1979. Toward an interdisciplinary, pragmatic philosophy of technology: Technology as a focus for interdisciplinary reflection and systems research. *Research in Philosophy and Technology* 2:15–52.

LePair, C. 1980. Switching between academic disciplines in universities in the Netherlands. *Scientometrics* 2 (May):177–91.

Lieberman, J. E. 1976. The pathology of innovation. *Liberal Education* 62(3):380–84.

Logan, R. L., and M. McKendry. 1982. The multidisciplinary team: A different approach to patient-management. *New Zealand Medical Journal* 95 (722):883–84.

Luszki, M. B. 1957. Team research in social science: Major consequences of a growing trend. *Human Organization* 16(1):21–24.

McCool, J. P. 1980. Cybernetics and general systems: A unitary science? *Kybernetes* (U.K.) 9(1):67–73.

McKendry, M., and R. L. Logan. 1983. The multidisciplinary team. *New Zealand Medical Journal* 96(731):359.

Martin, B. 1979. Interdisciplinary approach to dairy-herd health and productivity. *Veterinary Record* 105(9):186.

Mead, M. 1969. Crossing boundaries in social science communications. *Social Science Information* 8(1):7–16.

Meadows, A. J. 1976. Diffusion of information across the sciences. *Interdisciplinary Science Reviews* 1(3):259–67.

Meinwald, J., et al. 1978. Chemical ecology: Studies from East Africa. *Science* 199 (17 March):1167–73.

Michaelis, A. R. 1978. Great problems and interdisciplinary solutions. *Interdisciplinary Science Reviews* 3(1):1–2.

———. 1979a. Interdisciplinary freedom. *Interdisciplinary Science Reviews* 4(2):87.

———. 1979b. Interdisciplinary science policy. *Interdisciplinary Science Reviews* 4(1):1.

———. 1979–1980: Interdisciplinary debate. *Interdisciplinary Science Reviews* 4(4):263–264.

———. 1980. Interdisciplinary biotechnology for nutrition. *Interdisciplinary Science Reviews* 5(1):1.

Miller, J. G., and J. L. Miller. 1981. Systems science: An emerging interdisciplinary field. *Center Magazine* (September–October):44–55.

Montgomery, E. B., ed. 1968. *The foundations of access to knowledge,* Syracuse: Syracuse University Press. See especially N. Storer and T. Parsons, The disciplines as a differentiating force, pp. 101–21; and D. Barr, Encouraging an interdisciplinary dialogue: The sciences and the humanities, pp. 203–6.

Morecki, A. 1983. On the study of the standardization of terminology in interdisciplinary sciences. *Mechanisms and Machine Theory* 18:255–77.

Morris, H. L. 1980. Structure and function of interdisciplinary teams. In C. F. Salinas and R. J. Jorgenson, eds., *National Foundation March of Dimes birth defects: Original article series,* Vol. 16, p. 5. Dentistry in the interdisciplinary treatment of genetic diseases. Symposium, Charleston, February 28–March 1. New York: Alan Liss, pp. 105–10.

Moser, A. 1982. Integrating strategy: A basis for bio-technological methodology. *Biotechnology Letters* 4(2):73–78.

Nagi, S. Z. 1975. Teamwork in health care in the United States: A sociological perspective. *Millbank Memorial Fund Quarterly* 53:75–91.

Nanus, B. 1979. Interdisciplinary policy analysis in economic forecasting. *Technological Forecasting and Social Change* 13(4):285–95.

Neeley, J. D., Jr. 1981. The management and social science literatures: An interdisciplinary cross-citation analysis. *Journal of the American Society for Information Science* 32(3):217–23.

Nilsson, S. 1978. Aerobiology: Its international and interdisciplinary significance. *Scandinavian Journal of Respiratory Diseases* (s. 102):115–18.

Pantin, C. F. A. 1968. *The relations between the sciences.* New York: Cambridge University Press.

Parker, A. W. 1972. *The team approach to primary health care.* Berkeley: University Extension, University of California. Neighborhood Health Center Seminar Program, monograph series no. 3.

Parker, M., and R. C. Hindle. 1983. Multidisciplinary team. *New Zealand Medical Journal* 96 (728):224–25.

Pearson, P. H. 1983. The interdisciplinary team process: Or the professionals' tower of Babel. *Developmental Medicine and Child Neurology* 25(3):330–95.

Pfeiffer, S. I. 1981a. The multidisciplinary team and non-discriminatory assessment. *Arizona Personnel and Guidance Journal* 7:22–23.

———. 1981b. The problems of multidisciplinary teams: As perceived by team members. *Psychology in the Schools* 18(3):330–33.

Popper, K. R. 1965. Unity of method in the natural and social sciences. In D. Braybrooke, ed., *Philosophical problems of the social sciences.* New York: Macmillan.

Porter, A. 1971. Reflections on the nature and design of systems. *Philosophy of the Social Sciences* 1 (September):233–43.

Purschwitz, M. A. 1983. National dairy housing conference attracts wide interdisciplinary support. *Agricultural Engineering* 64(5):15.

Rae-Grant, Q. A., and D. Marcuse. 1968. The hazards of teamwork. *American Journal of Orthopsychiatry* 38:4–8.

Rapoport, A. 1978. General systems theory: A bridge between two cultures. Third Annual Ludwig von Bertalanffy Memorial Lecture. *General Systems* (Yearbook) 23:149–52.

Regazzi, J. J., B. Bennion, and S. Roberts. 1980. On-line systems of disciplines and specialty areas in science and technology. *Journal of the American Society of Information Sciences* 31(3):161–70.

Reiger, H. 1978. *A balanced series of renewable resources, with particular reference to fisheries.* Seattle: Washington Sea Grant (University of Washington Press).

Richardson, J. G. 1980. Science and technology as integral parts of our culture: Interdisciplinary responsibilities of the scientific communicator. *Journal of Technical Writing and Communication* 2:141–47.

Rogers, E. S., and H. B. Messinger. 1967. Human ecology: Toward a holistic method. *Milbank Memorial Fund Quarterly* 45(1):25–42.

Roller, M. B. 1978. Thermostat and coatings technology: The challenge of interdisciplinary chemistry. *Abstracts of Papers of the American Chemical Society* 175 (March):45. See also: 1979. *Polymer Engineering and Science* 19(10):692–98.

Rouse, W. B. 1982. On models and modelers: N cultures. *IEEE Transactions: Man, Systems, and Cybernetics* 12(5):605–10.

Schulmeister, R. 1977. Methodological issues in evaluating interdisciplinary studies. In *Interdisciplinarity.* Papers presented at the SRHE European symposium on interdisciplinary courses in European education, City University, London, September 1975. Survey: SRHE at the University of Surrey. ERIC document ED 165-512.

Science and synthesis. 1967. New York: Springer-Verlag.

Scott, P. 1981. The rediscovery of the liberal university: Popular higher education in a post-industrial world. *Soundings* 64 (Spring):5–28.

Simas, P. W. 1971. A new supra discipline, policy sciences, aims to "integrate intelligence and action." *Chronicle of Higher Education* 5(16) (January 25):1, 5.

Simonton, D. K. 1976. Interdisciplinary and military determinants of scientific productivity: A cross-lagged correlation analysis. *Journal of Vocational Behavior* 9(1):53–62.

Singleton, R., Jr. 1983. Interdisciplinary teaching with humanists: Reflections of a biological scientist. *Perspectives in Biology and Medicine* 26(2):304–14.

Smith, R. O., C. P. Moore, and L. Gilson. 1983. Development of interdisciplinary team effectiveness. *Archives of Physical Medicine and Rehabilitation* 64(10):492.

Smolicz, J. J. 1970. Paradigms and models: A comparison of intellectual frameworks in natural sciences and sociology. *Australian and New Zealand Journal of Sociology* 6(2):100–119.

Snyder, S. H. 1984. Neurosciences: An integrative discipline. *Science* 225 (September 21):1255–57.

Spalding, I. J. 1984. Laser applications. *Physics Bulletin* (U.K.) 35(10):425–27.

Studdert-Kennedy, G. 1975. *Evidence and explanation in social science: An interdisciplinary approach.* London: Routledge and Kegan Paul.

Thurber, J. A. 1981. The Battelle Memorial Institute's human affairs research centers. *PS* 14(3):584–89.

Tichy, M. K. 1974. *Health care teams: An annotated bibliography.* New York: Praeger.

Trent, J. E. 1978. Internationalization? Interdisciplinarity? Development? The social sciences from 1952–1977: A report on the 25th anniversary round table. *Social Science Information* 17(2):337–42.

Trow, M. 1984–85. Interdisciplinary studies as a counterculture: Problems of birth, growth, and survival. *Issues in Integrative Studies* 4:1–15.

Valletutti, P. J., and F. Christopolos, eds. 1977. *Interdisciplinary approaches to human services.* Baltimore: University Park Press. See especially Valletutti and Christopolos, Interdisciplinary approaches to human services: An introduction and overview, pp. 1–11.

Walsh, W. B., G. L. Smith, and M. London. 1975. Developing an interface between engineering and the social sciences: An interdisciplinary team approach to solving societal problems. *American Psychologist* 30:1067–71.

Whitehouse, F. A. 1951. Teamwork: A democracy of professions. *Exceptional Children* 18.

Wiebe, P. 1982. Knowledge, the disciplines, and the university. *Soundings* 65 (Fall):292–315.

Wilson, R. S. 1973. Bridging the gap between technology and the humanities. *Engineering Education* 63:349–51.

Winthrop, H. 1978. Policy and planning programs as goals of scientific work. *American Journal of Economics and Sociology* 34(3):225–45.

———. 1979. *Education and culture in the complex society: Perspectives on interdisciplinary and general education.* Tampa: University of South Florida Press.

Wise, H., et al. 1974. *Making health teams work.* Cambridge: Ballinger. See also: 1974. Making health teams work. *American Journal of Diseases of Children* 127:537–42.

World Population Society. 1974. *Multidisciplinary approaches to population problems: Global dialogue of the disciplines on population.* Washington, D.C.: World Population Society.

Yanitsky, O. 1982. Towards an eco-city: Problems of integrating knowledge with practice. *International Social Science Journal* 34(3):469–79.

Participants

Donald R. Baldwin
Assistant Provost for Research
University of Washington
Seattle, Wash.

John M. Barnes
Principal Plant Pathologist
Cooperative State Research Service, U.S. Department of Agriculture
Washington, D.C.

Philip H. Birnbaum-More
Professor of Management and Organization
School of Business Administration, University of Southern California
Los Angeles, Calif.

Alok Chakrabarti
Dean and Distinguished Professor
School of Industrial Management, New Jersey Institute of Technology
Newark, N.J.

Israel Dror
Chief Engineer
Ministry of Defense, State of Israel
Haifa, Israel

David J. Etzold
Professor of Management
University of Southern Mississippi
Hattiesburg, Miss.

P. Fric
Computer Center of the Slovak Academy of Sciences
Cabinet for the Theory of Science and Forecasting
Bratislava, Czechoslovakia

Renee C. Friedman
Institute for Policy Research and Evaluation,
Pennsylvania State University
University Park, Pa.

Robert C. Friedman
Director
Institute for Policy Research and Evaluation,
Pennsylvania State University
University Park, Pa.

F. Gal
Computer Center of the Slovak Academy of Sciences
Cabinet for the Theory of Science and Forecasting
Bratislava, Czechoslovakia

Donald J. Grace
Georgia Tech Research Institute, Georgia Institute of Technology
Atlanta, Ga.

John W. Hooper
School of Electrical Engineering and Microelectronics Research Center,
Georgia Institute of Technology
Atlanta, Ga.

Masahiro Ikejima
Professor of Management
Department of Business Administration, Asia University
Tokyo, Japan

Julie T. Klein
Associate Professor of Humanities
Interdisciplinary University Studies, Wayne State University
11 Linden Court
Ypsilanti, Mich.

Mary Nichols
Associate Director
Strategic Management Research Center, University of Minnesota
Minneapolis, Minn.

Heinrich Parthey
Institute for Theory, History and Organization of Science,
Academy of Sciences
Berlin, German Democratic Republic

Alan Porter
Professor of Engineering
School of Industrial and Systems Engineering, Georgia Institute of Technology
Atlanta, Ga.

Frederick A. Rossini
Professor of Physics and Social Science
and Director of the Office of Interdisciplinary Programs
Georgia Institute of Technology
Atlanta, Ga.

Martha Garrett Russell
Institute of Technology, University of Minnesota
Minneapolis, Minn.

W. T. Sackett
Associate Dean
Institute of Technology, University of Minnesota
Minneapolis, Minn.

Ana Marie Sandi
International Center of Methodology for Future and Development Studies, University of Bucharest
Bucharest, Rumania

Richard W. Schneider
Vice-President, Research and Academic Affairs
Drexel University
Philadelphia, Pa.

C. Richard Schuller
Research Scientist
Battelle Seattle Research Center
Seattle, Wash.

V. Uhrova
Computer Center of the Slovak Academy of Sciences
Cabinet for the Theory of Science and Forecasting
Bratislava, Czechoslovakia

Eduardo Vasconcellos
Planning Director
Management Institute, University of São Paulo
São Paulo, Brazil

Ilan Vertinsky
Professor and Director
Centre of International Business Studies and the Consortium for Strategic Management, University of British Columbia
Vancouver, B.C., Canada

Patricia Vertinsky
University of British Columbia
Vancouver, B.C., Canada

Index